Jasper
Wolfe
of Skibbereen

Wolfe and men like him *are* modern Ireland . . . It is [his] humanity, born of natural warmth of heart and long mingling with the simple folk of the country that, together with his immense talents, has made Jasper Wolfe an epitome of the natural unity of Irish life; to be remembered and quoted by everybody who knows West Cork.

Seán Ó Faoláin

Jasper
Wolfe
of Skibbereen

JASPER UNGOED-THOMAS

The Collins Press

PUBLISHED IN 2008 BY
The Collins Press
West Link Park
Doughcloyne
Wilton
Cork

British Library Cataloguing in Publication Data
Ungoed-Thomas, Jasper
Jasper Wolfe of Skibbereen
1. Wolfe, Jasper
2. Lawyers - Ireland - Biography
3. Politicians - Ireland - Biography
4. Cork (Ireland : County) - Biography
I. Title
941.5'082'092

ISBN-13: 9781905172719

Typesetting by Carole Lynch
Typeset in Goudy
Printed in the UK by MPG Books Limited

Jacket photographs
Front jacket (clockwise from top): see pp 222, 48, 75, 7;
Back jacket (l–r): see pp 262–3, 51, 256, 187;
Back flap: see pg 53.

CONTENTS

ACKNOWLEDGEMENTS

My brother Fergus had always kept in close touch with the Irish side of our family. A few years ago he suffered a fatal fall while pursuing his favourite activity, mountain climbing. It was while his wife Angie, my sister and I were sorting out his papers that the idea of looking seriously into our grandfather's life began to emerge. So this book, in its origins, is Fergus'. I hope that, if he were able to read it, he would approve.

I am deeply grateful to all those who helped me in writing about Jasper Wolfe's life and times. The following, in conversation and often also correspondence, shared their memories, offered invaluable information and insights and frequently suggested fruitful further lines of enquiry.

My relations: Dr Margaret Baylis, Katherine Cameron, Barbara Clark, Janet Connell, Elma SRA, John, Peter, Reg and Jeremy Murphy, Helen Sale, Daisy Swanton, Jerome Ungoed-Thomas, Derek and Val Walton, Penny and Arthur Weir, Aine Wolfe, Moya Wolfe, Val Wood and Jane Wright.

The people of Skibbereen and County Cork: Tim Cadogan (executive librarian, Cork County Library), Pat Culleton, John Barry Deane, Katherine Field, Julie Glanton, Mary Hegerty, Kevin McCarthy, Pat O'Donovan, Finbarr O'Driscoll, Dermod O'Brien, Gerald O'Brien, Kevin P. O'Flynn (of J. Travers Wolfe & Co.), Jim O'Keeffe (TD), Liam O'Regan (editor of the *Southern Star*), Philip O'Regan, the Very Reverend Dean Peters, the Reverend Robin P. Roddie (Honorary Archivist, Wesley Historical Society in Ireland).

I owe particular thanks to Gerald O'Brien and Philip O'Regan of Skibbereen, who generously shared their great local knowledge with me, thus saving me from many errors of fact and judgement and opening my eyes to much of which I had been unaware. I am similarly indebted to John Murphy and his brothers, my second cousins, who revealed whole sagas of Wolfe family life and of my grandfather's activities which were all news to me. My first cousin, Helen Sale, helped me to investigate further aspects of Jasper Wolfe and his family by discussing with me, and encouraging me to explore, the substantial family papers that she had inherited from her mother. My sister Katherine Cameron, as she had done for many years, welcomed me to her house near Rosscarbery, so giving me an essential and hospitable base for my extended visits to West Cork. My wife Caroline, being Welsh, understood and remained actively interested in my typically Celtic, and near obsessive interest in tales of family and history. Each of the above five, in addition to all their other contributions, read and commented on a late draft, so greatly improving the final version. Without them, and their warmhearted support over a good number of years, the telling of Jasper Wolfe's story would have been much impoverished, and indeed might never have come to fruition. Finally, a great family friend, Poppy Carden, coming fresh to Irish history, went through the text in detail. She made various valuable suggestions that should help to make the story easier to follow for more general readers. To her, to all those mentioned, and indeed to many others, my thanks for everything.

I am very grateful to Fintan O'Connell, Philip O'Regan, Gerald O'Brien, John, Reg and Jeremy Murphy, Helen Sale, Daisy Swanton, and my son Roland for their help in researching photographs. I also thank the National Library of Ireland for permission to reproduce the portrait of Thomas Johnson, and Roland for his graphic work on the maps.

West Cork

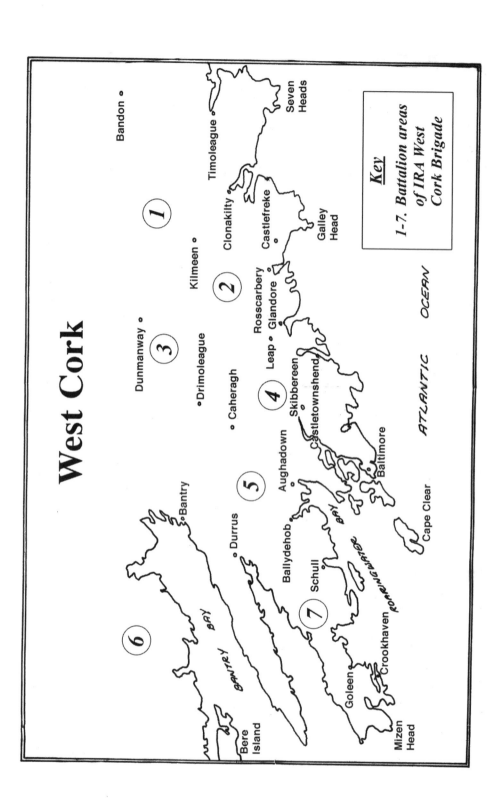

Bandon

Timoleague

Seven Heads

(1)

Kilmeen

Clonakilty

Castlefreke

Galley Head

(2)

Dunmanway

Drimoleague

(3)

Rosscarbery

Glandore

Leap

(4)

Caheragh

Skibbereen

Castletownshend

Baltimore

ATLANTIC OCEAN

Bantry

(5)

Aughadown

Durrus

Cape Clear

Ballydehob

ROARINGWATER BAY

(6)

BANTRY BAY

Schull

(7)

Goleen

Crookhaven

Bere Island

Mizen Head

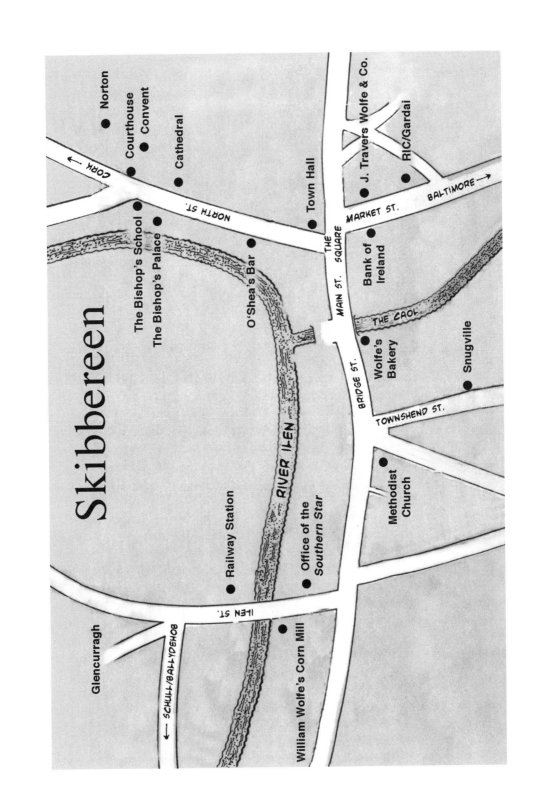

Skibbereen

INTRODUCTION

I started looking into my grandfather's life as a result of fond memories and considerable curiosity. The family knew that Jasper Wolfe had led a remarkable and dangerous existence and that, in his day, he had enjoyed the reputation of being a great character. I began to make enquires, initially of relations and then of others with connections to West Cork. Unexpectedly, trails opened up and fascinating papers of all sorts began to surface. I settled down to exploring. Visits to archives and libraries followed; I arranged specific interviews; and so it went.

Soon the fragments of stories that I had heard over the years started to fit into a picture that made sense. I began to see how it had happened that a Nonconformist shopkeeper's son had become first a highly successful local solicitor, then, as Crown Solicitor for Cork City and the West Riding of Cork (in effect, public prosecutor), perhaps the local IRA's top target during the Troubles of 1918–1923 (see Glossary). Finally, I came to understand how, in a remarkable twist of fortune, he had emerged as an Independent member of the Dáil, topping the poll within five years of having escaped for a third time from an IRA death sentence. When he eventually died at the age of eighty, Jasper Wolfe had crowned his career by being elected president of the Irish Law Society, the country's top honour for solicitors, and had lived to be a highly respected citizen – all but an institution – in the new Irish Republic.

The story of Jasper Wolfe's life only gradually emerged as a book. Investigations and thoughts required recording and structuring. Out of this process, naturally but without original intent, crystallised a biography. Having commented on a late draft of the book, one of my second cousins, the Murphys from Cork, remarked, 'Of course, you realise that if my mother had read this you would have been chased out of town?' To which I answered, 'And what do you think my mother would have said?' The truth is that this story could never have been written while family members, both Protestant and Catholic, who had lived through the early twentieth century were still alive. But equally, it had to be written while there were those, like myself and many others, who had known players from those historic times and who had a feel for the high emotions, the beliefs, attitudes and behaviours of an era now rapidly disappearing below the horizons of personal memory.

When I first started to think of possible publication, I hoped such a book would, with luck, be read by those who were in some way related to, or already knew of, Jasper Wolfe, together with those who were interested in the history of Skibbereen and West Cork. I also thought that my grandfather's, and indeed his family's, experiences during the Troubles were, in themselves, a story worth telling.

However, as I talked with a widening range of people, read further and uncovered more about Jasper's career, I began to realise that his life could be seen as having a wider significance. After the Troubles were over, his legal work in the new Irish Free State and his political career made him a player in the turbulent, national events at a time when Ireland was struggling to establish itself as an effective, democratic independent state. I could now see that, taken together with his earlier years, Jasper's life formed a trajectory through one of the most critical periods of Irish history, not only throwing fresh light on some of the key events of those times, but illustrating what it was like for many ordinary people, whatever their religion or background, to find themselves having to survive in an era of upheaval and dislocation. Viewed like this, Jasper's life was more than simply of local interest.

Finally, I came to realise that two themes in particular emerged from the telling of Jasper's story which, while offering their own insights into the past, could also be of particular contemporary relevance. First, there was his identity as one of Ireland's middle-class Protestants. Previously such lesser members of the Protestant faith had hardly registered on the radar of historical enquiry as attention concentrated on the clashes between ascendancy Protestants and native Irish, as well as between the hierarchies of the Church of Ireland and of the Roman Catholic Church. Now, however, their existence, and significance, were beginning to be noticed. Jasper Wolfe, a Wesleyan Methodist descended from shopkeepers and tenant farmers, was an almost archetypal representative of the relatively widespread numbers of what, in an earlier age, could have been called the 'middling' sort of Protestants. From the reactions of many people with whom I spoke, it seemed as if the outlook and experiences of my grandfather and his like, living embedded in the wider Catholic and native Irish community, might not only be of interest in themselves, but could offer new perspectives on the Ireland of the late nineteenth and early twentieth centuries.

One theme, however, emerged as crucial. I, and nearly every member of my family, whether close or distant, had in some way been hurt by the events through which my grandfather and his contemporaries had lived. The same seemed also to be true, to a greater or lesser extent, for significant numbers of others, living in Ireland or of Irish origin, with whom I spoke. But now, in contrast with people of my parents' generation, there seems to exist a growing, if not exactly universal, need to make one's peace with the past. And it is in this context, perhaps more than any other, that Jasper's life may be seen to matter in today's world.

Jasper was a peacemaker. He respected his adversaries, was virtually never bitter and was always willing to shake hands with them, or, even better, share a drink. Above all, he appreciated that, whatever the different ideals or methods of those involved in the struggles for Ireland's future, they were all united in one powerful emotion: a great passion for their native land. The story of Jasper shows how a spirit of reconciliation and generosity animated many, from all sides, even in the most desperate moments of Irish conflict. This is surely a healing message from the past which remains worth recalling.

I have come to share my grandfather's view of the world in which he lived. It seems to me that his was a remarkable generation of Irish men and women. During the armed conflicts, and indeed after these had formally ended, they lived through, or in some cases failed to live through, turbulence, fear, anxiety, shootings and unjustifiable atrocities as participants on all sides from time to time slipped the leash of personal conscience. But many, and ultimately the most influential, retained their original vision, their innate decency, their sense of honour and their commitment to building a just society. When war-war gave way to jaw-jaw, many of those same patriots who had fought with, and in some cases against, each other showed a remarkable tenacity, nimbleness and wit in securing a democratic state; and, as they put their revolutionary pasts behind them, they revealed also an equally admirable graciousness in giving way, or at least leaning backwards, when out-manoeuvred, or out-voted.

If those men and women who led Ireland to independence could return now, while I suspect few would agree that modern Ireland – which is largely their creation – is wholly good, they would surely accept that it is good in most parts, and better by far than the world that they inherited.

PROLOGUE

REMEMBERING NORTON, 1939–1952

JASPER AND MINNIE WOLFE

Minnie Wolfe, my grandmother, used to keep a shotgun in her bedroom. It was for frightening the crows, the pigeons, and the occasional jackdaws. Which it did. And not only them. Passers by used to duck – wisely. However, by the time I started arriving on my holidays, peace had been declared.

Norton, my grandparents' home, was strategically placed on a low hill overlooking the eastern and northern approaches to Skibbereen. It was a substantial, well-proportioned mansion, with its own out-buildings and grounds.

Norton was Grandma's imperium. She was assisted in her rule by Jerry – groom and factotum, together with a house-keeper and maid. However, the dominant personality amongst the Norton staff, and Grandma's natural soulmate, was Cadogan. A mighty man, he was at once fearsomely loyal, and ferociously independent. His formidable personality was embodied in an equally awesome physique.

Cadogan and Grandma, between them, formed the joint high command of Norton. While Grandma held sway indoors, outside Cadogan ruled. For him, gardening was fighting by other means. Every living thing was battled into submission. A former neighbour said to me that, 'the place was very nice, kept it lovely.' And that is how it deserves to be remembered.

And how did Jasper Wolfe, my grandfather, fit into this universe? It was clear that he was important. Although why was not at all obvious from anything I could see. True, he was given formal status, at least by Grandma. When talking, for instance, to Cadogan or Jerry she invariably referred to him

Norton.

as 'The Master'. But then, I was called 'Master Jasper'. This game of belonging to the Ascendancy class was played by Grandma with great vigour and conviction. But game it was. It was many, many years since the landed gentry had enjoyed much more than a toe-hold in Skibbereen; and, anyway, we had not belonged to them.

Grandpa remained sharp, but he was undoubtedly old. He may not have been whiskered, as Grandma was from time to time, but his teeth were black, brown and infrequent; he was partially, albeit on occasion intentionally, deaf; and he tended to droop and shuffle. His fingers were stained with tobacco. Like most of the men in his family, he had started to go bald from an early age. He was always dressed in a dark, three-piece suit. Across his waistcoat stretched a gold watch chain. On his finger was a gold signet ring, embossed with a wolf. He had the enormous, long ears that were a characteristic of the family.

Within Norton there were a few enclaves that were Grandpa's territory, and where Grandma's writ did not run. Upstairs, next to the main bedroom, was Grandpa's dressing room. Here, amongst the usual paraphernalia, was a group photograph of several young men. My mother explained that this had been taken in Dublin, of Grandpa with some student friends. She added that they were now all dead, mostly of drink.

Grandpa himself, as I later learned, had also been a very serious drinker. At nearly seventy, and on approaching two bottles of whiskey a day, he was given a stark warning by the doctor.

'Jasper, if you don't cut down on the whiskey, to say a glass a day, you'll be dead within months.'

Grandpa reflected. A day or two later he had another appointment with the doctor, and told him his decision.

'If I can only have one drink a day, I might as well stop altogether.' And he did.

Downstairs was Grandpa's study. A small office gave off this. 'The study' was really a misnomer. It still smelt of whiskey. Smoking was another indulgence Grandpa had surrendered. Among the room's treasures was a large silver ball made of wrappings from cigarette packets. It was in the study that Grandpa used to meet with his men friends, drink, play cards, and scheme political schemes.

Nowadays, Grandpa's way of life was mostly quiet. He read the papers, played patience, and on most mornings walked down town to his office, near the centre of town . Sometimes I went with him. Murty, an Irish terrier who was very much part of the household, also occasionally turned up for the trip, or at least part of it. An old man, a boy, and a dog, we would turn left out of the front porch, pass the conservatory, and make our way to a door in the high wall which marked the western boundary of the Norton gardens.

Once through the wall door we were in a steep lane, with high stone walls on either side. The left-hand wall, facing Norton's periphery, defended the property of the convent and school of the Sisters of Mercy. This was one of several imposing religious or public buildings, including the courthouse and pro-cathedral, all erected in the years not long before or after the Famine, which gave the northern approach to Skibbereen a real sense of space, civic confidence and style.

At the foot of the lane we turned left down North Street. As this approached the town centre, it narrowed, becoming a place of shops, private houses, and pubs. Unknown to me, at number 23, was a bar, often referred to as 'Mam 'Shea's', run by Mam O'Shea, the widow of a former town clerk,who had been one of Grandpa's greatest friends. On John O'Shea's death, a memorial window had been erected in the pro-cathedral by sub-scription; Grandpa had been one of the major contributors. At this bar,

Minnie Wolfe.

Grandpa would invariably pause on his return journey.

As we went down North Street, young boys of about six or seven, sometimes without shoes, would come up to Grandpa. A transaction would take place, which seemed to satisfy all concerned. Grandpa would offer some coins, which he had ready prepared, the boys would politely thank him, and that would be that. Particularly during, and for some years after the war, there was poverty in Skibbereen, and indeed in West Cork generally, of a sort I had never seen elsewhere.

Murty was by no means a faithful companion. He was not only unreliable in his attendance, but also had a delinquent side.Not long ago I was walking along the bottom of what used to be the Norton garden. I started chatting with a man who was passing by with his dog. It turned out he lived, and had done so for many years, in Cadogan's old home, Norton Lodge. He told me the following story about Murty and my grandfather.

On one occasion, Murty, bored as so often with his outing, sniffed and trotted his way ahead of Grandpa, along North Street, where he observed, and helped himself to, some lamb chops which were on display at a butcher's. Pursuit proved in vain.

'You know whose dog that was?' said a customer.

'No, by Jesus, no,' said the butcher, who had been inside his shop at the time of the theft.

'T'was Jasper's, I'd say.' (Grandpa was universally known as Jasper. It was not something Grandma would have wished.) 'You could,' added the customer, 'claim for that.'

'Is that right?' commented the butcher, thoughtfully.

A few days later, not entirely by chance, the butcher met Grandpa in the street.

'Good day to you, Mr Wolfe.'

'Good day to you.'

'I wonder, will you give me some advice?'

'And what might be the problem?'

'Well, just supposing some stray animal stole a piece of my meat. Could I sue the owner?'

'That you could.'

'You're sure now?'

'Of course, of course. You're in your rights altogether. The law is on your side. You go ahead and sue.'

'Thank you, sir. Thank you indeed.'

The next day there arrived at Norton, from the butcher, a claim for stolen property and damages, amounting to eighteen shillings. Which, incidentally, was rather more than the original value of the chops. Statements of witnesses who observed the incident, and who would swear to identify the guilty party, were attached.

Shortly after, the butcher was delighted to receive a cheque for the amount demanded. However, also attached was a bill from J. Travers Wolfe and Co., solicitors. This was in respect of legal advice provided, and the charge was one guinea, or twenty-one shillings.[1]

Four generations: (l–r) Dorothy Ungoed-Thomas holding Jasper, Rachel Wood Wolfe, Jasper Wolfe.

PART ONE

'I AGREE NOT TO SMOKE TOBACCO', 1872–1887

2

PAPA AND MAMA

My grandfather, Jasper Travers Wolfe, was born to Willie John Wolfe and his wife Rachel Wood on 3 August 1872. Why he was named Jasper is unclear, but Travers was the surname of an uncle by marriage on his mother's side who was probably also his godfather. To distinguish them from the many other Wolfes, Jasper and his family were to become known as the Travers Wolfes. His birth took place above the family shop in Bridge Street, Skibbereen. There were already two older children, both boys. These were good times for the young Wolfe family. Looking back, Rachel remembered, 'I was happy then.'

Jasper's parents were Methodist, Anglo-Irish Protestants. There had been Wolfes in Ireland for a very long time. One branch, the Old English, Catholic 'Woulfes', had arrived with the Anglo-Norman twelfth-century invasion. A second branch, known as 'Wolfes', had come as part of the Elizabethan Protestant settlement and seem to have been founders of the West Cork town of Bandonbridge (later known as Bandon). Jasper was descended from one or other of these branches, but more probably from the sixteenth-century colonists.

Jasper's grandparents kept a shop in Ballydehob, a few miles to the west of Skibbereen. Here, the family had been tenant farmers for generations. However, when the Famine struck, Ballydehob was very badly hit. Shortly afterwards, in the early 1850s, Jasper's father, impoverished and unable to find work, came to Skibbereen. According to family tradition he walked the few miles barefoot, with his one pair of shoes hanging round his neck. An uncle, William Wolfe of Ilen House, who had established a successful milling and corn business, helped his nephew to set up as a baker.

Willie John rented, and before long bought, premises in Skibbereen. These faced onto Bridge Street and consisted of a very presentable three-storey building, with ample retail space on the ground floor and adequate living accommodation above. Behind were a yard and plenty of storage facilities. The building's greatest advantage, however, lay in its position. Not only was it near the centre of town but it faced, just across the road and a small square, the river Ilen. Where the square edged the river was a quay, together with warehouses, in at least one of which William Wolfe of Ilen House had an interest. All this was extremely convenient for Willie John. His uncle's boats would unload flour at the quay and from here, a matter of a few yards, Willie John could carry his sacks and get baking.

Jasper's mother was twenty-four years old when she married Willie John Wolfe. The bride was ten years younger than her husband, but such an age difference was not unusual. The youngest daughter of a large family, and her father's favourite, Rachel had been brought up at Seaview, a tenant farm of about 100 acres. A mile or two inland from Rosscarbery Bay, the farmhouse was situated on a shelf of land near the summit of Knockfeen Hill. The view, from Galley Head in the east to Toehead in the west, was breathtaking. So, in a different way, were the winter gales which blew in, unimpeded, from the open Atlantic. Rachel loved the place, and her life there.

The Woods, like the Wolfes, were originally English settlers and had become substantial owners of farmland during the seventeenth century. Since then their fortunes had gone up and down, although mainly down. Nevertheless, Rachel's father, 'Big Billy', was quite comfortably off.

The Woods were Church of Ireland. This did not prevent John and his wife, Mary 'Polly Child' Bryan, sending Rachel to Miss Brodrick's Wesleyan Ladies' School in Skibbereen. This was one of those small, private establishments which flowered and faded in the somewhat haphazard garden of local Protestant education.

Rachel was a striking figure. Slim, upright, red-headed, attractive and poised, she would certainly have caught the eye. While still at school, or very shortly after, she had converted to Methodism. Her religious convictions were to sustain her for the rest of her life. She was also highly intelligent, with a mind both penetrating and diamond-sharp. In addition to all this, she was extremely determined and a more than capable manager of practical affairs. In a later time she would surely have been a very successful professional woman.

Willie John and Rachel's marriage, whether or not it was made in heaven, most certainly was much approved of in earthly circles. The two, who had met in the Methodist community of Skibbereen, married on 24 August 1869. Rachel's sister's wedding had taken place a few years earlier, just down the hill from the Wood family farm at the Church of Ireland church at Castleventry. Rachel herself, however, was determined that her wedding would be according to 'the usages of the Methodist Church in Ireland'. The pair were married at the Wesley Chapel in Cork. The witness for the bridegroom's side was his uncle, William Wolfe of Ilen House.

3

THE CAOL

By the time Jasper was three he was just about able to join in and play with his two older brothers, Willie (later known as Willie Wood Wolfe) and Jack, aged four and five respectively. He now also had a younger sister, May, who was nearly two years old.

The boys played in the back yard, the store sheds, and even ventured into the shop. From time to time they also managed to cross Bridge Street, doing their best to avoid the horse-drawn carts, traps, dogs and occasional stray animals, not to mention the inevitable dung. Once safely across, they could watch boats loading and unloading at the quay and no doubt get in the way of the men, including their father, who were hauling and stacking various goods in the warehouses.

This happy existence was not to last for long. In each of the next two summers, in 1875 and 1876, a baby sister was born. Sarah Emily died of infantile cholera within three months. Her mother later remembered these days in her diary as the time of 'my first great trouble'. The following July Rachel Francis arrived. She survived for only a few weeks.

All of this, dreadful though it was for their parents, would probably not have affected the boys very much. However, the events of 1877, when Jasper was five, changed everything. Things actually started well. In August another boy, Thomas Edward (Eddie), was born. However, in December Jack fell ill. He died three days after Christmas of typhoid. Jack was Rachel's favourite – 'my precious first born, and best beloved' – and she mourned him for the rest of her life, always remembering his birthday and imagining how he might have been. After Jack died, his parents had a full-length portrait painted of him copied from a studio photograph. In this he is dressed in a blue suit, hair neatly parted, leaning against what looks like a stile. This picture was to hang in the main living-room of the Wolfe family throughout their lives, and so the memory of Jack lived on. My mother told me that he had been the brightest of all the brothers and sisters.

Jasper had lost his big brother, and the leader of his gang. He was at the funeral when Jack was taken to the family vault in Aughadown, the graveyard of a ruined church overlooking the mouth of the river Ilen. When the chamber

THE FAMILY OF WILLIE JOHN AND RACHEL WOOD WOLFE

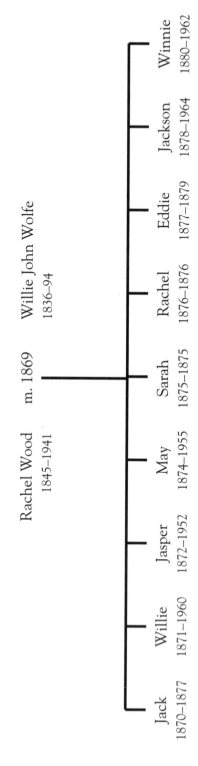

Rachel Wood   m. 1869   Willie John Wolfe
1845–1941   1836–94

Jack   Willie   Jasper   May   Sarah   Rachel   Eddie   Jackson   Winnie
1870–1877   1871–1960   1872–1952   1874–1955 1875–1875   1876–1876   1877–1879   1878–1964   1880–1962

Note. Rachel Wolfe's nine children were all born within 12–18 months of each other, the first within a year of marriage. Shortly after the birth of the last, her husband started to suffer from progressive paralysis.

was last opened, for a grandson of Willie's, Jack's coffin and those of his baby sisters were still in their places.

For a while, it might have seemed to Jasper as if life, though lonelier and less fun, continued much as before. In less than a year, another son, Jackson, was born, but within four months there was a further infant mortality when Eddie died of dysentery. Rachel gave birth to her last child, Winnie, nine months later.

Jasper's parents became convinced they knew what was causing the deaths of so many of their children, unusual in their frequency even in those days. Alongside their home and shop, Bridge House, ran the Caol stream. It flowed under the street (hence its name,

A Wolfe child, almost certainly Eddie, on his deathbed.

'Bridge Street') and into the Ilen. The trouble was that, since Skibbereen had no drainage system, the Caol was little more than an open sewer. It stank, rats infested its banks, and excrement, debris and the decaying remains of dead animals floated in it. It was apparent, even in the later nineteenth century, that these waters, at some times stagnant, at others in spate, were likely to carry disease and death.

Rachel and Willie John decided that they would have to move their family away from the banks of the Caol as soon as possible. For a start, they sent Willie, aged seven and now the eldest, to live with his Wood grandparents and his aunt Rebecca. Big Billy, having moved from Seaview, was now farming at Kilkeran, near Rosscarbery. Willie settled down quickly. He did well at school, attending the nearby Church of Ireland St Fachtna's College in Rosscarbery, and he helped on the farm, where he learned to speak reasonable Irish.

It is possible that Jasper was also intended to live at Kilkeran and may even have done so for a short while. Certainly Dorothy remembered stories of her father having to walk in the direction of Rosscarbery to go to school, but maybe it was just to visit Willie and his grandparents. Anyway, for whatever reason, he was soon settled back in Skibbereen.

Jasper's parents now set about house-hunting in earnest. In fact, a move would have suited them well at this time, as living above the shop with a growing family was hardly ideal. There was also the small matter of status. The Wolfes naturally desired to be respected in the community, and the most obvious way of establishing that one was a citizen of substance was to live in a well-appointed residence.

4

SNUGVILLE

Around about the time when Eddie died Jasper noticed, as did others, that his father sometimes dropped things in the shop and could have difficulty lifting the sacks of grain. Occasionally, too, his father seemed to drag his feet. However, nobody was particularly concerned. Willie John was now definitely prospering. Apart from running the shop, he seems to have had various other business ventures, including lending money, on security, to his clients. He was well placed to do this, since he spoke Irish and understood well the world of small farmers and merchants, whether Protestant or Catholic. In effect, he became, as a sideline, a 'gombeen' man. While he seems to have avoided the unpopularity suffered by many of these characters, providing cash advances seems to have involved rather more than the occasional venture.

So Jasper's father could now afford to live somewhere better, and healthier, than above the shop, beside the Caol. Buy or renting an ascendancy mansion near Skibbereen, with its own agricultural land, was one idea which, initially at least, seemed attractive. His uncle, William Wolfe of Ilen House, owned just such a dwelling. So it was that Willie John set out on his house-hunting expeditions. However, residences of the sort he was looking for did not come on the market often.

In the end, the Wolfes ended up owning three properties; Willie John acquired, in rapid succession, a family home, a farm and a holiday house. Jasper was seven years old when his family moved. Snugville, a name which came to be a bit of an embarrassment to younger members of the family, suited the Wolfes very well indeed. It was within a couple of hundred yards of the shop and it was in Townshend Street, a relatively quiet neighbourhood favoured by the Protestants. Equally importantly, it was, although it hardly looked it from the road, what a later owner called 'a fine town house'. Set back from adjoining houses on either side, it was separated from the street only by some iron railings and a modest gravel forecourt. However, behind its grey, quite elegantly decorated, façade was a very substantial dwelling, containing large well-proportioned rooms, a considerable conservatory and a good number of bedrooms. There was also a walled, if only medium-sized, garden. After a few years, the Wolfes were able to buy an adjacent yard and outbuildings, together with a large kitchen garden and orchard which ran down as far as the Caol.

Almost as suitable as Snugville was the farm. Whether through his gombeen activities or otherwise, Willie John managed to acquire the tenancy of Licknavar, just outside Skibbereen on the road to Baltimore. Benefiting from the generous terms of the Irish land laws (actually designed to help the Catholics, not the Protestants), this farm remained in the family for many years. With a manager installed and supervised by Rachel, it provided not only a good source of income, but was highly convenient for daily life. Here lived the horses which pulled the family trap and wagonette, the pigs which provided pork, bacon and sausage meat, the poultry which gave eggs and meat and the cows which gave milk.

And finally, like many other prosperous Skibbereen families, the Wolfes also purchased a holiday house by the sea. The most popular sites were at Baltimore and, even nearer, Tragumna. However, so as to be close to Rachel's relations in Leap, Kilkeran and Seaview, Willie John found a place at Glandore. The family, often with friends and relations, was to spend a good deal of time here, although occasionally, if cash was running short, the house was let out during the holiday months.

When the Wolfes moved into Snugville, they were hoping for a new beginning, but it soon became clear that their troubles were by no means over. Something, and it could no longer be ignored, was clearly wrong with Jasper's father. Willie John's symptoms came and went, but his condition was undeniably worsening. Though he often had difficulty walking, suffered from bouts of depression and was sometimes in pain, Willie John refused to give up and went on managing his business as best he could.

Jasper's mother now became the dominant figure on the home scene, and she found herself very stressed. In particular, her relationship with her invalid husband deteriorated. In her diary, which she wrote up every day, she wrote: 'Only that his mind is so weak, I often think the fearful contrast between what he is and what he has been, particularly with regard to his care and attention, would drive me distracted.' Rachel and Willie John began to argue. When Rachel came home with the new baby (Winnie had been born at Glandore, whether by choice or not is unclear), she was installed in the marital bedroom and before long Willie John moved to another room. There were to be no more births. However, Rachel, like her husband, battled on.

With his father ailing and his mother more or less in sole charge of the family, life was not easy for Jasper. When his brother Willie was around, things were not too bad. The two collected stamps together (unfortunately, as I found many years later, using glue to stick them in place, thus ruining some quite valuable items) and they found plenty to occupy them in and around the town. However, Willie was away most of the time at Kilkeran.

Jasper did not find his other siblings particularly congenial. May was astringent and humourless – and a girl! As for Jackson and Winnie, not only were they too young, but he had little in common with them either. Jackson was somewhat lacking in guile, and altogether too straightforward a character for Jasper's taste. As for Winnie, she was little more than pretty and conventionally nice (the latter a characteristic which, in the view of many family members, wore noticeably thin as she grew older).

Unfortunately, Jasper could not look to his mother for much in the way of understanding or tenderness. Rachel had little use for either Jasper or Willie. The main, irreparable, failing of the two boys was that neither of them was Jack. Her favourites were Jackson ('a fine, big, strong boy') and Winnie ('she is such a comfort to me, and a real help with her careful energetic ways, and her thoughtfulness for my comfort'). These two youngest, only born around the time of the move, belonged to the new life of Snugville and did not remind her of the painful times at Bridge House.

Jasper might not have been cherished by his mother, but at least she fulfilled her parental duties, like all her other moral obligations, with faithful conscientiousness. Although the Wolfes, like all but the most impoverished Protestants, had servants (indoors there was Ellie and, outside, the groom, gardener and odd-job man Mick Walsh), the lady of the house had a great deal of work still to do. Nearly all Jasper's food was prepared and cooked by his mother ('made cakes, pudding and apple pie'), his clothes were mended by her and a good many of them were made by her as well, including flannel shirts. His hair, too, was 'clipped' by her. Then there were birthdays and Christmases. Jasper's parties, as with those of his brothers and sisters, were all organised by his mother. She bought him presents (once, a penknife). She even played draughts with him.

Meanwhile, as earlier in the family's life, disease remained a real threat to the children. True, the Caol was no longer right next to the house, but it was nevertheless not more than a couple of hundred yards away. The occasional rat still managed to penetrate into the kitchen. Also to fear were the frequent epidemics of childhood illnesses. Jasper and Winnie both caught measles. Their mother wrote in her diary: 'There are many children dying all over the town. Jasper has been heavy and sick all day. I feel so tired and worn out.' Winnie started to recover, but Jasper's condition continued to fluctuate. 'Jasper is better today', but, twenty-four hours later, 'Jasper was very ill until about 11 o'clock, but is much better since. I stayed up nearly all last night, and was rather anxious about him.'

As well as illnesses threatening the children, there were accidents, which could be lethal. Child safety was not generally given much thought. Both from necessity and from a belief that they should learn to cope for themselves, boys, if not girls, were given a good deal of freedom. However, they could get themselves into dangerous situations. On one occasion Jasper nearly succeeded in shooting himself: 'Jasper had a most providential escape. The gun went off in the hall, but did no more damage than smashing a plaster bracket and a saucer.' Another time, Jasper practically burned to death when he and his brothers and sisters were left alone in the Glandore holiday house (Jasper was sixteen at the time) and managed to set the building alight. When Rachel arrived by trap with Mick Walsh she 'found them all alright, and after having a most wonderful escape from being burnt to death'. And then there were the considerable dangers of the road: stray animals, 'upsets' in the trap and so forth. Once when Jasper was driving with his mother, the horse shied. While Jasper escaped with a few grazes, Rachel was badly hurt, suffering nasty head and hand injuries. Another ever-present danger was the sea. The Wolfes had their own boat at Glandore and, on at least one occasion, this capsized a good distance from land, leaving Jasper to swim for it.

Jasper, and Willie especially, were not always models of good behaviour. On his own, Jasper was quite manageable. He soon learned to go his own quiet way, dissembling as necessary, but when his older brother was around it was a different matter. Willie was altogether a more open character than Jasper. He seldom attempted to hide his feelings and tended to do what he wanted, when he wanted.

What the two growing lads required every now and then was some firm handling. Normally such a task would have fallen to the father of the family. However, with Willie John for most practical purposes an absentee parent, it was left to Rachel to do what she could. She worried a good deal about the boys' behaviour and the difficulty of keeping them under control: 'I found it rather hard today to manage my boys. I need more grace and wisdom to guide me in my training of them.' Evidently she was not alone in thinking she could do with more divine support. An old friend and Methodist minister, the Reverend Hadden, was particularly critical. 'He is', said Rachel, 'so truthful and outspoken. It is very evident he has not a high opinion of my management of my children.' Rachel, as was her wont, battled on. Her fierce temper, 'her old foe' as she described it, turned out, when it came to disciplining Willie and Jasper, to be a valuable ally. They did not willingly provoke outbursts from their mother and, when they did, they usually retreated chastened. 'The boys were disobedient today, but I trust they got a lesson which they will not soon forget.'

5

METHODISTS

Jasper was brought up as a strict Methodist. Every day started and finished with family prayers led by Rachel. On Sundays, without fail, the whole family went to church. This was within easy walking distance, just up the road from the shop. As they left their house and walked along Townshend Street wearing their best clothes, they would have been joined by several other families similarly well turned out.

John Wesley had won converts to Methodism during his frequent visits to Bandon and from early in the nineteenth century the numbers of his followers were increasing in West Cork. This new denomination, originally no more than a society within the Anglican communion, seemed to many Irish Protestants a welcome, even inspiring, alternative to the Church of Ireland. The latter predominantly served, reflected and represented a static, hierarchical agricultural community of Anglo-Irish settlers. It was much concerned to preserve its privileges and, like Anglicanism in Britain, had become distinctly worldly. As the nineteenth century progressed, the Church of Ireland faced ever greater problems. As first Catholic emancipation and later disestablishment arrived, the Church, while failing to reform, began to see its influence and its wealth slipping away. The Church of Ireland had begun its long, and sometimes reluctant, retreat from arrogance to niceness. At best, it was treading water in the often unpredictable seas of Irish religious life. At worst, it was in danger of being swept away.[1]

By contrast, Victorian Methodism appeared to many as a dynamic and attractive faith. Wesley preached personal and social responsibility, friendship, toleration and respect for the law. At the heart of Wesley's teaching, however, lay the message that God cherished each and every soul, offering to all believers the gift of salvation in Christ. Methodism, above and beyond everything else, was concerned to help individuals experience and develop an inner holiness, and ultimately to be blessed by spiritual union with the divine presence.

In Ireland, all this had clear practical consequences. Methodists were independent of mind in a society dominated by civil and ecclesiastic authoritarianism. They did their best to support others when necessary and to live on good terms with their neighbours, whether Church of Ireland or Catholic. They observed and maintained the rule of law and the vision of a just society. At best, these were God-fearing, decent and principled people.

In Skibbereen, the foundations for the success and local ethos of Skibbereen Methodists had been laid by James H. Swanton, JP, who had been the leading figure in the local Methodist community for a quarter of a century, from 1840 onwards. 'The Governor', as he was invariably known, came from the Wolfes' home town of Ballydehob and belonged to a family that had produced converts to Methodism from the earliest years. Through his religious leadership (he was a very active lay preacher) and his business acumen (he made a fortune in the corn trade and became a major landowner), he ensured that the Skibbereen church was spiritually well conducted, properly funded and competently managed. He established good relations with the Irish Catholics and he was prominent during the Famine, planning relief measures, setting up soup kitchens, initiating a public works programme of road building and importing and distributing grain. He supported Nationalist candidates in elections, sympathising with their demands for Land Reform and Home Rule. Following a general election in 1847, a triumphant crowd of 5,000 carrying lighted tar barrels and green flags marched through Ballydehob and halted in front of the Governor's house, 'for the purpose of cheering that worthy and patriotic gentleman' (*Southern Reporter*, 19 August 1847). It was largely thanks to J. H. Swanton's example and influence that, from their early days, Methodists managed to establish a secure base in the Skibbereen area.

By the time Jasper began attending services, Methodism in Skibbereen was thriving. In the church, he and his family, like other regular attenders, had their own pew. This not only signified faithful membership, but secured reserved seats in a place of worship which was nearly always full. Conversely, if a family started to ration its attendance, its empty pew would be obvious.

Most of the congregation would have been familiar to Jasper. Several of the pews would have been occupied by relations, mostly various families of Wolfes. Other worshippers were neighbours and many were, like Jasper's father, involved in shopkeeping, trade, or similar activities. The members, almost without exception, came from the middle or lower middle classes, were of Anglo-Irish origin and had connections of one kind or another with the settler farming community.

These Methodists, mostly making their livings in a competitive, entrepreneurial world, included both the very well off and some who were close to real poverty. At one end of the scale was Jasper's great-uncle, William Wolfe of Ilen House. He gave the church £400 a year and even kept this up when he lost two uninsured ships of grain and had to relinquish his plans for building a conservatory. (From the mid-nineteenth century until about 1914 £1 was roughly worth €75). At the other end of the scale were many of the less successful traders and women managing on their own. Overall, those for whom survival was a bit of a struggle seem to have been in a clear majority. Certainly, when the collection plate came round copper coins predominated over the silver. To help address this little problem, a card was regularly hung in each pew: 'This being the first Sunday in the month, you are requested to increase your contributions.'

Methodists ran their own show, and that was perhaps their greatest appeal. For a start, everyone had his or her own hotline to the Almighty, and then congregations, as societies of believers, were more or less self-governing. For much of Jasper's boyhood, a successor of James H. Swanton as Circuit Steward (the chief official, who enjoyed great authority) was John Wolfe, son of William Wolfe of Ilen House. Other lay members (many of them related to Jasper, like the great James H. Swanton himself) helped run the myriad activities of the church. And at the same time, as ever, more worldly matters could also be attended to, the men quietly furthering mutual business interests. All this was a considerable, and welcome, contrast to the practices of the Church of Ireland. For Methodists, there was no episcopal hierarchy laying down religious dos and don'ts from on high. Almost equally importantly, there was no permanently ensconced vicar or rector, the source of all local authority. On the contrary, Methodist ministers had to move on every few years and so never stayed long enough to dictate the spiritual, moral or practical agenda. And finally, there was no rigid social hierarchy, where all the real levers of power were in the hands of the big landowners. Methodists did not kowtow. They practised a faith which provided for the needs, not of traditional rural society, but of the new, mainly urban, lower middle and middle classes who were emerging, even in a place like Skibbereen, in response to the demands and opportunities created by the Industrial Revolution.

Methodism offered much, and expected much. Apart from the religious highlight of the week, the Sunday service, for the younger members there were also the Wesleyan Methodist Sunday School Union and the Band of Hope, a sort of Protestant Christian youth club that covered the whole of the United Kingdom and included amongst its multitudinous activities the publication of the *Boy's Own Paper*. Jasper was registered as member number 478 of the Sunday School, where he was duly 'entitled to compete for all honours and prizes of the order'. He was likewise signed up for the Band of Hope. Jasper's presence was required at meetings of both these organisations, not to mention Sunday worship and various other get-togethers and festivals which occurred from time to time.

Very soon, Jasper must have encountered that great Nonconformist endeavour, the battle against drink, or 'Drink' as it was often written. This was quite as necessary in Skibbereen as anywhere else in Ireland or Great Britain. The town was the site of a first-rate brewery, owned by the wealthy Catholic McCarthy family, and was more than adequately supplied with public houses. Here the men could drink 'McCartie's Porter', as well as various other liquors. Women were not permitted in bars, but got over this without much difficulty. On market days especially, farmers' wives would come in from the surounding countryside with eggs, chickens, vegetables and other produce for sale; they would return with bottles of beer, or something stronger, safely secreted under their black cloaks, 'singing', as someone in Clonakilty museum told me, 'like larks'.

As a matter of the strongest principle, no alcohol was available at Snugville. And hardly fifty yards up the road was the Temperance Hall, site of the first Temperance Society in Europe. Rachel Wolfe was a dedicated member of this association and it was one of the few places where she would have co-operated with Catholics, many of whom, including priests, were quite as strongly and actively opposed to the evils of drink as she was. Rachel's children, like nearly all other youngsters from Victorian Nonconformist families, were recruited early as foot soldiers in the crusade. Jasper, being a Band of Hope member, would have signed a 'Pledge Card' (a solemn undertaking to abstain forever from alcohol), or it might even have been signed for him if he was too young to write for himself.

Finally, Jasper and his brothers and sisters were expected to lend a hand to their mother when she required help in her various good works for the Methodists. For them, as indeed for her, the most onerous demands probably came with preparations for the twice-yearly bazaars. These were major money-making events which could raise as much as £100. They were also considerable social occasions. Visitors came from as far away as Cork, not forgetting to bring contributions for the stalls; and the local ladies themselves took care to dress up in 'very swell costumes'.

Rachel had her own stall at the bazaars, which were held nearby at the 'Lecture Hall' in Mardyke Street. She spent weeks preparing her goods for sale. The boys were required to make their own offerings, on one occasion a few painted objects by Willie and a large cork frame by Jasper. On the great day itself, they were also required to be in attendance, fetching, carrying, helping to sell. Winnie even had her own Penny Stall.

Jasper, like Willie, was not a naturally religious individual. The two of them, it is true, never, throughout their lives, showed any serious inclination to stray too far from the Methodist Society, but they clearly saw themselves as camp followers rather than as captains of the godly enterprise. In truth, while they were indeed decent and honourable in their own way, active participation in a community of faith and the demanding business of following specific moral rules was not really for them; nor, indeed, was inward holiness. They preferred to seek both inspiration and consolation from more worldly sources.

As they grew older, to their mother's dismay, all this became ever more evident. Jasper and Willie grew less and less interested in 'pressing to enter the Kingdom'. Willie was the more openly rebellious. 'I fear the old sceptical spirit is seizing hold of Will again . . . I do wish he would turn his attention to the things that would last for both worlds, and not spend his youth in carelessness and sneering at what is good and right.' Jasper, as was his custom, was more diplomatic, but when it came to action, or rather lack of it, he proved just as reluctant to conform as his brother, something of which Rachel was well aware. 'I find that the boys have gone back so much. I cannot get them to stay for our Bible reading even, and only with difficulty can I get them to preaching or to Sunday School.' On one particular occasion a visiting minister held a series of special meetings and services. Again, Jasper and Willie failed to be counted among those anxious to accept the gift of salvation. 'I felt disappointed my boys seemed so careless.' And, later in the week, 'This has been a day of fasting and prayer. My boys did not go tonight. I fear very much they still scoff.' The recurring visits of ministers from overseas could also cause tension. 'Got the tea and went to the Missionary Meeting. I tried hard to get Jasper and Will to come, but could not induce them – I feel very sad to see how utterly careless they are about the means of grace or the means of improving themselves in any way.'

By the time the two boys were about to leave school, Rachel had reluctantly come to recognise that neither of them were really cut out for the Lord's work. She had to fall back on prayer. With Jasper in mind she wrote in her diary: 'May the Good Lord change his heart.' And then, much more specifically, there was the question of his smoking. She trusted that he could be kept from Drink by the Pledge, but tobacco, an evil closely allied to alcohol, now threatened. With great reluctance, she felt constrained to resort to bribery. Hoping for a promise of abstemiousness, she entered into negotiations with Jasper, offering cash. The result was a document which read as follows:

I agree not to smoke tobacco in consideration of getting a weekly sum of 6 pence from this date to be paid in advance on the 29th day of every month, and this agreement will remain in force as long as the above weekly sum is regularly paid.
Dated this 29th day of October 1889.

Jasper Wolfe

In any event, it was not long before Jasper broke the agreement – permanently.

THE WOODS

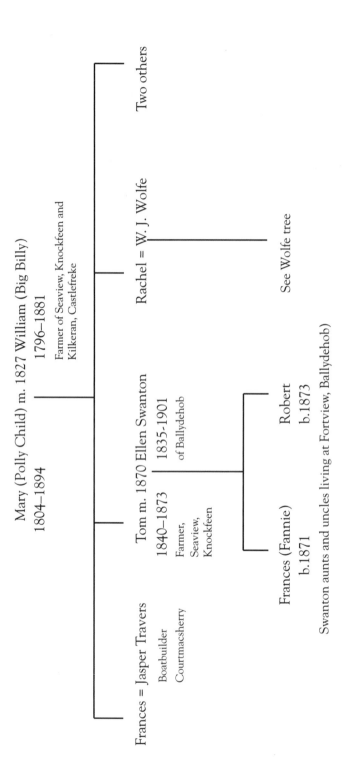

Mary (Polly Child) m. 1827 William (Big Billy)
1804–1894
1796–1881
Farmer of Seaview, Knockfeen and
Kilkeran, Castlefreke

Frances = Jasper Travers
Boatbuilder
Courtmacsherry

Tom m. 1870 Ellen Swanton
1840–1873
1835-1901
Farmer,
of Ballydehob
Seaview,
Knockfeen

Rachel = W. J. Wolfe

Two others

Frances (Fannie)
b.1871

Robert
b.1873

See Wolfe tree

Swanton aunts and uncles living at Fortview, Ballydehob)

6

SEPTS

If Jasper had been condemned to live much of his life confined within the damaged nucleus of his own family, he would no doubt have suffered a fairly miserable existence. However, things were not at all like that. Jasper lived in an extended family. Indeed, a family so extensive that hardly anyone knew how everybody related to everybody else. Almost all the inhabitants of West Cork, settler and native Irish alike, enjoyed similar kindred arrangements. The Irish word for such constellations was a sept and, to all intents and purposes, it was a sept to which the Wolfes, and most other families, belonged.

The Wolfes had always been inclined to congregate together in clannish alliances. As early as the fourteenth century, the Old English Woulfes of Kildare had formed a sept. A fairly formidable crew, they had their own coat of arms, a wolf passant (i.e. walking) in front of an oak tree, beside a river with a couple of salmon. They also had their own immodest motto, in Gaelic, 'Cuilan Uasal' (which roughly translates as 'Shining Paragon'). The West Cork Wolfes were aware of their historic heritage. On special occasions Jasper, like everyone else at Snugville, ate with forks and spoons carrying the image of a wolf passant. Rachel had had her best silver engraved with the family emblem. Cleaning the silver was a significant household duty.

Septs endured, whether or not they were called such, because they were useful. Families often found themselves in difficulties. On the whole, people were tough and knew they mostly had to rely on themselves. But help was sometimes welcome and the wider family was by far its likeliest source. In the virtual absence of public welfare and employment rights, the sept provided a vital, if broad-meshed and not necessarily reliable, network of support and influence.

Jasper's extended family stretched from Schull in the west to Clonakilty in the east. In Schull, which was part of the Skibbereen Methodist district, or 'circuit', Wolfes were mainstays of the Methodist church (a William and a Robert Wolfe were Society Stewards). To the east, the Wolfes owned or leased various farms. Just below the Woods at Seaview, at the foot of Knockfeen Hill, there were Wolfes who farmed at Coolcraheen. Jasper's mother was close to Ellie Wolfe of Coolcraheen, 'my lifelong friend and companion'.

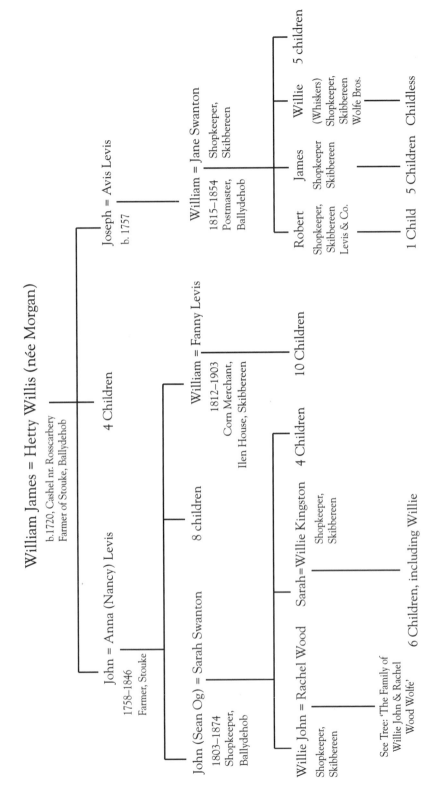

THE WOLFES OF BALLYDEHOB AND SKIBBEREEN

William James = Hetty Willis (née Morgan)
b.1720, Cashel nr. Rosscarbery
Farmer of Stouke, Ballydehob

John = Anna (Nancy) Levis
1758–1846
Farmer, Stouke

4 Children

Joseph = Avis Levis
b. 1757

John (Sean Og) = Sarah Swanton
1803–1874
Shopkeeper,
Ballydehob

8 children

William = Fanny Levis
1812–1903
Corn Merchant,
Ilen House, Skibbereen

10 Children

William = Jane Swanton
1815–1854
Postmaster,
Ballydehob

Willie John = Rachel Wood
Shopkeeper,
Skibbereen

Sarah = Willie Kingston
Shopkeeper,
Skibbereen

4 Children

See Tree: 'The Family of
Willie John & Rachel
Wood Wolfe'

6 Children, including Willie

Robert
Shopkeeper,
Skibbereen
Levis & Co.

1 Child

James
Shopkeeper,
Skibbereen

5 Children

Willie
(Whiskers)
Shopkeeper,
Skibbereen
Wolfe Bros.

Childless

5 children

Wolfes were thick on the ground In Skibbereen itself. They had all arrived within the previous two generations (most, like Jasper's father, from Ballydehob) hoping to better themselves. Like many other inhabitants of Ireland, they were usually up for a bit of excitement and were always ready to take a chance, and to move on if it seemed a good idea.

Jasper only had to look over the garden wall and there he might see another member of the sept. This would be a lugubrious-looking figure universally known as 'Willie Whiskers'. The gentleman in question, complete with a long straggly beard, was married but childless and ran a stationery, toy and knick-knack shop in Main Street known as 'Wolfe Bros'. It was from here that Jasper's birthday penknife and many other presents were bought. The 'Bros' referred to Willie Whiskers himself, Robert and James, although the latter two had departed to set up their own shops. Robert ran a drapery, 'Levis & Co', in the centre of town, which he had bought from his father-in-law. James owned a hardware shop up the street from Bridge House. Robert and James both had a number of children, all distant cousins of Jasper's. The brothers were recalled by one of their daughters as being 'very upright, honourable, dependable and hard-working', as well as being 'great readers'.

Willie Whiskers, Robert and James were three of the eight children of yet another William Wolfe of Ballydehob (fairly distant cousins of Jasper's father) and Jane Swanton from Gortnagrough House, Ballydehob. William had been postmaster in his home town and also did some farming. Unfortunately, he died at the early age of forty, dropping dead in a field from a heart attack. He left no will, just a destitute family. Normally, help from relations would have been forthcoming, but everyone, Swantons and Wolfes alike, looked the other way. Why? It looks as if Jane's first child was born well before she was married. Such transgressions were seldom forgiven, not least by the women in a family. Jane was left to cope on her own. She moved to Skibbereen (at about the same time as Jasper's father, Willie John) and set up a very modest shop in Bridge Street. Her last child was born after her husband's death and died aged three months. Jane lived to old age, her hair still glossy brown, wonderfully good looking, formidable, but certainly loved by at least some of her grandchildren.

Opposite James Wolfe's hardware shop in Bridge Street lived Jasper's aunt Jane, sister of Jasper's father Willie John and wife of William Kingston. Aunt Jane and Uncle William had four daughters and two sons, including Willie Kingston, all first cousins of Jasper's. The father of the family, William Kingston, was a delightful, gentle and kindly man. He ran what was, to begin with, a successful grocery and bakery business. He also hired out sidecars, covered cars and brakes. Unfortunately, allegedly prescribed whiskey for a weak stomach, he took to drinking. Well before midday, he could be found staggering upstairs to collapse drunk on his bed. His wife and daughters tried to cure the man of the family by buying patent drugs guaranteed to cure drunkenness and slipping them into his tea, but to no avail.

Jane, understandably, got very stressed. Fiery by nature, she frequently abused her husband. Her son Willie once saw her attack him, pulling a bottle of whiskey from his pocket and smashing it against the wall. As her temper worsened, the children suffered too. When angry with her sons, Jane Kingston would assault them with a whip. However, they usually managed to escape, hiding underneath the dining-room table or elsewhere. The storm would pass as quickly as it had erupted.

William Kingston's fortunes deteriorated until, when he died in agony of a 'twisted gut' (appendicitis), he was virtually bankrupt. Fortunately, the Kingstons were a resilient and resourceful family. With money running out, the eldest daughter, Daisy, started to take in pupils. Before long she was in great demand and set up a small school in some rooms in her uncle Willie John Wolfe's premises at Bridge House. In due course her three sisters joined her, and their 'Ladies' School' (which also took boys) thrived for years.

The final troops of Jasper's relations in Skibbereen lived just outside the town. At Ilen House was Jasper's great-uncle William, the successful corn merchant and devout Methodist who had helped his nephew, Jasper's father, get started as a shopkeeper. Nearby, at Grove House, was William's son John. Both these men were married with numbers of offspring, providing a further rich source of cousins for Jasper, some of whom overlapped with him in age. Even these, the most successful and prosperous of the Wolfes, had their own difficulties and tragedies. Of the children of William and his wife Fanny Levis, one died in infancy, a daughter became seriously deaf following scarlet fever as a teenager and lived at home all her life, while a third daughter, married with five children and living at Ballydehob, died early ('a lovely young mother', as Jasper's mother recorded).

Each extended family interacted with, overlapped with, and was almost inevitably multiply related to other such families in the locality. As far as the Wolfes were concerned, for generation after generation, some of the same names kept recurring in the family tree, in particular Swanton and Levis. Occasionally, if for instance a family came from the periphery of the usual marital catchment area, a new name, such as Wood, might be entered on the family honours list.

The Wolfes of Snugville had as close links with Rachel's Wood as with Willie John's Wolfe relations. Apart from his Wood grandparents, Jasper, his brothers and sisters saw most of two Wood cousins, Robert and Fannie, and their mother Ellie. These children were almost exactly the same age as Jasper. Their father, Tom Wood, Jasper's uncle and Rachel's brother, had married Ellen Swanton of Gortnagrough House, Ballydehob. On his marriage, Tom had taken over his father's farm at Seaview (which is when Big Billy moved to Kilkeran). Rachel had been close to Tom, the next youngest in the family. However, within three years of his marriage he died of typhoid. His widow, Ellie, with the help of a few workers, continued to run the Seaview farm.

Rachel did what she could for her nephew, niece and sister-in-law. They frequently dropped in, and sometimes stayed, at Snugville. Fannie even lived with the Wolfes for a while. She was probably, as Rachel had done, going to school in Skibbereen. However, Rachel found that carrying out this particular family duty was not without its challenges. Robert, a decent, straightforward, hard-working boy, she was very fond of ('we are very glad indeed to have Robert'). His older sister Fannie was a rather different matter. In fact, Rachel quite despaired of her:

> I have been thinking of how useless poor Fannie will be if she should grow up so slow and lazy as she is at present. I wish I could make a change. I fear I cannot train others to be smart and active . . . It irritates me to see a dull, stupid person. It is so much better to go through life with smartness, able to help others and make a home nice and comfortable, than to lie down in idleness and have untidy, careless habits, to make oneself disgusting all round.

Rachel also found her sister-in-law, Ellie, the children's mother, far from easy.

> I feel more than ever how I cannot get on with some people, no matter how much I try. It is the third or fourth time I have offended E. Wood without the least intending it. I have done my very best to help her. And somehow I know my efforts are not appreciated.

All these relatives were forever visiting and being visited: 'I had a visit from W. Wolfe of Schull'; 'Robert and Lizzie Wolfe [of Levis & Co., drapers] came down from town [to the Glandore cottage] after tea'. Rachel, perhaps driven by sons Willie and occasionally Jasper, would take a drive or walk to visit Fannie Wolfe, William's wife, at Ilen House, or Marion Wolfe, John's wife, at Grove House ('Had a lovely drive round the Grove'; 'walked to Ilen House, and spent about two hours there').

Rachel and her children also made longer visits, particularly to the unmarried Swanton brother and sister of Ellen Wood, who lived outside Ballydehob, at Fortview, near the main Swanton residence of Gortnagrough House ('Went to Fortview by car, Willie driving. Had a most enjoyable day and returned in safety'). The Snugville Wolfes also, on occasion, visited Fortview over Christmas ('May, Jasper and I had to go by train. Will came out after us. The boys as usual enjoyed themselves very much').

As well as all this, there was plenty of life at the holiday cottage at Glandore. A good deal of family activity seems to have involved preparing for departure, leaving, sorting things out once arrived and then returning: 'I prepared for Glandore. Fannie [Wood] packed up her things and we started at about 10.30. Will and I followed in the wagonette, with Daisy, Sarah [Kingstons] and May Levis.' Also on board was Minnie Vickery, about the same age as Jasper and one of a large Methodist family who lived just down the road from the Wolfes. On this occasion, as quite often happened, Jasper walked on ahead. He may well have preferred to do so, since he suffered all his life from various allergies, and horses probably caused an allergic reaction. Certainly, as an adult he was seldom seen near one.

From Glandore, there were frequent visits to the Wood grandparents at Kilkeran, and to see the Wood cousins at Seaview. On one such occasion, Rachel wrote in her diary: 'Robert Wood was here for May, and after tea we sent May, Jasper and Jackson with him to Seaview'; the Wolfe children spent the night at Seaview and the next day they were collected by Willie. A merry family evening followed at Glandore: 'We stayed up until 11 o'clock, and had such a pleasant time. The boys are getting more entertaining as they grow older.' Altogether, Glandore was much enjoyed by Jasper and the rest of the family: 'The cottage at Glandore is a great boon to the children.'

Finally, outings of one sort or another, as a rule involving an assortment of cousins and friends, featured prominently in the social calendar. Sunday School trips were large-scale affairs; one photograph shows fourteen accompanying adults, all dressed up to the nines. Castlefreke was a favourite destination, and conveniently close to the Woods at Kilkeran. The nearest, and so most frequent spot for Wolfe days out was Tragumna ('We went to the strand and met the Kingstons there. How happy we would be now but for W. J.'s health'). Another time, Annie Wolfe – either the deaf daughter from Ilen House or the wife of Willie Whiskers, both called Annie Wolfe – was in the party. At 'Trag', as it was popularly known, men and women bathed on separate beaches, the men naked. It was a great moment when Willie, Jasper and the other boys were able to leave the children and the ladies' beach and join the gentlemen. Lough Ine was another favourite.

> I got Mike [servant] to drive the children, Ellie [servant] and me to Lough Ine. There we picked blackberries, had tea, and I read some of Miss Yonge's book [*Dynevor Terrace*]. I enjoyed this quiet evening in the open air, and was glad to have such a place to take the children to; it cannot but educate their tastes and give them a love of nature. It may be that in after life they will look back on these days spent blackberrying with mother with pleasure and a wish for innocent pleasures.

So Jasper grew up in a climate where there was much to do and enjoy, but always against a background of various sudden or continuing disasters. These, however, were simply taken as part of the natural order of things. A few people went under, but the majority got on with life as best they could and enjoyed it when and where possible. Neither blame nor self-reproach, and certainly not self-pity, featured much in the psychology of the Methodist Anglo-Irish in West Cork. Jasper would not have been explicitly taught how to deal with life, but, as children do, he undoubtedly observed, marked and inwardly digested. Like many others of his generation, he learned to be self-reliant, uncomplaining and ready to have a good time whenever the opportunity presented itself. Perhaps most important of all, he recognised that to survive, and if possible prosper, you had to get on with people, stand by your relatives and friends and maintain good contacts.

7

TRIBES

As a Wolfe and a Methodist, Jasper belonged to the tribe of Anglo-Irish Protestants. However, despite being comfortable within his ancestral skin, what really attracted and fascinated him was that other, and considerably larger tribe, the Catholic Gaels. With them he felt an affinity, and perhaps even a sort of kinship.

Growing up in Skibbereen, Jasper would have been in contact with the Catholic Irish from his very earliest days. To begin with, like almost all Protestant children, he lived in close proximity to the Irish servants who worked in and around the house. Ellie was in Snugville every day, went on outings with the family, stayed at the Glandore cottage and was part of the general set-up. Similarly, Mick Walsh was ever-present, helping in the garden, carrying Willie John or pushing him in his bath chair, catching the horses, driving and maintaining the 'cars', looking after the animals and doing every imaginable sort of outside job.

Jasper left no record of his experiences, but fortunately his younger cousin, Willie Kingston, did. Willie was brought up in very similar circumstances to Jasper and his memoirs give a very good idea of what life for a small boy growing up in a Protestant/Catholic world must have been like. He recalls:

> a dirty old woman, known as Kitty Pheasant, who used to get free dinners in the kitchen, and I remember gleefully leaving the dining-room for the kitchen, there to be fed by her with potatoes peeled with her nails, and pieces of meat torn off with her dirty hands . . . it was during this period that the maids used to terrify and subdue me by tales of spooks and ghosts, to which grown-ups added tales of a like nature.

Once he was able to go about town on his own or with companions, Jasper would certainly have encountered Catholic boys. On such occasions it was customary, provided nothing much else was going on, to exchange ritual insults. The Catholic gang would call out:

> Proddy waddy greenguts, never said a prayer,
> Catch him by the long legs, and throw him down the stair.

Similarly, the Protestants lads would shout:

> Catholic, Catholic, go to Mass,
> Riding upon your old jackass.

Protestant and Catholic boys also engaged in hostilities at rugby. Here, having far fewer numbers to call on, the Protestants almost invariably lost. At one time they suffered particularly badly due to the ruthless and frequently illegal activities of a particularly rough member of the Catholic team. Finally, a formal complaint was made to the Catholics and the boy was removed. Furious with his own people for not standing by him, he accepted an invitation to play for the Protestants and created havoc among his former teammates. A draw, which could hardly have been described as honourable, was achieved.

Jasper would also have known of more serious tensions. There were a few in Skibbereen who were implacably opposed to any sort of British presence in Ireland. A man who was to become one of the iconic Republican leaders, Jeremiah O'Donovan Rossa, was well known to Jasper's father. O'Donovan Rossa, who was descended from a family that had been displaced by English planters, had settled in Skibbereen; he had been brought up near Rosscarbery, not far from the Woods' Knockfeen farm at Seaview. Shortly after the Famine, O'Donovan Rossa set up an agricultural and seed business on Bridge Street immediately opposite the Wolfe premises at Bridge House. In short order, he founded the Phoenix Society (a sort of nationalist debating society), then signed up to the Irish Republican Brotherhood and took part in guerrilla training so as to be ready for revolt against British rule. When he was arrested for a few months he had to close his shop, but he subsequently reopened for trade a short distance away. His life as a Fenian, his trial, time spent in gaol and years of American exile belong to history, but O'Donovan Rossa's ideas of revolutionary republicanism continued to pulse through many hearts and minds in Skibbereen – if with varying strength and with unpredictable results.[1]

Normally, the inhabitants of Skibbereen got on with each other more or less peaceably. However, it was not unheard of for voices to be raised and fists to be shaken. Shortly after the Wolfes moved to Snugville a riot erupted in Bridge Street. The turbulence, as often happened, had blown in from the agricultural world. In 1879 wet weather, crop failures and falling prices had threatened financial disaster for multitudes of small landholders. In this crisis, an elderly landlord from near Clonakilty, William Bence Jones, had caused hardship and outrage by raising the rents of his tenant farmers to impossible levels. A local parish priest, John O'Leary, led the opposition. Amongst other things, he published a series of influential articles in London journals attacking Bence Jones in particular and Irish landlordism in general. Bence Jones, a month before the Skibbereen riot, responded in kind, writing his own attack on O'Leary. The tenantry then organised a boycott, as a result of which their landlord soon found himself unable to secure income, or indeed the general necessities of life.

During this spot of bother, a 'menial' of Bence Jones arrived in Skibbereen, which seemed a safe distance from Clonakilty, to obtain supplies. Having managed to get what he wanted, he called in at a local public house for refreshment, but, unfortunately for him, he was recognised. And attacked.

Jasper, if he had been watching from his father's shop, would have seen people rushing down Bridge Street towards Main Street to alert the police. Shortly after, from their barracks on the other side of town, the Royal Irish Constabulary, perhaps three or four in number, uniformed, with truncheons at the ready and trotting as fast as dignity allowed, would have come into view making their way towards the fight. The main action was just out of sight of Bridge House, up the street and around the corner, where the fighting was growing ever fiercer. Even 'the gay and pretty ones', reported the *Cork Examiner*, joined in. One who had her head cracked open by a policeman seized his baton and gave it as a souvenir to the doctor who treated her. Eventually, order was restored. It is believed that William Bence Jones did not get his supplies. He died a few months later.[2]

More organised agitation, both peaceful and violent, was on the way. Land Reform was rapidly moving to the top of the Irish agricultural and political agenda. An early sign of this in Skibbereen was the formation of a local branch of the National Land League, which had been founded a couple of years previously in 1879. Soon after the Bence Jones riot, a vast inaugural rally was held on the Fair Field, just behind the Methodist church and adjacent to the Church of Ireland church. In contrast to the earlier events, this was a relatively tranquil occasion. The *Eagle*[3], although generally loyalist in its sympathies, was quite capable of taking an unprejudiced, even sympathetic attitude towards Irish nationalist aspirations. On this occasion, having failed to report the earlier disturbance, it pulled out the stops for the Land League rally. As ever, when it was a question of demanding reforms, it seemed that local priests and neighbouring rural people were in the vanguard of proceedings: 'Father McCartie's devoted brass band played sweetly . . . while romantic Leap won the admiration of the populace by a three hundred strong muster of some of the finest specimens of bold peasantry.'

THE BISHOP'S SCHOOL

Where should Jasper go to school? His parents, like nearly all Nonconformists, took education very seriously indeed. 'What a boon it is to be properly educated, and refined, and cultured', mused Rachel. However, when it came to finding a suitable secondary school, which in principle should have been, if not specifically Methodist, then at least Protestant, there were difficulties. Normally, the educational free market in Skibbereen could be relied on to come up with an acceptable establishment, but unfortunately, as Jasper approached his early teens, there was very little on offer. Earlier, Mr Sproule's Collegiate School had flourished and, before long, Mr Longmore, succeeded by Mr Storey, would run classes in the old Methodist schoolroom. After that would come the Miss Kingstons' Ladies' School. But in the early 1880s there was virtually nothing.

So, what to do? The obvious answer was to look further afield. Willie was already attending St Fachtna's College at Rosscarbery, so clearly it might have made sense for Jasper to join his brother there. However, since Willie had become a pupil, the Wolfes had begun to have doubts about St Fachtna's. The old head, or 'the Master' as he was known, the Reverend James O'Callaghan, kindly, scholarly and much loved, had retired. His successor came and went in a year. The next in that post lasted longer. Nevertheless, the school now started a slow downward slide, which eventually was to end in closure.

However, the real difficulty for the Wolfes was not so much the state of the college, as its ethos. The current Master was a high church man, educated at Keble College, Oxford. He appears to have seen himself as carrying the flag of St George in an outpost of the empire. The college's pupils were predominantly offspring of the Anglo-Irish gentry and its curriculum was mainly geared to preparing boys for entry to institutions and careers in England. A later prospectus made things fairly clear. The college offered 'a sound preparatory education, more especially for English schools; . . . preparation for the universities, professions, civil service; a few pupils may read for Sandhurst and militia preliminary exams'.[1]

Jasper's father, in particular, was emphatic that he wanted his children, first and foremost, to grow up as Irish men and women. He did not want them to be encouraged to look towards a future across the Irish Sea. When he and

Rachel discussed their family he spelled out his wishes. 'He warned me', she wrote in her diary, 'never allow the children to leave Ireland if I was spared longer than him. He said he would leave provision for them so that they may be able to live at home in comfort.'

It was, eventually, exams, and one exam in particular, which decided matters. Until very recently, the question of examinations for their offspring had not much troubled the minds of Protestant parents. They did their best to leave whatever land, business and capital they might be fortunate enough to possess distributed as helpfully as possible amongst their children. This was the policy of Rachel's parents. If a father wanted to find some salaried or professional position for a son, then he used what influence he had to secure what was desired.

Now, however, a great change was taking place. The British, tardily following the example of the Germans and the French, were introducing open competitive examinations for entry to higher education, and to a whole range of professions. The age of meritocracy was approaching and, as they swiftly realised, amongst the greatest potential beneficiaries would be the middle and lower middle classes. Here were self-respecting, hard-working people who had struggled to climb up from, indeed sometimes even to stay in, the world to which they had been born. Now, if they had the ability and money was provided to fund their studies, young men (and in due course a few young women) could make lucrative and prestigious careers for themselves.

In Ireland, the key which opened entry to this new world of opportunity was the prosaically named Intermediate (secondary) exam. This had been established in 1878 by an Act of Parliament, with its own board and rules for qualifying schools. It was mainly paid for by funds released by the disestablishment of the Church of Ireland. Any candidate passing this exam would qualify to apply for university or professional courses.

In Skibbereen, the Catholic Church, which in Ireland took education very seriously indeed, was quick to seize this opportunity. Dr FitzGerald, Bishop of Ross, founded a school, the main purpose of which was to prepare boys for this new exam and for exams which secured entry to universities and professional courses. The school, even though the first, short-lived head was a disaster, rapidly proved to be a great success.

The Wolfes now faced a difficult decision. They were hardly in a position to ignore what exam success could offer. While Willie was looked after, as he was destined to inherit the shop, there were still two other boys and two girls to provide for. The farm at Licknavar, even though the Wolfes were only tenants, could probably give a living for one son, or perhaps a daughter, but that was just about it. At least some of the children, whatever Willie John's hopes of enabling his children to 'live at home in comfort', would in fact have to make their own way in life – or live as rather impoverished dependants.

And so it was that Willie John and Rachel contemplated sending Jasper to the Bishop's School. In nearly every way it provided all they wanted. It was on the doorstep, it was rooted in the Irish world and, above all, it trained pupils, with excellent results, for the Intermediate exam. There was just one problem: the school was Catholic. In other times, or in other places, for a Protestant to attend such an institution might have been out of the question. But not so in the Skibbereen of the 1880s. The truth was that neither the Catholics nor the Church of Ireland nor the Methodists (though they were rather less competitive) had been able to establish themselves locally as undisputed religious champions. One consequence of this was that none of the denominations was able to control its followers as tightly as it would have liked.

Amongst the liberties enjoyed, and on occasion taken, by the citizens of Skibbereen was the freedom to choose where to educate their children, irrespective of religious affiliation. A few years before the Wolfes entered the educational market place, Skibbereen had boasted a Protestant, but no Catholic, secondary school. Then Sproule's Collegiate School was well attended by Catholics. Now the tables were turned. Although there was still only one secondary school, this time it was Catholic. The Wolfes, with just one or two other local Protestant families, swallowed their religious reservations and entered their son for the Bishop's School. As was to happen so often with the middle classes, belief in the value of education trumped most other principles.

Jasper definitely wanted to go to the Bishop's School (or the University and Intermediate School, as it came to be known). His parents may even have taken his wishes into account. Every morning Jasper would leave Snugville and walk through the centre of town, up North Street, to the school. On the crest of a low rise just above North Street stood St Patrick's Cathedral (technically, the Pro-Cathedral), which overlooked both Prospect House – the bishop's palace, a long, low, elegant building – and the adjacent Bishop's School. Jasper had passed this way many, many times before, for instance when on his way to visit his Wood grandparents or to stay at the holiday cottage in Glandore, but now he was not simply passing by. For the first time, he was entering the world of the Catholic Gaelic Irish and leaving behind his Anglo-Irish, Protestant tribe.

As Jasper approached the school, he would have been accompanied by a good number of younger children. These entered the substantial main entrance to attend the National School, which was housed on the ground floor. The school had originally been built in the early years of the Famine, at the instigation of the then administrator (in effect, the parish priest). The building, as no doubt was intended, appeared solid and imposing, although, from the outside at least, it looked rather more like a gaol than an educational establishment. This was because all its windows were covered with wire netting. These defences had proved necessary because evidently not everyone loved and respected the place as no doubt they should have. The problem, as one former pupil of the Bishop's School later recalled, was caused by 'the stone-throwing proclivities of evil disposed mischief-makers, big and small'.

Jasper and the other boys of the Bishop's School did not enter through the main door but had instead to go round the side of the building and climb two external flights of stone steps to their classroom on the first floor. This was the only way in, as there were no internal stairs in the school. It was generally believed that the architect had simply forgotten to have them built. However, from the pupils' point of view there was a great compensation. The external stairs had a polished iron safety rail, down which it was possible to slide.

The teachers at the Bishop's School – both of them – knew their trade. The principal was Edmond L. Hogan, 'one of the best teachers I ever met', one old boy commented. He taught Latin, Greek, French, English and History (including Irish history). To keep discipline (and the boys could reduce a class to anarchy and chaos if they were given half a chance), he relied on personality and a vicious tongue. He was also the sort of natural pedant who takes pleasure in forever correcting the pupils' errors of speech. 'He was delighted when one gave him an opening to give a lesson in the use of "will" and "shall". If a pupil asked, "Will I do so and so?" he sarcastically answered, "I am sure I do not know. I do not know what you intend to do."'

Mr Hogan was assisted by Daniel Emmet McCarthy, a very different character, though he also was remembered as 'a very good teacher'. Mr McCarthy looked after the science and practical subjects, teaching mathematics, physics, hygiene, animal physiology and navigation. To aid him in his work, Mr McCarthy built a little laboratory. His lessons could be remarkably memorable. Not many forgot his story about the wounded Canadian soldier who had a hole blown in his stomach through which the experts could watch the process of digestion of all kinds of food, from tripe to pork. Mr McCarthy's approach to discipline was physical rather than psychological. He was abusive and personally rude, he used his fists and he beat the boys frequently and hard. However, when the larger and older boys sometimes answered him back, massive slanging matches could blow up. Mr McCarthy did not necessarily always win.

For a brief period, a part-time teacher, Mr Harrington of the Young Men's Society, was employed to prepare boys for the Intermediate exam in Irish. However, 'the classes died of inanition'.

Jasper's fellow pupils came from a variety of very different backgrounds. First, and most numerous, were sons of the emerging Catholic middle class. Religion apart, these boys mostly came from families with aspirations and values not very different from those of Jasper himself. The parents often were descended from small tenant farmers and were now making a living in trade or similar occupations. Next there were able boys from more or less poor rural backgrounds who had been spotted by their teachers in National School as having potential. And finally, there were the few Protestants, in the main like Jasper, from the 'merchant' class.

It would hardly have struck a visitor seeing the handful of unruly boys jostling their way towards the school building that this group was intended to form a future elite, but so it was, and indeed so it worked out. They certainly more than met the first characteristic of an elite: there were precious few of them. Throughout Ireland hardly more than five per cent of children attended secondary school. As for West Cork, the Bishop's School was the only establishment systematically preparing students for the Intermediate exam. In the year that Jasper sat the exam, just five West Cork candidates passed, all from the Bishop's School. In later life, many of the old boys duly progressed to successful careers. The sons of the middle classes mostly went on to become lawyers, doctors, civil servants and businessmen; and the boys from the country, whose families could not afford to pay for professional training, predominantly went into the Church, where they often enjoyed distinguished careers. Many of these men and others like them were in positions of local influence when the great crises of Irish history erupted in the early twentieth century.

Two of Jasper's fellow pupils were to be of particular significance in his life. Jim Burke came from the rising Catholic middle class. An odd shambling figure with a squeaky voice and endlessly talkative, he was astonishingly clever. In due course he was called to the bar, winning a top scholarship and subsequently, with his brothers and other family members, becoming highly influential in the life of Skibbereen.

While Jasper knew Jim Burke well, he was hardly friendly with him – in fact, the two were to be rivals – but it was very different with Florence McCarthy. From the start, he and Jasper hit it off. Florence, the son of a small tenant farmer from near Clonakilty, was one of those bright country boys whom the Catholic Church had earmarked for great things. Strongly built, handsome and charismatic, he stood out as a natural leader. He was just the sort of son that devout Irish mothers from poor backgrounds prayed would honour (and advance) their families by becoming a priest. Florence went on to attend Maynooth and to be ordained. For neither Jasper nor 'Father Mac', as he became known, were their differing religions ever the slightest hindrance to their lifelong close friendship.

The boys at the Bishop's School were passionate about politics and sport. This was just before the dramatic flowering of Gaelic games, which occurred in West Cork and elsewhere from the late 1880s on (the Skibbereen branch of the Gaelic Athletics Association was founded at a meeting in the Town Hall on 8 November 1887). So, for the lads of the Bishop's School it was cricket and handball in the summer and rugby in the winter. However, bowling took place throughout the year, and it was this which really stirred the blood. The favourite course was along the road beside the railway line leading north out of the town. Whether, like their elders, the boys placed bets is not recorded, but, like their elders, they certainly did quarrel and fight: 'bitter were the rivalries, and many were the acrimonious discussions and disputes that took place about scores and marks'. And those are the words of a man who later became a 'distinguished ecclesiastic'. The highlight of the bowling year was May Day. On this originally pagan festival the boys took their iron bowls and, in defiance of law, order, shopkeepers, shoppers and the Royal Irish Constabulary itself, bowled through the streets of Skibbereen. In practice, however, the whole affair was probably indistinguishable from the various minor affrays which were a more or less normal part of daily life.

The really serious action, however, was to be found in politics. Jasper's time at the Bishop's School coincided with the tremendous upsurge of the Land Reform and Home Rule movements. In 1879 Charles Stewart Parnell had taken over the leadership of the Irish Party in the House of Commons. Already popular in Ireland, and hated in England for his hard-headed pursuit of Irish interests, he rapidly became 'the Chief', 'the uncrowned king of Ireland'. As the agricultural crisis of the early 1880s erupted, Parnell was also appointed president of Michael Davitt's newly founded Land League. In rapid succession there followed the election of a Liberal government under William Gladstone, ever more violent rural agitation, the stick of a Coercion Act and the carrot of the 1881 Land Act. However, hayricks still blazed, evictions continued and killings did not cease. Irish anger, suffering and resentment could not be instantly dissolved by panaceas from Westminster. Gladstone held Parnell responsible for the violence and had him arrested and put in Kilmainham Gaol. As predicted by Parnell and others, his place was taken by 'Captain Moonlight' (as various secret, violent groups of Land Reformers were collectively known), and the outrages, far from easing up, increased. After a few months Parnell and Gladstone agreed the 'Kilmainham Treaty', Parnell was released, the Land War ended and the two leaders agreed to forward 'principles and measures for general reform'.

However, as so often is the case, good intentions were scuppered, and rapidly, by the events that followed. Four days after Parnell left gaol (2 May 1882), Lord Frederick Cavendish, the new Irish Chief Secretary, nephew and trusted cabinet colleague of Gladstone's, together with T. H. Burke, the head of the Irish civil service, were walking in Phoenix Park, Dublin, when they were approached and murdered by a group of ex-Fenians known as 'The Invincibles'. Despite Parnell's denunciation of the killings, the British government introduced a new Coercion Act. Although both Irish and mainland politics now drifted, the Representation of the People Act of 1884, which nearly quadrupled the Irish electorate, greatly enhanced Parnell's power. The general election of 1885 gave the Nationalists 86 seats and the balance of power at Westminster. The next year Gladstone, now convinced that only a measure of self-government could bring real peace to Ireland, introduced his first Home Rule Bill. With its defeat vanished the last realistic opportunity for a generation of securing a constitutional settlement of the Irish question.

In Skibbereen, the pupils of the Bishop's School were high on politics, and there was very little dissension. Most, including Jasper, were in the Nationalist camp. 'We were', wrote Jim Burke many years later, 'enthusiastic Parnellites. We were saturated with Davis, Mitchel, and Speeches from the Dock'. Apart from absorbing themselves in the history of the struggles for Irish liberty, Jim

Burke, Jasper and the rest were able to keep up with current events in the press. From the *Skibbereen Eagle*, through the *Cork Constitution* and the *Cork Examiner*, to Dublin's *Freeman's Journal* and the London *Times*, the boys could follow events blow by – often literal – blow. With the exception of the Nationalist *Freeman's Journal*, these papers reported what was happening from a Protestant viewpoint. However, the coverage was astonishingly detailed and it was perfectly possible to winnow out bias, or indeed to see things in the light of one's own beliefs. All this must have done wonders for the pupils' skills in literacy and textual analysis.

The boys were avid attenders, and at times participators, in meetings. On one occasion, a couple of years after Jasper had left, the Bishop's School pupils even went as a group to a meeting in the Town Hall. This had been called to condemn Parnell, after the Nationalist Party had split when his affair with Kitty O'Shea became public knowledge. The boys, however, were, without exception, full-blooded Parnellites. There were many others of a similar persuasion present and matters got fairly lively. The Bishop's School contingent, amongst others, made their presence felt by loud interruptions. Although 'severely censured' and threatened with expulsion, they all survived.

The masters of the Bishop's School, too, became actively involved in the Nationalist cause. From the beginning, Mr McCarthy was a highly visible Parnellite and 'took a prominent part in the land agitation'. If there was a Nationalist meeting, or a confrontation with evicting landlords, or any gathering to challenge the powers of the ascendancy, he would be there, a 'powerfully built man, with a rude exterior, ready with his fists, and by no means afraid of the police in stormy times'.

Mr Hogan, on the other hand, was initially rather cautious in his support of Parnell and the Land League. As a member of the rising bourgeoisie and an elitist, he had little natural sympathy for the small farmers and labourers of the countryside. He despised the lads in the school who came from struggling rural homes and was never short of 'quips and sneers at the farmers . . . nor ever in want of a gibe at the expense of some country boy about the League'. He also had to worry about the attitude of the Catholic hierarchy. He was dependent upon the Bishop of Ross for his job, and Dr FitzGerald, like almost all of the Church's leaders in Ireland and throughout Europe, was deeply anxious about any movement with a gleam of republican or revolutionary fervour in its eyes.

However, for reasons which were never revealed, Mr Hogan eventually emerged as a Parnellite. In the general election of 1885 the Nationalist candidate for South Cork (Skibbereen's constituency) was a certain Dr Kenny. He was introduced for the first time at a huge meeting of the Land League at Drimoleague. A large contingent of boys from the Bishop's School attended the great occasion. To their absolute amazement, who should they see, prominent on the platform and 'decked out in a voluminous green and gold scarf', but Mr Hogan himself. Nothing was said by anyone, but from that day on the principal's taunting of country boys and the Land League entirely ceased.[2]

So, how did Jasper, as a Home Rule enthusiast, fit into all this? Actually, very comfortably. Supporting Parnell was not unnatural for a boy with Anglo-Irish origins. After all, the great leader was a Protestant, even a landlord; nor was he a one-off. He belonged to a great tradition of Protestants who had advocated, and sometimes fought for, the liberty of the Irish people. From Wolfe Tone and Robert Emmet onwards, there had always been free-thinking radicals of settler origin who had identified themselves with the sufferings and aspirations of the Irish nation.

Jasper had few, if any, problems with his fellow pupils. Amongst the boys there was little religious or ethnic intolerance. In their attitudes, they reflected an outlook shared with many of their elders. In and around Skibbereen, numbers of the Anglo-Irish had come to believe not only that the Irish tenant farmers deserved a better deal, but that Ireland, in some form or other, could not in justice be denied a greater control over its own affairs. As for Skibbereen Catholics, many recognised that at least some local Protestants were men and women of goodwill. Several of the leading figures fighting the evils of the Famine had been Protestants, such as the Church of Ireland vicar the Reverend Richard Boyle Townsend, who visited the sick and dying without cease and himself perished of famine fever; and such as Jasper's distant relative, James H. Swanton. These men, and others like them, were no more forgotten in Skibbereen than those ascendancy landlords who exploited their privileged positions.

For all the tensions and injustices in Irish society, in Skibbereen at this time there was a degree of mutual tolerance amongst many Protestants and Catholics and a slowly growing sense of shared citizenship. These were values to which Jasper, and most of those educated at the Bishop's School, would remain committed, whatever the difficulties, throughout their lives.

PART TWO

'ALL WEST CORK FOR HIS CLIENT'
1888–1915

9

Solicitor's Apprentice

When Jasper reached sixteen, a great deal began to change for him, and for his family. There was one particular crisis which shadowed and distorted everything else. It seemed that Willie John, although he had ups as well as downs, was deteriorating. Rachel was very worried: 'I scarcely saw W. J. looking so very feeble, and evidently suffering. I do not think he can hold out much longer . . . He thinks he is nearly at the end of his journey . . . Poor Papa is failing fast.'

How to keep the shop running, on which the Wolfes' livelihood mainly depended, was becoming a very serious concern. The family found themselves having to spend hours and hours keeping things going. 'Jasper and Will', their mother reported, 'worked hard in the shop today'. Rachel herself had always lent a hand when necessary, but now she spent more and more time on the business. So, for example, she dealt with preparing the pig meat which was sold in the shop. Pigs were kept and slaughtered on the farm and from there Rachel took over: 'After tea went to the shop to attend to the salting and cutting of two pigs. I spent two very busy hours there . . . After breakfast I went sausage filling, and had all finished by two o'clock. I felt quite done up, and as tired as ever I could be.' And she had to deal with customers: 'I went to the market, and then stayed in the shop until it was nearly one. Then I came and got a drink for Will' – who was just catching measles – 'and went back and stayed until teatime. I worked hard at the desk, and took over £40.'

But things could not carry on like this. To make matters worse, the shop assistant for several years, Johnny Roycroft, left to set up on his own, a common problem, so steps had to be taken to replace him. Another assistant, Mr Bustard, was appointed. Rachel had initial reservations about him – 'Somehow I feel a little doubtful. May I be mistaken'. Fortunately, she was.

The key question, however, was who should take overall responsibility for the business? There was only one possible solution: Willie would have to take charge as soon as possible. He was the eldest son and, although he was only just seventeen, he was bright and capable and already understood quite well how things were managed. With help from his parents, and quite possibly Mr Bustard, he should soon be able to take over the reins.

In earlier generations, Willie would no doubt have thought of himself, even though the circumstances were unhappy, as very fortunate, a young man who had drawn one of life's long straws. He was set to take over a successful business, a good name and a respected position in the town. He looked, to the world as it then was, made for life. Always provided that he did not, for whatever reason, manage to scuttle his inheritance. There was only one problem: Willie himself was not best pleased. For him, as for others of his background and generation, various prospects for making one's way in the world were opening up. He enjoyed his academic work and would have liked to pursue his studies, possibly training for a profession. However, the bottom line was he had no choice. He had to leave St Fachtna's, return to live at home full time and settle down to making sure that the family stayed solvent.

Next, the family's living arrangements had to be dealt with. Not only was room getting tight, even in the spacious Snugville, but relations between Willie and Jasper and their mother were already strained. For them all to remain under the same roof did not seem a particularly clever idea, and so it was decided that the two older boys would now live above the shop. Rachel made the necessary arrangements: 'I got paper ready for the boys' room in Bridge House . . . I had a man to paper the boys' room.'

Willie John's illness was raising yet further difficulties. Was it sensible, was it even practicable, to have an apparently dying man, with heavy-duty nursing needs, in the same house as younger children? In the end, only Jackson remained at home full time. May and Winnie were sent away to board in the Ladies' College on Jersey. This establishment was attractive to Rachel because it was originally a Methodist foundation. The girls, initially at least, were less enthusiastic. They found the long sea journeys a nightmare and missed Ireland. Nevertheless, the two settled down. Winnie was an average pupil, causing little excitement or trouble. May, on the other hand, who was nearly sixteen when she arrived, shone. She was, the school reported, the brightest girl they had ever had there. Unfortunately, all the relevant academic records were destroyed during the Nazi occupation of the Channel Islands, so the truth of this family story cannot be confirmed. There is no doubt, however, that May, like her mother, grew up to be an exceptionally intelligent woman.

Jasper meanwhile was picking his way, unobtrusively but purposefully, through the evolving dramas of family life. His main concern, and one shared with his parents, was what should he do with his future? Careers guidance was not on the curriculum of the Bishop's School. However, almost immediately opposite was the courthouse. Here, Justices of the Peace held petty sessions and a judge (unlike in England) presided over quarter sessions. All the proceedings were open to the public and, as Jim Burke later recalled, boys from the school across the road, including Jasper, often 'stole into court to gaze in awe on County Court Judge Ferguson robed in wig and gown'.

Jasper decided that he wanted to become a lawyer, or, more specifically, a solicitor. A necessary first step was to pass his Intermediate exam. He was, to his mother's considerable surprise, well thought of at school. When she went to pay Mr Hogan she was, as she put it, 'shocked to hear Mr Hogan's opinion of Jasper' ('amazed' is the equivalent word today). 'What a blessing', she added, 'when boys so conduct themselves as to gain the good opinion of all with whom they come in contact'. In June Jasper took his exams and the results came through at the end of August. He had safely passed, although, unlike his cousin Daisy Kingston and Jim Burke, he did not win any of the official exhibitions or prizes that were on offer.

Next, Jasper needed to be accepted as an apprentice in a solicitor's office. Until quite recently the leading firm in Skibbereen had been that of Timothy McCarthy Downing, MP. This gentleman, described as 'lynx-eyed, wiry, keen, made of steel, with an eye like an eagle, and a face that was the terror of equivocating witnesses',[1] had successfully plugged into virtually all the local power circuits. Building on the foundations of his successful legal practice he became a Justice of the Peace and entered the world of politics as Nationalist Member of Parliament for South Cork. He also allied himself with the local Catholic gentry when one of his daughters married Florence McCarthy, JP, of Glencurragh House, a member of the brewing and landowning dynasty. He acquired, too, a clutch of influential local posts, becoming first chairman of the Town Commissioners and Deputy Lieutenant of County Cork. Finally, he was an active member of the Catholic Church, earning the enduring gratitude of the hierarchy when, on his death, he bequeathed his residence, Prospect House, as a palace for the Bishops of Ross.

The practice, and to a large extent the mantle, of McCarthy Downing was inherited by his partner. Thomas Downes was also a very distinguished personage and it was quite helpful, at least in some people's eyes, that he bore a marked resemblance to the Prince of Wales, later Edward VII. Like his predecessor, he became one of the leading citizens in Skibbereen. He too was appointed chairman of the Town Commissioners and there were few local undertakings which he was not well placed to influence: he was a governor and founder of the Baltimore Fishery School, solicitor to the Schull and Skibbereen Tramway Company and a commissioner of the Skibbereen and Baltimore Harbour Company. He also enjoyed considerable reflected glamour from his wife, who was a granddaughter of Daniel O'Connell, the Liberator.

It was Mr Downes whom Jasper's parents now approached about taking their son on as an apprentice. Evidently neither side was in the least concerned about the religious difference between the Wolfes and the solicitor and it was agreed, in principle, that Jasper would be taken on, provided of course the usual fee was paid. However, before Jasper could start work, he had to pass his Law Society preliminary exam, which required a visit to Dublin. In October 1888, accompanied by his mother, Jasper set out. The journey was not uneventful. From Cork the carriage, as Rachel recorded in her diary, was 'bad', since one gentleman insisted on smoking. Dublin itself turned out to be full of crowds attending the Kildare races and it was only with the greatest difficulty that Rachel and Jasper managed to find places on a bus. However, eventually they reached Ballard's, their hotel.

The next day, having been bought a new coat by his mother, Jasper went to the Four Courts to sit the first of two days of exams. Rachel, meanwhile, spent her time shopping and visiting the Mount Jerome cemetery to look for the graves of friends, mostly without any luck. A few weeks later the exam results arrived in Skibbereen. Rachel was friendly with a family called the Deanes, who had been near neighbours of the Woods at Seaview. Various Deanes had gone into law and it was Bob Deane who sent a telegram from Dublin to report that Jasper had passed.

Jasper was very pleased with himself and his results. His mother, however, felt ambivalent. She was relieved that Jasper had secured the opportunity of enjoying a successful future, but law was far from being her first choice. She would much have preferred her boy to become a Methodist minister (like one of the sons of the Governor, James H. Swanton). She had strong moral reservations both about the legal profession and about her son's character. When the news of Jasper's exam success came through, she wrote in her diary: 'This will influence his whole life for good or evil. God grant', she added darkly, 'it may be for good'. A few weeks later, as he left to sign his indentures and start work, she commented: 'in five years he will be finished, if it be God's will to spare him. I fear the temptations will be very great. I often think how much more noble to proclaim the gospel than to plead in a Law Court.'

Jasper, together with Willie, now settled down to life above the shop in Bridge House. While Willie only slowly came to terms with having to be his father's successor, Jasper was in his element. He took to the legal life like a bird to the air, receiving an excellent training in the Downes practice. Then, shortly after Christmas 1893, he departed for Dublin to study for his final law exam. The finals, when they came, opened with a nasty surprise. One of the first papers was a French unseen, which began with the phrase, 'Au commencement des siècles' (literally, 'at the beginning of the centuries'). 'Siècles', as it happened, was not a word which featured in the French vocabulary taught at the Bishop's School, so Jasper guessed it meant 'vehicles', and his translation started, 'When vehicles were in their infancy'. He managed, however, to ensure that the rest of the piece made sense. Unfortunately, not the right sense.

Luckily, it turned out that the examiners did not consider a fluent command of French to be an essential qualification for a budding solicitor (although in this they were partly mistaken, as many years later Jasper had to deal with some French-speaking fishermen in court and his daughter Dorothy was employed as an interpreter). In fact, Jasper's unsatisfactory attempt at translation seems to have been entirely overlooked, for he secured first place in the finals, together with the award of a gold medal and a scholarship. Since he was in competition with ambitious young men from all over Ireland, many educated at rather more prestigious establishments than the Bishop's School, this was a remarkable, and largely unexpected, achievement.

10

J. TRAVERS WOLFE & CO.

Willie John fought his illness every inch of the way and survived far longer than anyone expected. Until the very end he insisted on being wheeled to the shop in his bath chair every day. His nephew, Willie Kingston, remembers seeing him 'very grey in the face, his clothes powdered with flour and meal'. Eventually, what he officially died of was pneumonia. The actual complaint could not be diagnosed at the time, but the various symptoms suggest it was multiple sclerosis.

Willie John at least had the comfort of knowing that, by his and Rachel's efforts, he was leaving behind him a family properly provided for and well able to face the future. Jasper, having won his gold medal, appeared to be all set for a successful legal career and Willie was managing the shop and the family's business affairs with growing confidence. May, now well educated, was back at home and being wooed by the Reverend Bob Haskins, a Methodist minister who had been based in Skibbereen for the last three years. To Rachel's intense satisfaction, this highly desirable relationship soon led to marriage. Winnie seemed well able to look after herself and Jackson, it was already clear, not only had his fair share of the family brains, but was also interested in becoming a lawyer.

Rachel took steps to honour the past and mark the new circumstances of herself and her family. In memory of her husband, she presented a fine stained-glass window to the Methodist church, which, conveniently, was being refurbished. At about the same time, she gathered her surviving family about her for a formal photograph in the doorway of the Snugville conservatory. Hanging on the dining-room wall in the background it is just possible to make out the portrait of Jack. Rachel and her children, all in their best clothes, each of the boys complete with waistcoats and watch chains, make a determined and confident-looking group.

Shortly after qualifying, sometime around 1896, Jasper set up on his own. Such an initiative was not as rash as it might seem. Going it alone was in the spirit of the time, as the chances of getting a well-salaried legal post or even a partnership were slight, since few firms consisted of more than a couple of solicitors. More importantly, Jasper had excellent contacts. After five years

The Wolfe family at Snugville. Standing (l–r): Jackson, Jasper, May; seated (l–r): Willie, Rachel, Winnie.

with Downes he knew very well which clients might be dissatisfied and ready for a move, particularly since Downes himself was not getting any younger. Then again, Jasper had useful family connections. From the west, where there were Wolfes in Schull and Swantons in Ballydehob, to Clonakilty and Rosscarbery in the east, homeland of Woods and yet more Wolfes, Jasper's new outfit was at the centre of a web of relations, all of whom, at fairly frequent intervals, required legal services of one sort or another.

J. Travers Wolfe & Co., as the new firm became known, was a Protestant concern. Despite the growing influence of the local Catholic middle class and the mutual goodwill which mostly prevailed in Skibbereen, this provided Jasper with a further advantage. The Anglo-Irish were stationed on an inner circuit of power. A Protestant solicitor, even a Methodist (a member, as Rachel put it, 'of the much maligned dissenting ones'), could hope for favourable treatment when it came to looking for business. Furthermore, as everyone knew, Jasper did have his gold medal. Whoever put work his way could be sure he was backing a winner.

Jasper took nothing for granted. He was a famously hard and diligent worker and looked after his clients' interests conscientiously. At that time, there was a craze for cycling and Jasper and Willie, who won medals for his prowess, would ride huge distances. Jasper himself regularly cycled all over West Cork, even as far out as the Mizen Peninsula, in search of clients. When in his office or in court, he did his utmost to look the part. He grew a moustache and dressed with the greatest sobriety, such that his appearance announced him as a reliable, orthodox Victorian professional gentleman. This impression of conventionality was something to which he adhered for the rest of his life.

Jasper was fortunate in another respect. He came on the scene during a golden age for Irish lawyers. In 1881 Gladstone's Liberal government had passed a Land Act designed to give tenants the 'three Fs': fair rents, fixity of tenure and free sale. A decade later, Balfour introduced a further act, designed to encourage landlords to sell to their tenants. Only three years after Jasper went solo, the local Castletownshend lands, over 10,000 acres in all, were auctioned off in 87 lots. Many of the purchasers were tenants, borrowing the necessary capital from the Land Commission (which had been set up to deal with land disputes and transfers), and so becoming 'peasant proprietors'. All this involved much drawing up of deeds, disputes over fixed assets, disagreements over boundaries, negotiations over sale of livestock, and so on. From the lawyer's point of view, the whole mouth-watering bonanza was even further enhanced because the complex drafting of both acts gave rise to the need for yet more legal advice and disputes. Work was flooding into solicitors' offices all over the county.

Jasper rapidly established himself as an expert in land law. Many years later, on 19 April 1928, he recalled in a speech to the Dáil that, throughout his legal career, he had frequently dealt with the Irish Land Commission.

I have appeared in many land purchase cases, and I have experience of
every branch of the Land Commission . . . I have had something like forty
years' experience of the Commission. I think I have appeared for more
tenants in the County Cork than any other living advocate, and perhaps I
could say the same of the landlords. (Dáil Éireann, 19 April 1928)

It was not long before Jasper was securely established. He rented an office in
North Street, on the opposite side of the road from the Bishop's School and
residence. For a short while he was joined by Jackson, as an apprentice.
Jackson, like his older brother, had secured first place and a gold medal in his
solicitors' finals, but he was anxious to move on. First he took a doctorate in
law and then he qualified in England as a barrister. Jasper's response to all this
was quite scathing. Jackson, he would remark dismissively, was born with an
exam paper in his mouth. Nor did Jasper think highly of his brother's legal
skills. When, in due course, Jackson considered applying to take silk
(becoming a King's Counsel), Jasper commented that any client to be defended
by Jackson would be well advised to save everyone trouble and plead guilty in
the first place.

Hardly had Jackson departed than Jasper's young cousin, Willie Kingston,
son of Jasper's aunt, Sarah Kingston, joined the practice. Since his family, after
the death of his father, was very impoverished, Jasper waived the apprentice
fee that would normally have been payable. Although never dedicated to the
law, Willie showed the characteristic family aptitude and in due course, like his
two cousins before him, came first in the All-Ireland Law Exam Finals.
Although Jasper found Willie regrettably lacking in both guile and ambition,
he offered him, once qualified, the position of assistant solicitor in the office
and he worked there, on and off, for the rest of his long life. Meanwhile, copies
of Willie's and Jackson's gold medal certificates joined Jasper's on the wall,
well placed to catch the eye of prospective clients.

In addition to his apprentices, Jasper employed two or three junior clerks
and a senior clerk. One of these, a Mr Whittaker from Dublin, who had a large
family, turned out to be an aggressive drunkard and Jasper eventually had to
throw him physically out of the office. Shortly after this incident came another
crisis, when fire gutted the ground floor of the office. Fortunately, no one was
hurt and the fire was extinguished before reaching the upper floor, where most
of the important papers were kept. Badly shaken, Jasper decided to move,
taking on new offices, including a strong room, in Market Street. The junior
clerks and Willie, who was still an apprentice at the time, did most of the
moving, with Willie wheeling the firm's safe through the streets on a truck, a
task the clerks considered beneath their dignity.

Within a few years, Jasper was doing sufficiently well to be able to consider
marriage. He had a girl in mind and she lived almost next door. Minnie
Vickery could not have been a more suitable bride. She and her family were
active Methodists; her maternal grandfather was a distinguished Methodist

Staff at Jasper's North Street office. Willie Kingston and (almost certainly) Dollie O'Shea, second and third from right.

minister. Her father ran a shop in Main Street, which in due course was taken over by Minnie's youngest brother Robert. She had two other younger brothers, both of whom were training to be doctors, and a younger sister who married an English civil servant.

The Vickerys had rather unusual –exotic even – origins for Anglo-Irish settlers. In about 1740 a John Vickery was shipwrecked off Bantry Bay when returning from Antigua in the West Indies, a naval base mainly inhabited by slaves working sugar and cotton plantations. It seems likely that John Vickery was involved in the trading, or more likely the agricultural management, of slaves. He decided to stay on in Ireland and started to farm on Whiddy Island, just off the coast from Bantry itself.

Minnie was a powerful, practical personality, good at managing things and not averse to giving orders. She was also splendid to look at, full of vigour, reminding people, as one relation put it, of 'a ship in full sail'. While in no way putting on airs and graces, she was endowed with many of the gifts which Victorians valued in a young woman; not least, she could play the piano and act and sing. She also had some of the virtues, and vices, traditionally associated with those the native Irish sometimes called Saxons. She was brave, loyal, hard-working, forthright and tough. At the same time, she was unimaginative, not naturally sympathetic to others and, as a nephew once said, 'a narrow-minded woman'. She was, though, the right woman for Jasper.

Over the years she would provide a safe haven, emotionally and operationally, from which he could venture forth on his often risky ventures. It was a very traditional marriage, but it worked well for both of them.

All through the night before the marriage, which took place on 18 August 1898, there was thunder and lightning. However, the day itself was fine, all went well and the bad omens of the night had no effect, at least not immediately. Jasper and Minnie moved into a terraced house opposite the North Street office. It had plenty of room, a garden that stretched down to the Ilen and an arched opening which led from the street to outhouses and stabling. Ellen Brien joined the household as a maid and stayed for more than two decades. Within a few years Dorothy was born and Minnie started to want a bigger house.

Most conveniently, Downes died at this point and his house, Norton, came on the market. In 1908 Jasper rented it and some years later he bought it. The Travers Wolfes were now well placed to claim a position as a leading local family. Minnie was not only active in the Methodist church (she played the organ for many years) but she also performed in the various entertainments which were a regular feature of Skibbereen life. Every year Daisy Kingston, one of Willie's sisters, mounted a 'Children's Concert'. This was a considerably more substantial affair than the title suggests. The audience arrived from miles around and a special tram (running on the Skibbereen–Schull Light Railway) was arranged for taking people back to Ballydehob and Schull when the fun was over. Both adults and children featured in the concert. Once, Mrs J. Travers Wolfe sang a solo, 'Call Me Back', and a couple of duets with her younger sister Lillie, including Mendelssohn's 'Song from Ruy Blas'. A lighter note was struck by child solos such as 'Yawning' and 'The Tardy Scholar'. At other concerts Minnie sang alone, songs such as 'Bantry Bay' and 'Who'll Buy My Lavender?' and duets such as 'Madam Will You Walk?' with her brother Robert, a very good-looking young man with a splendid voice. Light opera, especially performances of Gilbert and Sullivan, were particular favourites, and Minnie and Robert excelled in these. Nearly all these events took place in the Town Hall and a great deal of trouble was taken over them. Minnie was always dressed up, complete with basket of lavender or seductive fan, as appropriate. Almost without fail, she wore the most astonishing hats. All these entertainments, despite occasional Irish names among the performers, had an overwhelmingly Anglo-Irish flavour. Irish music and songs only appeared rarely, and then merely as a sort of exotic extra.

Shortly after moving to Norton, another daughter, Rachel, always known as Ray, was born. Several years later, the last child arrived, a much longed-for boy, baptised Travers. His grandmother Wolfe was delighted when he was brought to see her:

Had a very pleasant visit from Baby Wolfe of Norton, my eldest grandson, the dear little chap . . . Who can tell, but he may yet be living here when

The Wolfes at Norton, 1911 (l–r): Jasper holding Travers, Ray, Minne, Dorothy.

I shall have long lain in the quiet grave. May he live to be a good man and become a great blessing in his day and generation.

Minnie's life now centred more and more on managing house and family. Her widowed mother came up for a meal twice a week, although the visits of Jasper's mother were much less frequent. The girls, apart from school, had extra lessons in various desirable accomplishments. Dorothy had piano lessons with Willie Kingston's sister Daisy: 'I can play my march without a stop now I think, and cousin Daisy said "Capital".' She also visited her grandma Wolfe at Snugville for further music lessons. Nevertheless, Dorothy and Ray, who did not always get on, mostly led a fairly carefree life. Norton, with its sizeable grounds on the edge of the countryside, offered plenty of space for the activities of the children and their friends. Writing to her mother, who was away at the time, Dorothy gives a picture of the sort of life the children led:

Jean was up playing with us yesterday, and she and I decorated Gangway House, a tree in the avenue, with all sorts of shrubs and flowers and ferns. I trimmed a good deal on the branches, and would have done more only Ray got the 'sulks' and we had to go up to the house. When we got there we commenced to paint.

Walks also did not necessarily turn out quite as planned:

We went for a field-boreen-ditch walk about half an hour ago. That is, we ran over the potato garden, squeezed through the gate, and we were in the boreen. Jean and I stained our hands red with blackberry juice, but Ray did not. There was lots of water on the boreen, and we could not walk on it, when suddenly Jean fell off right into the water. Oh! such a state she was in, all her knickers and dress were simply awfully muddy, so she had to go right over the fields home. We were afraid she would get a cold, but she did not after all.

Needless to say, Jasper wanted to prove himself worthy to follow in the footsteps of the late McCarthy Downing and the late Thomas Downes. Like his predecessors, he began to accumulate memberships of various significant organisations. He became a director of the *Eagle*, a member of the governing body of University College Cork and a member of the Management Committee of the Schull and Skibbereen Light Railway.

Any public recognition Jasper might achieve would depend on his success as a solicitor. At just about the time he moved to Norton, he must have been feeling a little anxious. The surge of activity which had been generated by the great Victorian Land Acts of Gladstone and Balfour was beginning to subside. However, disturbed by the slow progress of land reform, the Irish Secretary at the time, George Wyndham, passed an act through parliament designed to provide a further, massive, stimulus to the transfer of land ownership from landlord to tenant. Once again, and from Jasper's point of view with excellent timing, new waves of work flowed into solicitors' offices throughout Ireland, and not least into J. Travers Wolfe & Co. Willie Kingston recalled that, from 1904 on, business rapidly increased. Willie remembered that when he started his apprenticeship the office was dealing with a high court action relating to title of land in which three counsel were to be briefed. Since, among other things, this required three copies to be made by hand (typewriters not yet having arrived in Skibbereen) of all deeds, even one major case could provide plenty of work.

11

'A THIN, RESTLESS YOUTH, WITH EARS LIKE THE HANDLES OF AN URN'

West Cork made much use of its legal system. Since private quarrelling and minor infractions of the public peace were often seen as an art form rather than a crime, many were more than ready to appear in court, in pursuit, as a rule, not so much of justice as of their own interests. Furthermore, as the costs of litigation were quite low, private individuals did not have to worry greatly about the expense.

The courthouse, although officially only an arena for the dispensation of justice, was also, in practice, and almost equally significantly, a centre of public entertainment. Much conspired to produce this situation. There were, as yet, no radio or cinemas. Plays and musical entertainments, although they existed, bordered on the genteel and never on the bawdy – religious opinion of all shades saw to that. Meanwhile, in the courthouse there were real-life dramas – featuring violence, treachery, cunning, deceit and even sex – and members of the public, abetted by the lawyers, were more than willing to play starring roles. Maurice Healy, in his memoir, *The Old Munster Circuit*,[1] put it like this:

> The Englishman goes into a court of law unwillingly, fearfully, and especially apprehensive of cross-examination. No doubt there are occasional witnesses of that kind in Ireland too; but [for] the vast majority . . . each is confident he will not be [out] until he has knocked up a good score . . . The witness would settle himself in the chair with which every Irish witness is accommodated, and would turn upon the enemy 'a glance serene and high' . . . He would answer his counsel condescendingly; and every now and then he would turn to the judge in a friendly way and explain the effect of his last answer so as to make it easy for him . . . At other times his eye would sweep around the galleries, much as Mr Gladstone might have emphasised a point by turning a flashing glance towards his supporters. To attempt to overthrow the testimony of such a highly skilled partisan by the usual 'I suggest you are wrong' kind of cross-examination would be to court disaster.

All that was needed to turn the legal show into a hit was an audience, and this not only existed, but its needs could be more than met. In Skibbereen, the courthouse itself provided a fine setting. Somerville and Ross, ascendancy ladies from nearby Castletownshend, spent many hours watching proceedings, notebooks at the ready. The courthouse of 'Skebawn', as they called Skibbereen in their best-selling *Experiences of an Irish RM*, they likened, with its 'tall windows . . . pews and galleries', to 'a dissenting chapel'. Since they also wrote that 'the reek of wet humanity ascended to the ceiling', they could equally convincingly have compared it to some civic meeting place. Actually, more than anything else, the courthouse resembled a small theatre. On one side were tiered benches rising up towards the roof, with room, at a squash, for nearly a hundred spectators. This auditorium, lit from behind by some of the windows referred to by Somerville and Ross, faced towards the seats of the magistrates, or the judge, while to left and right, as it were flanking the stage, was accommodation for clerks, laywers, jury (if required) and witnesses. The latter, and indeed any other participants, only had to half turn to play, as if to the gallery (except for the magistrates or judge, who were already eye to eye with the audience).

Not everyone could get to court, so their need was met by the *Eagle* and the *Southern Star*, journals with acres of space to fill and a readership avidly anxious to follow the wit, wisdom, doings, misdoings and fates of their neighbours. For many years, until well after the Troubles, reports of court proceedings were frequently the most substantial – and probably the most popular – items on the menu offered by the local press.

Appearing in court took up much of a solicitor's time. In Ireland, he could plead (that is, defend) and prosecute. It was vital to the success of his practice that a solicitor was skilful in cross-examination and argument, and all the other dark skills of the advocate. If he was clever and entertaining, he would be talked about locally. If he won his cases, he would get clients. If stories were told locally of how a solicitor bamboozled the opposition, if his quips made people laugh, if he usually emerged the victor, then he would gain both local fame and prosperity. This was the career path Jasper now began to travel.

Jasper often appeared in court several times a month. He features, quite recognisably, in one of Somerville and Ross's Irish RM stories. The authors wrote that 'the services of the two most eloquent solicitors in Skebawn had been engaged'. One of these was called McCaffery and described as 'a thin, restless youth, with ears like the handles of an urn'. This was Jasper, who was indeed noted for his remarkably long ears. In the story (about a fight amongst women over fish), McCaffery is described as subjecting one witness to a 'pelting cross-examination'. This particular case ended in an honourable draw, with all concerned being bound 'to the Peace'.[2]

Fighting, together with drunkenness, took up much of Jasper's time in court. In one particular case, the magistrates at the petty sessions in Skibbereen heard how, towards closing time, a large crowd, estimated by some witnesses at 300, had gathered outside Mrs Mary O'Brien's public house in North Street. She was charged with permitting drunkenness on her premises. There were different views of what had occurred inside. The alleged cause of the trouble was John Crowley. The King, represented by the Royal Irish Constabulary, said that Crowley was drunk and fighting. Crowley and various witnesses admitted that he had 'drink taken' but claimed he was not drunk. Nor was he fighting. He simply had an argument, 'some words with another person'. The policeman who went in to sort matters out declared that he had seen 'men having hold of Crowley as if he wanted to fight'. Mr Wolfe, defending, said, 'It was the constable kicked up all the row', a remark to which the presiding magistrate objected. John Crowley alleged that the constable 'caught him by the back, and said, "Master John, dead or alive you will have to go to the barrack"'. The bench decided by a majority to give Mrs O'Brien the benefit of the doubt and dismissed the case against her. John Crowley, however, was found to have been drunk and fined five shillings. The judgement, as the prosecuting advocate pointed out, was hardly consistent, but no doubt it made sense in the circumstances (*Southern Star*, 23 January 1904).

Maritime incidents provided another rich source of disputes. A case that was much relished at the time was remembered for many years after (I was told the story well over half a century later).[3] On this occasion, Jasper found himself up against his brother Willie. The facts were these. A ship with engine failure had put into Baltimore for repairs. The job done, it set out again, only for the problem to recur. The captain returned to the port, the difficulty was again sorted out, the ship sailed once more and once more came to a halt. In due course, the owners of the vessel sued the mechanic who had carried out the repairs for losses incurred. Jasper appeared for the complainant. The defendant's case was simple: he had performed miracles in getting the engine of such an ancient vessel to go at all, and not once but twice. The truth was that the motor was beyond all hope or prayer.

William Wood Wolfe was called for the defence. Since Willie, by this time, was both a member of the Baltimore and Skibbereen Harbour Board and a Justice of the Peace, he appeared as both an informed and a principled witness and he duly testified to the technical competence and probity of the defendant. Jasper, as prosecuting attorney, commenced his cross-examination. He fastened onto the experience and qualifications of the defendant and the witness for the defence, his brother Willie.

Jasper asked the defendant, 'And I suppose you specialise in boat work?'

'Sure, I know about boats. I'm after patching up every sort of engine. And I'll be doing all sorts of work with iron.'

'But you are qualified to repair marine engines?'

'I know as much about them as anyone, I'd say.'

'But you're not actually qualified?'

'Not as you mean, perhaps not.'

Jasper then cross-examined Willie.

'Now, Mr Wolfe, can you tell us your qualifications to reassure us that as good a job as possible was done on this engine?'

'I am very experienced as a member of the Harbour Board.'

'Yes, but are you actually qualified?'

'Not in this particular technical field.'

'Ah! But you do have some qualifications. Could you tell us what they are?'

Willie hesitated. Jasper pressed. 'You are, I understand, a grocer. Perhaps you have some qualifications in that field?'

'Well, yes. I am trained to blend tea.'

Jasper then called the main witness for the prosecution. The man, in answer to questioning, stated that he was a trained engineer of many years experience with the Royal Navy. 'And are you properly qualified?' he was asked. The witness reeled off a list of letters, standing for various professional qualifications. He then gave it as his opinion that the only thing wrong with the engine in question was the quality of the repair.

In summing up, Jasper said: 'Well, there we have it. The engine was mended by an unqualified blacksmith, and his competence vouched for by a certificated tea taster. On the other hand, in the view of a fully qualified and experienced marine engineer, the job was botched.' Jasper won his case.

Some cases provoked particular interest in the local community. One such, heard at Drimoleague Petty Sessions, involved salmon poaching. Mr Wolfe was defending. The Conservators of Fisheries of Skibbereen District charged James Dempsey, a postman, that 'he used a light with intent to take salmon or other fish from the river'. On the night in question, Constable Griffin was alone in the police barracks, his colleagues all being out on patrol. Seeing some men acting suspiciously, and equipped as for a fishing expedition, he left the barracks (which, since he was in sole charge, was against the rules) and hid himself by the river. Shortly, he saw a light approaching in the river and recognised the man holding it.

'Is it here you are, Dempsey?' called the constable. No reply.

The policeman then caught hold of the torch (a burning oil brand), but was himself pulled off the bank and into the water. A struggle ensued. The two eventually ended up on the side of the river. Dempsey grabbed a stone and hit the constable, who stated that the accused 'put a lump the size of my fist on my head'. Though partiallly stunned, Constable Griffin fought back and eventually knocked the fisherman out.

'I held him down there until there was not a puff of wind left in his body.'

The policeman then left the accused flat on his back and unconscious by the river and rushed back to town. He ran through the main street, his truncheon drawn, had a drink at a couple of pubs and eventually returned to the still-empty barracks.

Cross-examining, Jasper did his usual best to discredit the witness. 'If there was a picture painted of a wild constable rushing through the village with a baton in his hand, this constable would not be Constable Griffin?'

'It would.'

'With a baton in your hand?'

'Yes.'

'Why?'

'For fear I would be attacked.'

'I will ask one other question,' said Mr Wolfe. 'Did a prisoner escape from the barracks a few weeks ago, when again you were alone, and again left the barracks without authorisation?'

'A prisoner attempted to escape, but was re-arrested.'

Jasper, having suggested the constable was over-excited, disobedient and unreliable, then called a host of witnesses, all of whom swore that Dempsey had been washing out porter bottles in a pub throughout the relevant time and that no one had seen the accused in wet clothes. Dempsey himself denied having the slightest idea that the constable might have been alone on duty in the barracks. He added, that while 'I could kill a brown trout, I never killed a salmon'. It did not take the magistrates long to reach a decision. 'The majority of the bench', said the RM, 'believe that the constable was telling the absolute truth.' So this was one occasion when Jasper lost his case (*Southern Star*, 23 January 1904).

At Bantry quarter sessions there occurred another case which, as the *Eagle* reported (3 February 1912), 'occupied a great deal of public interest, and the court was crowded'. A Miss Theresa Morrissey of Cork was suing Dr Kearney, GP, of Rosscarbery for bills left unpaid when he and his brothers were students and her lodgers. Jasper represented the defendant, Dr Kearney. The barrister acting for Miss Morrissey said that 'the lady was extremely kind to these young men. As a matter of fact they had voracious appetites, because sometimes they ate six meals a day. They also had fire and light.'

Questioned by her lawyer, Miss Morrissey said: 'I sent the defendant several bills, but I never got a divil of a bit of payment. I kept the account in a pass book, and gave it to my solicitor. But he lost it. I then wrote to Dr Kearney several times, and sent the items out of my head.'

Mr Wolfe said: 'Our case is that all the figures claimed are out of your head' (laughter).

Jasper then cross-examined the lady. It turned out that she had sent several large postcards to Dr Kearney, open for all to read. Jasper, who no doubt knew the judge well and had a good idea of how he might react, did little more than read out excerpts from these.

Jasper (reading): '"I am now showing up to the public in your own locality the respectability of the sponging, cheating Kearney family." You wrote that?' enquired Jasper.

'Yes.'

Jasper read on: '"Every day of my life, at the rising of the Sacred Host and Chalice, I will beseach God to send his curse and vengeance on your child, and on your family, and this will be my continual cry to God till I have the last of

your debts paid. May God's anger afflict you." Did you mean all that?' asked
Jasper.

The plaintiff replied calmly, 'Yes, I meant all that.'

Mr Wolfe, 'You're quite proud of it?'

'Yes.'

Mr Wolfe, reading: '"I suppose the people of Ross look up to Dr and Mrs
Kearney, but I will change their opinion." You wrote that?'

'Yes.'

After hearing further evidence, the judge rejected the plaintiff's case,
adding, 'That is the most appalling letter I ever read.'

Miss Morrissey's lawyer commented, 'Your Honour is not to decide the case
on a matter of religion', to which the judge replied, 'I didn't either.'

Although Jasper appeared for both plaintiffs and defendants, his court
reputation was above all made as a defence lawyer. He was particularly
successful in criminal cases. Many years later, in a Dáil debate on strengthening
protection for juries, which he strongly supported, he recalled the
unsatisfactory practices which had prevailed in Ireland under the British legal
system (Dáil Éireann, 11 June 1931). 'In the area in which I practised', said
Jasper, 'I was perhaps the chief friend of the dock'. He added that for sixteen
years, up until the Troubles broke out, not one alleged criminal that he had
defended had been convicted. However, he went on to make it clear that in
securing this remarkable rate of acquittal he had been greatly helped by the
way criminal law was practised. The system, in Jasper's words, allowed 'the
accused person a privilege of being entitled to see the jurors beforehand' and
'to square with impunity the jurors by whom he was about to be tried' (all
criminal cases were tried by jury).

Jasper illustrated by an anecdote the fact that the practice of helping juries
to make up their minds was all but universal:

> I remember a juror in my area stating that he had an objection to serve. He
> was pressed to state his objection. He was very slow in telling it, and the
> judge came to the conclusion that someone had been trying to square him,
> and that the honest man was objecting to serve on these grounds. At last
> the judge persuaded him to speak, and he recorded his objection in these
> words. 'Your Honour,' he said, 'I know nothing of either of these parties',
> the fact being that he had not been canvassed by either side.

And so, having been neither bribed nor intimidated, the potential juror saw
no point in turning up for jury service.

There was one case which, perhaps more than any other, helped to establish
Jasper's reputation, both in West Cork and more widely. It concerned
smuggling. This was a widespread and very lucrative practice along the coasts
of southwest Ireland, which, with its coves, high ground, good cover and sparse
population, was highly convenient for the secret landing of illicit goods.

The case against the alleged smugglers appeared absolutely damning. In the late spring of 1907 the navy learned that a suspicious vessel had been seen near Cape Clear, in West Cork. HMS *Skipjack*, under Commander Travers, was sent from Queenstown, Cork, in pursuit and, when the *Cosmopoliet* was sighted sailing away from the land, the *Skipjack* ran alongside and the suspect vessel was boarded. In the hold were found 100 boxes of tobacco and cigars, amounting to a ton and a half, and £306, £204 of which was in Irish bank notes, £80 in gold and £20 in silver, all United Kingdom coin. The tobacco was packaged in amounts that weighed less than the weight legally specified for import. The vessel was from Rotterdam and the captain, when asked where he was headed, replied 'Iceland', suggesting that he was somewhat off course. It emerged that two of the crew of five had previous convictions for smuggling.

The case was held in a special court in Skibbereen, presided over by the Resident Magistrate, who was accompanied by seven Justices of the Peace, including Sir E. Coghill and Mr W. Wood Wolfe. This exceptionally large bench was further reinforced by the president of Queen's College, Cork. The key question to consider was whether the *Cosmopoliet* had or had not been within Irish territorial waters, which extended three miles from the coast.

Appearing for customs was Jasper's former schoolfellow, Jim Burke, now practising as a barrister. Burke quickly established that, at the time of boarding the *Cosmopoliet*, the *Skipjack*'s navigating lieutenant had taken cross-bearings which showed the ship's position as 2.45 miles off land, that is over half a mile within territorial waters. Commander Travers stated under cross-examination that 'there could be no mistake about the bearings'. Jim Burke further showed that the 'bearings were taken with the best instruments that science can devise or money procure' and that they were estimated by 'men experienced in nautical matters'. It emerged that the captain of the *Cosmopoliet* also had a chart showing his position. However, the navy sailor who saw this chart when the alleged smuggler was boarded said that, at that time, it contained no relevant entries. A few days later the captain entered his ship (by then detained in Baltimore harbour) and was alone in the cabin for five minutes. After that, the chart contained bearings showing the *Cosmopoliet*'s position when it was boarded, apparently over four miles from land.

Jasper now set about demolishing the case Jim Burke had put forward. He concentrated on undermining the credibility of the prosecution claim that the *Cosmopoliet* had been within territorial waters. His main target was the navigating lieutenant who had taken the relevant bearings. Jasper suggested that Lieutenant Wigglesworth had knowingly given false evidence.

Mr Wolfe, cross-examining the officer: 'Anything you now say is correct?'
'Yes.'
'Tell me, have you sworn on the Bible to tell the truth?'
'I have.'
'So, did you kiss the Book?'
'No, if you mean did I press my lips to it.'

Mr Wolfe: 'This is a most disgraceful transaction. Everybody in the court saw him deliberately keep the Book half an inch away from his mouth.'

A member of the bench: 'We noticed it here.'

Mr Wolfe: 'When I see a man avoid the Book, I know what it means.'

Witness: 'I didn't want to kiss its dirty cover.'

Mr Wolfe: 'It is one of the most disgraceful performances I have ever seen on the part of an officer of His Majesty's navy.'

A member of the bench (a doctor): 'It is the microbes' (laughter).

Mr Wolfe: 'The microbes of untruth.'

Jasper went on to show that the lieutenant was inexperienced, having only been qualified a year, that he did not know the West Cork coast well, that he was irregular in his recording of bearings and that the weather when the *Cosmopoliet* was detained had been 'intermittently foggy', so that taking accurate bearings was difficult. Jasper so played on the lieutenant's self-confidence that he started to laugh contemptuously and to interrupt.

Jasper asked, 'Will someone keep him in order?' The chairman of the bench had to quieten the officer. 'I hope,' commented Jasper at another point, 'that there will be no more remarks from the sniggering gentleman across the table.' Altogether, the unhappy lieutenant was thoroughly discredited.

Jasper next turned his fire on the Royal Navy commander. Had he checked the relevant bearings? He had not.

Mr Wolfe: 'On detaining the *Cosmopoliet*, did you accuse its captain of being within the three-mile limit?'

'Yes.'

Mr Wolfe: 'What did he say?'

'I didn't hear.'

'Did you, or your navigating lieutenant, go on board the *Cosmopoliet?*'

'No.'

'Did HMS *Skipjack* accompany the *Cosmopoliet* into Baltimore harbour?'

'No.'

Then there was the question of whether the location of the capture had been marked. The commander admitted it had not.

Mr Wolfe: 'When the question of distance is raised, it would occur to any ordinary person to throw out a buoy.' Jasper next raised a blizzard of technical points about the movements of both ships, which created an atmosphere of utter confusion as to which had been precisely where and when.

In his concluding remarks, Jasper questioned, tactfully, the efficiency and probity of the navy and the customs. Taking bearings was not, he suggested the foolproof, scientific procedure that had been claimed.

Mr Wolfe: 'It is very easy to make a mistake in taking bearings. Most men are liable to make such mistakes. How otherwise are we to account for the number of terrible accidents which happen year after year, even around our own coast? Naval vessels are again and again driven on the rocks or sands around this coast. I assume, for the honour of the navy, that it is an easy matter to make a mistake in taking cross-bearings.'

The navy's motives were also open to question. The *Skipjack* crew, said Jasper, had a financial incentive for trying to secure a conviction. 'It is a fact that every year a sum of money is distributed amongst the crews of Royal Navy ships for services of this kind. Last year the amount distributed amounted to three times the gross amount of fines imposed for infringement of the rules.' Jasper further suggested that the navy had been less than honourable in its efforts to ensure conviction. It had, in an attempt to influence public opinion and the court, studiously circulated reports in the press that the defendants were carrying on a contraband trade and that the capture was due to the energy of the crew of the *Skipjack*. There had also, or so he alleged, been efforts by the police, which were successful, to intimidate the crew of a third vessel that had been in the area at the time and so ensure that they would not appear as witnesses for the defence.

The bench, by a majority, found the case not proved. The decision was greeted by applause in the court. Whether this was on account of relief that the smuggling trade had not been dealt a serious blow, or through admiration for Jasper's bravura performance, or simply from dislike of the British navy and the customs, was unclear.

The authorities were furious at the outcome and, despite the verdict, refused to release the *Cosmopoliet*, as apparently they were entitled to do. The affair now rapidly escalated. Questions were asked in parliament, the British Foreign Office and the Dutch government corresponded and eventually the case was heard again in the high court in Dublin, before the Lord Chief Baron and a special jury. Evidently a deal had been reached at governmental level, because no defence was offered: the crew was allowed to go free, but the ship was declared forfeit.[4]

After these events, it became widely assumed that, if Jasper was on your case, you would win. It was soon being said that he had 'all West Cork for his client'.

PROTESTANT HOME RULER

All his life, Jasper was a Home Ruler. Speaking in the Dáil he once said, 'I was associated with the National movement before the majority of the members of this House were born. I have remained connected with the movement ever since' (Dáil Éireann, 29 April 1932). Jasper was always interested in politics, although not in party politics. Fortunately for him, there was plenty of opportunity, at various levels, for independent-minded citizens to get involved in public life. He was twice elected as a Town Commissioner and then in 1898 the Conservatives passed the Irish Local Government Act, which introduced County, Urban and District Councils. This important measure shifted power across Ireland away from the landlord and ascendancy class towards professionals, farmers, shopkeepers and publicans. From now on local control would, with few exceptions, be in the hands of the Catholic and Nationalist majority.

The first elections took place amidst great excitement during the spring of 1899. The *Southern Star*, a Catholic paper based in Skibbereen, reported that 'Public interest is entirely absorbed in the forthcoming elections . . . nothing else is talked about'. Jasper stood for the new Skibbereen District Council. He was the only Protestant to secure a seat. His fellow councillors were all people he had known for most of his life. The concerns of the new body were, by definition, parochial.

John O'Shea in later life.

Jasper had to deal with such matters as street repairs and the fixing and collection of rents from council properties.

Jasper soon found himself in the midst of a protracted and animated dog fight over the election of a town clerk. He was the leading supporter of a candidate who happened to be one of his closest friends. John O'Shea, a few years older than Jasper, was a fellow Parnellite. He had, for instance, spoken out for Parnell at the Town Hall meeting when the boys of the Bishop's School had been so vocal. He was also a publican and his premises were conveniently close to J. Travers Wolfe & Co. in North Street. Here, according to his advertisements, 'John Jameson's, the celebrated and best whiskey in the world, can be had'.

The new council had inherited a clerk from the now superseded Town Commissioners. This gentleman, who was alleged not to have attended to his duties for two years and to have taken official documents home, now wished to resign. The questions that had to be addressed were whether he should be paid a pension, whether his successor should be interim while matters were sorted out and, above all, who should be his successor. A rival candidate to O'Shea was put forward. It soon became clear that personal loyalties were involved and feelings were running high. Jasper accused his opponents of 'grossly illegal' tactics and they responded by declaring they were 'not going to be put down by Mr Wolfe's little technicalities or nice points'. In the end, a vote was taken and O'Shea won. Thus Jasper had succeeded in securing a vital post for a close ally (*Southern Star*, 6 May 1899).

Jasper, still the only Protestant on the council, retained his seat in the next election. At this point controversy over another appointment blew up. It was the gentlemanly custom on the Skibbereen Town Council for the chairmanship to rotate annually, according to seniority, and in 1904 it was Jasper's turn. However, despite the tactful protestations of Mr P. J. Collins, the outgoing chairman, a rival candidate was put forward, and this was none other than Jim Burke. An unholy row now broke out. Jim Burke was proposed by Tim Sheehy, a man who, to the very end of his long career, was fabled for his loquacity, his skill in changing political horses and his ambition. Sheehy, who at this point was an ardent supporter of John Redmond's Nationalist Party, was opposed to Jasper taking the chair and made his case at great length. He emphasised, and there was no doubt of his sincerity, that 'There is no question here today as regards the candidates about religion . . . we never denied a fair representation to the minority . . . personally I have not the slightest objection to Mr Wolfe'.

Tim Sheehy objected to Jasper because he was not an active Nationalist:

No position in the trust of the people should be handed over to anyone except a faithful soldier in the Nationalist ranks. I will always cast my vote in favour of the Nationalist candidate, until the bright time when the flag of legislative independence waves over our native Parliament. I will always sustain the National traditions of the town, and I will cast my vote for none but a supporter of the Irish people.

Getting even further carried away, Tim Sheehy accused Jasper of being a Unionist:

> If any of the great leaders of the Irish people were to come to this town, what would our position be? A Conservative chairman of our Town Board; and what would our people say if our chairman did not come forward and preside at a National gathering? There is no question on the score of religion, but it is a question of a Unionist or a Nationalist.

Jasper demanded the right of reply, but Tim Sheehy objected: 'You are a candidate.' However, the chairman supported Jasper.

Jasper was actually quite vulnerable. While certainly no Tory, he was not a member of the Nationalist Irish Party either. Moreover, although a supporter of Home Rule, he also believed that Ireland should remain securely within the United Kingdom. It would not be difficult to misrepresent his position. In these circumstances, Jasper counter-attacked, hard. As a rule, he preferred to be courteous and reasonable, allowing carefully selected facts to win his arguments. However, in Skibbereen at this time, imaginative verbal violence was quite as common, and accepted, as physical pugnacity. When he put his mind to it, Jasper could be coruscatingly rude.

He opened with an attack on Tim Sheehy's verbosity: 'Mr Sheehy speaks in season and out of season, but very frequently out of season . . . the candidate whom he proposes today has said of him, in that classical style of his, "*Cacathoes loquendi*".' Jim Burke interrupted to put Jasper right on his pronunciation of *Cacathoes*, a correction which Jasper did not challenge (in fact, the Latin phrase, from the Roman satiric poet Juvenal, had been misquoted by Jim Burke, altering 'Cacathoes scribendi', meaning 'An inveterate itch to write', to 'An inveterate itch to speak').

Jasper next proceeded to attack Tim Sheehy's ambition. Whenever Mr Sheehy spoke, suggested Jasper, it was generally with a view to advancing himself. 'I am reminded', Jasper said, 'of that quotation [from Gilbert and Sullivan, very possibly culled from one of Minnie's song sheets, Jasper himself being no musical aficionado],

> If you want in this world to advance,
> Your position in life to enhance,
> You must stir it and stump it,
> And blow your own trumpet,
> Or bless me, you haven't a chance!'

Jasper then recalled how Tim Sheehy had canvassed the Tory Unionist, The O'Donovan of Lissard, to get himself appointed a Justice of the Peace, how he had proposed that himself and other directors of the Skibbereen and Schull Tramway Company should be 'made into busts and stuck into niches in the walls for the admiration of the world' and how he had appeared on 'the Parnellite platform and on the anti-Parnellite platform . . . a man who performs political somersaults'. Tim Sheehy, enraged at these attacks, interrupted with ever greater vehemence and frequency: 'I will not permit you to malign me in this way here, and I say it is very unfair of you Mr Chairman to allow it.'

The chairman proved to be remarkably lenient towards Jasper. Perhaps this was because he was a fellow solicitor. P. J. Collins ruled that 'Mr Wolfe is perfectly entitled to reply . . . You opened the ball.' Tim Sheehy refused to accept the chairman's ruling and the two took to shouting at each other. As one report of the proceedings put it, 'There was considerable excitement here, the Chairman and Mr Sheehy discussing heatedly the point of order'. Jasper did not help matters by exclaiming, 'I am not to be put down by the bellowings of a bull.'

When a degree of order had been restored, Jasper continued, still in fine form. Perorating, he finally dealt with the key question. 'I never at any time of my life said I had any objection to Home Rule. I am now, as I have always been, in favour of Home Rule.'

'You will show it by enrolling yourself in the organisation of the country,' demanded Tim Sheehy. Wolfe replied: 'You are a sham and a humbug . . . I said I subscribed to the National cause.'

After a good deal more of the same, a vote was eventually taken and Jasper lost by 4 to 3. He thanked the council for their patient hearing and added that if he had said anything in a heated moment to cause offence he was sorry for it and hoped that they would all be as good friends as ever. And so it turned out, for few of those present, and certainly not Tim Sheehy, were the sort of men to bear grudges. Jim Burke was duly elected chairman (reported in the *Southern Star*, 23 January 1904).

In normal circumstances it is more than likely that Jasper would have succeeded to the chair without any challenge. However, not only Tim Sheehy but Skibbereen Nationalists as a whole had a very good and specific reason for wanting one of their own as chairman in this particular year (1904). A statue, the *Maid of Erin*, dedicated to the men who 'fought and died for Ireland' in the rising of 1798, was being raised in the centre of Skibbereen. Paid for by public subscription, it had been the idea of the recently founded 'Skibbereen Young Ireland Society'. This group saw itself as a natural successor, in 'the cradle of Fenianism', to O'Donovan Rossa's original Phoenix Society. The society had, accordingly, asked O'Donovan Rossa himself to unveil the statue and the 'great patriot', planning to visit Ireland from his home in the United States, had accepted.

A tremendous occasion was in prospect, but what about the welcoming committee? As civic representative of the town, the chairman of the Urban District Council would inevitably be expected to play a leading part in the proceedings. Suppose, however, that the chairman was an Anglo-Irish Protestant? As Tim Sheehy had hinted ('If any of the great leaders of the Irish people were to come to this town, what would our position be?'), and as everyone in Skibbereen was well aware, an embarrassing situation was in prospect. Here was an event which would attract not only local but also national and even international attention. And what would the worldwide Irish Nationalist and Republican community think, and no doubt say, if Skibbereen, in welcoming the Fenian hero, did so in the person of a Methodist solicitor, a descendant of English colonists? The looming civic embarrassment hardly bore thinking about. In the circumstances, it was inevitable that Jasper should be opposed for the chairmanship.

In the event, the whole occasion was a great success. The entire local community, whatever its religious beliefs or political views, joined in the celebrations. Jasper himself contributed generously to the cost of the *Maid* (the names of all subscribers were published) and even the *Eagle* (3 December 1904), anti-Republican as it was, bestowed its approval, praising the monument as 'an eloquent reminder to future generations of the ideals for which their forefathers yielded up their lives in dungeon, and on scaffold and battlefield'. It complimented the members of the Young Ireland Society on 'their energy, earnestness, and persistency'. Above all, the *Eagle* commented approvingly, if somewhat condescendingly, that 'the manner in which contentious matters were discussed and decided at their meetings showed that individual members could sink their general feelings for the general good and tolerate views and opinions different from their own'.

As for Tim Sheehy and Jim Burke, they both enjoyed a starring role in the day's events. While special trains arrived from all over West Cork, they made their way to the courthouse, where they took their places in an open brake with various dignitaries, the local MP and O'Donovan Rossa himself. The vehicle then proceeded, in a long procession, down North Street towards the Town Square and the *Maid*, who, as luck would have it, stood just in front of the premises where Tim Sheehy ran a public house and shop.

The progress of the brake, reported the *Eagle*, was reminiscent of the return of a Roman conqueror. North Street, together with every other thoroughfare in the town, was festooned with green and gold banners showing harps, shamrocks and mottoes in Irish, and the Stars and Stripes of the United States of America. Flags floated from windows and, as the brake approached, ladies leaned forward waving their handkerchiefs in greeting to the aged Fenian, who was 'visibly touched'.

At the monument itself, the unveiling party mounted an extremely crowded platform. Tim Sheehy found himself a place right next to O'Donovan Rossa and a photograph survives to record the event. As for the chairman of the Town Council, Jim Burke's great moment had arrived. On behalf of all the citizens of Skibbereen he gave the speech of welcome to the town's returning hero. In a very popular gesture he proposed that money be collected for a testimonial to

O'Donovan Rossa. All in all, what could easily have become an excuse for sectarian flag waving was universally treated as a chance to celebrate a sense of shared Irishness, not to mention shared Skibbereen-ness.

Hardly more than a year after the unveiling of the *Maid of Erin*, the Liberals returned to power at Westminster and, for the first time since the days of

Unveiling of the Maid of Erin. *Timothy Sheehy and Jeremiah O'Donovan Rossa, second and third from left respectively.*

Parnell and Gladstone, it seemed that Home Rule might be enacted. While Jasper welcomed this political development, there was, for the time being at least, little that he could do to help things along. Although the Nationalist Party under Redmond was committed both to parliamentary democracy and Home Rule, it also included a strongly sectarian and Gaelic approach, led by the deputy leader John Dillon and promoted by the activist Ancient Order of Hibernians, or the 'Molly Maguires' as its tougher supporters were known. This was a political organisation unlikely to prove welcoming to the likes of Jasper, which was clearly one major reason why he had never joined.

However, things were about to change. The National Party began to lose support as it failed to secure progress either in achieving Home Rule or in speeding up the transfer of land from owners to tenants. At this point William O'Brien entered the fray, establishing his own political party and grass roots organisation, the All for Ireland League.

O'Brien, a charismatic figure who had quarrelled with Redmond, was a journalist, veteran Nationalist politician and Corkman. He was very well thought of in his native county, where his programme was instantly and widely popular, not only with Catholics but also with a good number of Protestants. He demanded an end to delay and prevarication over Home Rule, reconciliation with all Protestants, landlords and those from the North and a reinvigorated transfer of land from owners to tenants. Overall, he spoke for an inclusive, open, all-Ireland policy. His programme, in effect, offered an updated form of Parnellism. For the first time since Parnell, Home Rule Protestants had a political party which would welcome them as members.[1] Large numbers joined, especially in County Cork, and among those to sign up were not only Jasper, but his brother Willie.

While Jasper had been building up his legal practice and setting up as a married man, Willie had not been sitting on his hands. He too had been active establishing himself as a leading citizen. So far unmarried, the business he had inherited was doing well, as was his farm at Licknavar. He had been appointed a Justice of the Peace and held various other public positions. He had also been elected to the Town Council and, in 1910, been unanimously voted its chairman. Willie had, in effect, inherited Jasper's place. The latter, following his tussle over the chairmanship, had not stood again. There were no hard feelings on anyone's part; indeed, within a short time Jasper was appointed solicitor to the council.

Jasper became active in support of the O'Brienite cause. In the two general elections of 1910 he was electoral agent for the ageing but highly respected James Gilhooly, for many years Nationalist MP for Cork West but now converted to the All for Ireland cause. It was, however, Willie who emerged as the leading figure. He was voted president of the Skibbereen branch of the All for Ireland League and, as such, took a prominent part in meetings and rallies throughout West Cork.

The excitement of the time, and the part played by Willie Wood Wolfe, can be seen very clearly in the events of one particular evening (reported in the *Eagle*, 12 December 1910). A huge torchlit procession was held in Skibbereen during the second general election of 1910 to celebrate the successful return of William O'Brien for his Cork City constituency. Hundreds of people accompanied by a brass band marched from, and back to, the Trade and Labour Hall in Bridge Street. Here Willie, 'who was loudly cheered, addressed the assembled multitude':

> We want to bring back to Ireland an honest, united party, who will not be bossed by a clique in Dublin . . . We ask every man in Ireland, whether Catholic, Protestant or heathen, to come together and do their part for their native land. The time will come when we will reach out a friendly hand across the Boyne, and unite every Irishman.

The only sour note in the whole evening had been sounded by the Molly Maguires (the tough characters supporting the Redmondites), who had stolen some of the O'Brienite brass band's instruments. A resolution regretting this despicable action (which nevertheless does not seem to have silenced the band) was passed to loud cheers:

> Resolved that we the members of the Skibbereen Brass Band and All for Ireland League condemn in the strongest manner possible the low, cowardly and unprincipled action of the local Molly Maguires and their hirelings in purloining the instruments of the local band, and that we direct the attention of every respectable citizen of Skibbereen to keep aloof from that low clique which lowered their dignity to be party to such a base act. And furthermore we call on lovers of liberty and freedom of opinion at the forthcoming elections to record their votes in protest against such cowardice.

When all the election results came in Jasper saw that Gilhooly had been safely returned for West Cork, as had the All for Ireland League candidate for South Cork (Skibbereen's constituency). The O'Brienites had secured all but one of the Cork seats. They had not, however, succeeded in breaking out of their southwest stronghold.[2]

Nationally, the result of the election, with the Liberals returned to government, cleared the way for the introduction, in April 1912, of the third Home Rule Bill. This in turn triggered no-holds-barred opposition from the Ulster Unionists, the consequences of which for southern Protestant Home Rulers such as Jasper and Willie were potentially appalling. First, the Northern campaign apparently scuppered all hopes of securing agreement between Nationalists and Unionists on the future of Ireland through the O'Brienite policy of conciliation and consent. Athough the All for Ireland League struggled on for several years, it was essentially finished. Secondly, Ulster hostility threatened, if partition proved to be the only possible solution, to leave southern Protestants, including Home Rulers, a truly tiny minority amongst a Gaelic–Catholic multitude. Finally, because the Ulster propagandists raised fearful spectres of the Catholic bigotry and intolerance that the Dublin government would unleash, relationships between Catholics and Protestants in the south were at risk of being undermined by mutual suspicion and fear. At worst, the actions of the Irish Unionists seemed to southern Irish Protestants sympathetic to Home Rule to be a betrayal not only of their nation, but of their co-religionists.

It particularly irked Jasper that among the first Northerners to start shouting about the dangers of Catholic theocracy were certain Methodists. Three weeks before the Home Rule Bill was introduced in parliament, the Ulster Methodists mounted what was intended to be a 'Monster Demonstration' in Belfast. It was hoped, and believed, that around 60,000 would attend from all over Ireland. In the event, some 4,000 turned up, and the absentees were more notable than those who attended. The *Ulster Guardian*, a Liberal paper, reported on 23 March 1912 that 'The vast majority of the ministers in active work were not present. Methodists south of the Boyne ignored the demonstration.' The organisers, evidently out of embarrassment, even declined to publish a list of those on the platform, the normal practice at the time. The unexpectedly low numbers were partly explained by the support of some Methodists for Home Rule, but mainly, as the *Ulster Guardian* put it, by objection 'on principle to their Church being identified with party politics'.

One of the handful who did travel from the south to the demonstration was a recently appointed Justice of the Peace from County Cork. Mr John Willis was active, on behalf of a body called the Defence Union, in collecting and publishing evidence purporting to show how Catholic Nationalists in the south abused positions of public trust. In an address to the demonstration he declared:

> In the County Cork since the passing of the late Local Government Act not a single Protestant has been appointed to any position carrying pay. I have no patience with a Methodist minister who is a Home Ruler. I am an Englishman living in Ireland. The Israelites were 400 years in Egypt, and they were not Egyptians afterwards.

This speech and similar public pronouncements from various sources containing charges known to be false were not, for the time being, challenged. Jasper and others like him kept silent. It was months before any southern Protestant sympathetic to Home Rule fired more than the occasional shot back at the big Unionist guns. The *Ulster Guardian* (1 February 1913) declared that 'the spectacle of panicky hysteria which Irish Protestantism has been allowed unchecked to afford the world has been humiliating to the last degree'.

However, despite their apparent calm, Protestant Home Rulers in the south were becoming restive. The first public evidence of southern Protestants, other

than a few stray individuals, speaking up for Home Rule occurred in the far
west peninsula of the Mizen Head. It was a fair day in late October in the small
town of Goleen. In what was claimed to be an impromptu meeting, but which
showed evidence of careful planning and political savvy, various local
Protestants gathered together. A resolution was proposed and 'passed with
enthusiasm', which read as follows:

> We the Protestant people of the united parishes of Kilmoe, Crookhaven,
> Goleen and Toormore protest against the unjustifiable slanders and libels
> of the Catholic Nationalist people of Munster and Ireland, but particularly
> on behalf of our Catholic neighbours, from whom we have experienced
> nothing but the sincerest friendship, toleration and assistance. That we
> have no fear of Home Rule and believe it is urgently necessary for the
> welfare and success of Irishmen and the prosperity of our beloved native
> land. (*Cork Examiner*, 26 October 1912)

Copies of this resolution were immediately posted off to various influential
figures, including Asquith, the British Liberal Prime Minister, and John
Redmond, leader of the Irish Parliamentary Party, as well as to newspapers
throughout Ireland and Great Britain. It received widespread publicity, locally
and nationally, particularly in the Liberal press. Altogether the impression was
created that Goleen and its neigbourhood were deeply significant and
potentially influential centres of Irish Protestant thinking, and that what they
had to say ought to be listened to with the most careful attention.

Not everyone, however, was impressed. One individual who turned out
to be particularly upset was Reverend Carroll, the Church of Ireland rector
of Kilmoe. The letter accompanying the resolution had stated that he and
various others had only not been present at the meeting due to 'unavoidable
absence'. The incensed minister wrote to the papers to explain that he and
the others referred to, one of whom was digging potatoes, failed to attend only
because they had not been told of the meeting. And what is more, if they had
attended, they would have made their Unionist sympathies and their
opposition to the resolution as plain as humanly possible (*Cork Examiner*,
9 November 1912).

Jasper was in court in Skibbereen on the day of the Goleen meeting and
there is little to suggest that he was involved. Nevertheless, he, like his co-
religionists in Goleen, was ready to counter-attack. At about this time, in the
autumn of 1912, the first serious attempt was being made to found a movement
of southern Protestant Home Rule supporters.[3] It was in London, not Dublin,
that an Irish Protestant Home Rule Committee was established. The
honourable secretary was Herbert Z. Deane, now a London solicitor but
originally from near Rosscarbery in County Cork, and a member of the family
which had been close friends of Rachel Wood Wolfe since her childhood.
Herbert signed Jasper up as a supporter.

The new committee decided to organise a 'Great Meeting', at which Jasper was asked to speak. The event took place in the city of London in early December. It proved to be tremendously successful. Long before the doors opened, large queues formed: 'There was a great crush and much disappointment by the crowds who had to remain outside.' (Later, to cheer them up, several speakers spoke from a balcony.) The proceedings opened with a 'vocal concert' and various 'well known artistes sang national songs like "The Shan Van Vocht" . . . "The Wearing of the Green", and "Over Here".' The front of the platform was decorated with Irish and British flags.

Opening the meeting, the chairman said that it had been called 'to protest against the attempts being made by certain sections of Irish Protestantism to provoke religious rancour and intolerance'. Speaker after speaker reiterated this theme. The Reverend Canon Lilley, formerly a Church of Ireland minister and now vicar at Paddington Green and a well-known author, argued that fears of religious intolerance under Home Rule were 'absolutely without foundation'. As for Protestant Ulster, it was 'hag ridden by the prejudices of a bygone age. Self-government is the only solvent of religious bitterness in Ireland.'

W. B. Yeats had been booked to speak, but he wired to say that 'owing to a railway accident in the west of Ireland he was unable to arrive in time'. The first big name of the evening to appear was Sir Arthur Conan Doyle, famous for his Sherlock Holmes stories but also descended from an Irish Catholic gentleman. Sir Arthur described how:

> My great-grandfather, under the Penal Laws, could not own a horse worth £5 or join a learned profession. But I don't worry about that. If we would only let our grandfathers sleep in their graves, and turn our thoughts to the practical problems of the moment . . . People say Ulster blocks the way. But we should hold out the open hand, even though the closed fist comes back.

The main attraction was George Bernard Shaw, who proposed the motion 'That this meeting express its strong desire to see the end of racial and religious feuds in Ireland, and Irishmen of all creeds and classes working together for the common good of their native country'.

Shaw opened by saying, 'I am an Irishman. My father was an Irishman, and my mother was an Irishwoman. My father and my mother were Protestants who might be described, owing to the intensity of their faith, as sanguinary Protestants.' However, he went on to explain that his upbringing had not been exclusively Protestant in its influences. 'Many of the duties of my mother were shared by an Irish nurse. And she never put me to bed without sprinkling me with holy water' (this was greeted by roars of laughter). In a knockabout performance, Shaw at one point referred to his own career and success and someone in the audience quipped ''Twas the holy water that did it!'

Jasper had been recruited to speak at the end of the evening. His task was to illustrate the fairly general sentiments and arguments of the keynote

WINDOW & GROVE,
68A, BAKER STREET, LONDON.

Jasper Wolfe, 1912.

speakers with some hard facts from life as actually lived by Protestants in the south. It was the first time he had spoken at a meeting of such size and significance and, while it was believed he could be relied on to do a decent job, no one really expected great things of an unknown country lawyer from the far west. In the event, Jasper rivalled only Bernard Shaw as a star turn. According to the *Cork Examiner* (17 December 1912), he 'was one of the prominent speakers at the great meeting of Protestant Home Rulers . . . He delivered a convincing and eloquent speech which supplied a truly fitting climax to the remarkable occasion.' The voice of Nationalist Ireland, the *Freeman's Journal*, added that 'Mr J. Travers Wolfe spoke with great success on his experience as a Nonconformist of toleration in the south of Ireland.' Long afterwards, when they were both old men, Canon Lilley, whose own address had also been well received, wrote to Jasper sending him an article on Shaw. 'Looking back over the years', he wrote, 'my chief recollection of you was at that meeting in Farringdon Street when in my judgement you outshawed Shaw and outshone everyone else in the best speech of the evening. But I don't suppose Shaw would agree!'

Jasper, in his speech, had set out to demonstrate that Protestants, contrary to the Unionist scare stories, were treated fairly and decently by Catholics. In particular, he demolished the claims of Catholic discrimination against Protestants made by Mr John Willis, JP, at the Methodist Unionist demonstration in Belfast nine months previously.

I can bear testimony to the tolerant treatment meted out to Protestants by their Catholic neighbours. I have personally experienced it, as a private citizen, and in my profession as a solicitor, as well as on local government bodies, both rural and urban. When I am told that I am to be persecuted I do not believe it. (Cheers.) I particularly deplore the fact that a Protestant who is also a Methodist like myself, was found in the county of Cork willing to go to the Belfast Conference to tell them that Protestants in the South and South West were being persecuted by their Catholic neighbours. (Cries of 'Shame!') That gentleman had been dragged from Cork to Belfast to traduce and malign his fellow-countrymen. He and his fellow Unionists should fight this question fairly and not hit below the belt. (Cheers.)

Jasper gave examples, citing himself and others as examples, of Protestants appointed to salaried public positions by Catholics. When Jasper finished, the chairman asked if anyone was against the motion being debated. A shout came from the gallery, 'Divil a wan!' (The *Ulster Guardian*, 14 December 1912, reported the great occasion in detail.)

On a high after the success of the London meeting, Protestant Home Rulers swiftly got together in Dublin and set up an 'Irish Protest Committee'. They organised a demonstration to take place within four weeks, at the end of January 1913. Held in the Antient Concert Rooms in Dublin, the assembly was reported to be 'large and representative of all classes in the community. On the platform and in the hall were members, lay and clerical, of every Protestant denomination. The House of Lords and the House of Commons, Irish landlords and farmers, employers and workers, all the professions were all represented' (*Ulster Guardian*, 1 February 1913). Amongst those on the very well populated platform was J. Travers Wolfe of Skibbereen. Great numbers of people sent messages of support.

As in London, the purpose was 'to record a public protest against the statement frequently made from political platforms that the majority of Irish people would use Home Rule to oppress their fellow countrymen'. Again, the proceedings opened with music and the playing by a band of a 'charming selection of Irish airs'. These, as the *Ulster Guardian* commented, did not 'include "Kick the Pope" which roused Sir Edward Carson and his Covenanters on Ulster Day'. A whole array of speakers, chosen to represent the different interests of Protestant Ireland, each welcomed the prospect of Home Rule. This time, Yeats arrived in time and delivered a speech which was described as a 'fine literary effort'. 'The Ireland of today', orated the great poet, 'is like a stagnant stream in which float about tin cans, dead cats, and all manner of garbage. The advent of self-government will liberate the waters and sweep away the accumulated refuse of intolerant ideas.'

Amongst other Protestant speakers were two from County Cork, Jasper and the recently elected High Sheriff of Cork. On this occasion, the speaker who attracted the greatest plaudits was not Jasper but his fellow Corkman. The High Sheriff said:

This is an opportunity to vindicate the Christian and tolerant spirit of the Catholics of Ireland among whom we live, and of whom we have no fears. (Applause.) This meeting is called to spread the light, and discount the slanders against our Catholic fellow countrymen. It is now the duty of every man to say whether he is with his country or against her. (Applause.) I come as a young Irishman, proud of my country and as strongly imbued with the spirit of Irish Nationality as I believe any good Irishman should be. (Applause.) As a business man I pay warm tribute to the Catholics of Cork and the Catholic Corporation of the city for having, only yesterday, elected me High Sheriff.

In the aftermath of all this excitement, Jasper continued to do his bit. He received a deeply upset letter from John Willis, to which he replied courteously and at length, with a devastating, fact-based annihilation of Willis' charges of Catholic bias against Protestants in public life. Fortunately for the Justice of the Peace, the correspondence was private. Jasper also gave a number of talks in England, putting the case that Home Rule would result, not in sectarianism, but in enhanced mutual tolerance between the religious and racial communities of Ireland. What he had to say was reported, and widely appreciated, back in Ireland.

As Jasper and other Irish Protestants were at last speaking out for Home Rule, British Conservatives and Ulster Unionists were conspiring together to preserve the Union, if necessary by force. Eventually, although only after the war against Germany had broken out, the Government of Ireland Act, legislating for a devolved parliament in Dublin, was placed on the statute book. However, its implementation was to be suspended until after the end of hostilities; and there was a get-out clause for Ulster.

A MIXED MARRIAGE

Unlike Jasper, his older brother had remained unmarried, but this was about to change. The good neighbour policy with Catholics which Willie was preaching in public, he was practising in private. Willie had fallen in love with Dollie O'Shea. She was not yet twenty, a strong-willed, able, sumptuously attractive young woman, and the belle of Skibbereen. She was the daughter of Charles O'Shea and Annie Hourihan. Her father was the Skibbereen postmaster and also ran a pub in North Street, next door to Jasper's office before the move to Market Street. Her mother came from a farming family. While Dollie was still quite a young girl, Charles, who was well liked by the ladies, had walked out on his family and departed for New York. Annie was left to manage the pub and her six surviving children as well as she could.

Dollie had known the Wolfes since she was a young child, and from her early

Willie Wood Wolfe.

teens she was in and out of Jasper's office in North Street, where she used to flirt with Willie Kingston. Her affair with Willie Wood started when she was just seventeen. Before long the two were staying in a borrowed house in Baltimore overlooking the harbour.

Willie and Dollie were in love and determined to marry. From Dollie's point of view, Willie would make an excellent husband, a man who was established, respected and prosperous. As far as he was concerned, most men would be very happy to have as a wife a lovely-looking younger woman. Although he and his family were generally better off than hers, they both in fact belonged to the rising middle class of shopkeepers and business people with roots in tenant farming. The age difference itself, around twenty years, was of little concern to anyone. At that time men waited until they could afford to run a family and young women welcomed security and status. In fact, until well into the twentieth century, marriages could result quite as much from hard-headed deals as from love affairs. It was fairly common among the Gaelic Irish for marriages, together with dowries and other financial arrangements, to be negotiated by 'matchmakers' (Willie Kingston in later life was a greatly trusted matchmaker).

Nevertheless, the two faced horrendous difficulties if they were to get married. Willie's mother, Rachel, was viscerally and venomously hostile. Her opposition had deep and various roots. She resented the fact that Dollie was not a good match. In her eyes, this prospective daughter-in-law came from a lower social stratum than herself. She had been doing her best to match Willie with a respectable, well-connected young woman from Cork, but now such hopes looked like being dashed. And what was even worse for her as an active campaigner against 'The Drink', the O'Sheas kept a pub.

All this, however, was as nothing compared with fears provoked by Dollie's Catholicism. Many Protestant men, including the Wolfes, could have friendly personal, business and political relationships with the Catholic Irish, and might not be too worried about allegations of Catholics wielding excessive power in public life. There was little to suggest, whatever the hysteria of many Ulster Protestants, that Rome was interested in setting up an Irish theocracy. However, Protestant women, and not least Rachel Wolfe, were a different matter. Many were implacably against having anything more than the most superficial and fleeting contact with Catholics – unless they were servants.

Why were Rachel and others like her so fearful of mixing with Catholics? Their deepest anxieties concerned marriage and children. Women were seen as keepers of the hearth and defenders of the flame of Protestant family life. And this was directly threatened by Catholicism. When Rachel was a girl, the Catholic Church in Ireland was just emerging from many years of religious persecution by the British government and, in practice, recognised marriages between its members and Protestants and usually also accepted, if reluctantly, that the religious upbringing of children was a matter of parental choice. Now, however, under what has been referred to as a 'devotional revolution', this was ceasing to be the case. The archbishop of Dublin, Cardinal Cullen, pushing through the policies of his friend Pope Pius X, had initiated an increasingly strict interpretation of matrimonial law and it was becoming ever rarer for the Irish Catholic hierarchy to accept mixed marriages or permit children of such unions to be brought up as Protestants.

For Rachel, this meant that any grandchildren were in danger of being lost to the Methodism in which she believed so strongly. She, like others, was also profoundly concerned that, with children of a Protestant parent being brought up as Catholics, more than just the religious beliefs of one family was at risk. The Anglo-Irish in Cork, and particularly the Methodists, were few in number. Not many mixed marriages were needed (and Willie and Dollie's was not the only one to take place in the Wolfes' extended family) for the survival of the Methodist community to be under serious threat.

As if a furious Rachel was not enough to cope with, Willie and Dollie also had to face an even more fearsome adversary, the Roman Catholic Church itself. There would have been no problem if Willie had been prepared to convert, but he was not. He was hardly a devout Methodist, but the characteristically Protestant individualism, or bloody-mindedness, which had led him to 'sneer' at his religious upbringing made him utterly incapable of accepting the dogmatic teachings of Catholicism. However urgent his love for Dollie, however great the priestly pressure, he would not and could not sign up as a follower of Rome.

Most unfortunately for Willie and Dollie, just before they began their affair, Pope Pius X promulgated the decree *Ne Temere* (1907).[1] This aimed to remove various ambiguities which had emerged over the years concerning the Church's attitude towards marriage. Amongst other things, the rules concerning 'mixed marriages', as they were known, the marriage of Catholics with non-Catholics, were clarified and tightened. Various requirements were laid down concerning mixed marriages which in practice meant that the Church was extremely reluctant to recognise them, although it stopped just short of a total and absolute ban.

Unable to arrange a Catholic ceremony, in August 1911 Willie and Dollie travelled to London and got married at St Pancras registry office. However, contrary to what might have been expected, this was not to mark a decisive break for the Wolfes with the Catholic Church. It turned out, and this was recognised in the 1917 Code of Canon Law, that, although mixed marriages were 'severely prohibited', a dispensation could be obtained. It seems that the Wolfes managed to obtain such formal permission, or something very similar, no doubt once Willie had promised to respect Dollie's faith and allow the children to be brought up as Catholics. (It probably helped that the local priest was none other than Jasper's great friend, Father McCarthy.)

In the aftermath of these traumatic events, Willie Wood and Dollie settled down to family life, eventually producing a large and successful family, who were duly brought up as Catholics. Dollie became ever more devout as she grew older, and she and Willie remained happily married to the end of their long lives. When, well into his eighties, Willie started to lose his mind, Dollie finally succeeded in persuading him to convert. Their eldest son Brian, by now lapsed as a Catholic and living in England, rushed over to Skibbereen and protested strongly, but he failed to change his father's mind. 'That priest's a terribly good feller,' said Willie.[2]

Rachel, unlike the Catholic Church, was not prepared to give an inch. She neither compromised nor forgave. As a result, whereas the Pope gained members, she lost a son, a daughter-in-law and several grandchildren. When she learned that the marriage had actually taken place she was totally incensed, but her anger was not beyond words. 'Willie', she wrote, 'married a low, wretched barmaid, and cut himself off from his family and brought disgrace on his father's memory'. Rachel had hopes that Willie and her new daughter-in-law would emigrate, but this was not to be. Willie and Dollie settled themselves in Bridge House. Since Rachel was living only just around the corner from the pair, it was more than likely that they would occasionally bump into each other. The inevitable duly happened: 'Walked up to Ilen House. Coming back saw Willie and his barmaid; they went to play golf – how much more at home a barmaid would be behind the bar.'

Matters rapidly went from very bad to even worse. About a year after the marriage, Willie and Dollie welcomed their first child, a son. When out with a friend in her horse and trap, Rachel encountered the new family and she went straight past without acknowledging them: 'We met Willie and his nurse and baby and his wife out driving. He did not look very much at his ease. I do not think he felt at his ease either.'

Dollie was not one to put up with such treatment for long. She was also very well placed to retaliate. Rachel, in her rage, seems to have overlooked the vulnerability of her own position. Either that or she simply assumed that she would not be attacked. The weakness of her situation originated in the terms of Willie John's will. He had left Snugville to Jasper and Bridge House, together with the business and the tenancy of Licknavar farm, to Willie. The understanding was that Jasper and Willie would provide for their mother until her death, so she lived rent-free at Snugville and looked after the farm, drawing a good income from its profits. Most significantly, Willie John had also arranged that his widow should receive free provisions from the shop.

Left to himself, Willie would probably have made a few difficulties for his mother but would have been satisfied with simply annoying her. This was his usual style. As Rachel put it, somewhat dramatically, 'Willie can make life a great burden . . . How often has Willie given me a sad and sore heart since his father's death.' Now, as Rachel was to find out, she faced a far more dangerous adversary. One day, the grocery supplies stopped. Shortly after, a notice appeared in the *Eagle*:

LICKNAVAR, 1&¹/₂ Miles from Skibbereen

EXCEPTIONALLY DESIRABLE RESIDENTIAL TOWN FARM
FOR SALE BY PUBLIC AUCTION

Managing the sale was William G. Wood, a very successful 'Auctioneer and Farm sale expert'. Not only was he a cousin of Rachel's, but the advertisement also stated that details of the sale could be obtained from J. Travers Wolfe. It seemed as if her relatives were ganging up on her. Rachel now faced a catastrophic drop in her income, not to mention a very disagreable change in her way of life, as she got great pleasure from her farming activities.

Rachel got in touch with Jasper, who was not particularly supportive, and with various other relations. However, real help came from a most unexpected quarter. One of those interested in buying the farm (more precisely the tenancy of the farm), a Mr Attridge, received an anonymous note:

THE MAN ON THE LOOK OUT

Mr Attridge I hope that you were not foolis enough to buy from Wood Wolf the land grabber the robber that grabbed farm at Lick or Licknavar if so run from it if you value your life and the W.g. Woods now take this warning from one who knows yourself and your family and your friends for years and would wish them well as I am a loyal member of the Green White and Gold and must get fair play. This ruffan crew trew out the respectable famiily that that farm belonged to on Xmas eve and it snowing the Mother and eleven young children. So dont earn the vengeance of the man on the look out. Keep away from Wood Wolfe the trator to God and man.

Since Willie was popular with his Catholic neighbours and since the farm had been tenanted by himself and his father for around thirty years, it seems questionable whether the allegations made against him had much to do with fact. However, it was very evident that someone besides Rachel did not want the farm sold. The resident manager, who stood to lose job and home, was one possible candidate. Anyway, when the tenancy came up for sale, it did not reach its reserve price. Perhaps the threats had been taken seriously. Perhaps Jasper, in his usual style, had been quietly smoothing things over behind the scenes. Or perhaps Willie and Dollie were content to have given Rachel a bad fright. The matter dragged on for a while, but in the end Licknavar was not sold and free supplies from Bridge House to Snugville resumed. Nevertheless, relations between Rachel, Willie and Dollie remained stuck in deep permafrost. No reconciliation ever took place.

Rachel believed that Willie, through his marriage, had 'cut himself off from all his family', but this was not quite correct. What actually happened was that the Wolfes divided into two camps, with males mostly on one side and females on the other. Jasper and Willie stayed closely in touch, doing business, drinking

> The Man on the look out
>
> Mr Attridge I hope that you were
> not foolis enough to buy from Wood
> Wolf the land grabber the robber
> that grabbed farm at LICK or
> Lick navar ifso run from it If you
> value your life and the W.C. Woods
> now take this warning from one
> who Knows yourself and your
> family and your friends for years
> and would wish them well as
> I am a loyal member of the Green
> White and Gold and muse get fair
> play this ruffan crew out the
> respectable family that farm
> belonges on a Xmas. eve and is
> snowing the Mother and elevn youn
> children so dont earn the vengance
> of the man on the look out. Keep away
> from Wood. Wolfe the trator. so God and man

and playing cards together. Jasper would visit Bridge House and Willie would come to Norton, via the back door, to join in the all-male, all-night sessions of whiskey-drinking, talking and card-playing which Jasper held with great regularity in his part of the house. Jackson, too, kept up with the Wood Wolfes. He and they were all keen sailors and, when Jackson was over from England, great yachting parties would take place at Baltimore.

The women took an entirely different approach. Winnie and Jasper's wife Minnie were almost as hostile to the Wood Wolfes as Rachel herself. Minnie would invariably cross the road rather than acknowledge Dollie. Only May, independent-minded as ever, remained in touch with her brother and his wife. Before long, the next generation were involved. Jasper and Minnie's daughters, Dorothy and Ray, were implacably hostile, while their younger brother, Travers, was well-disposed. Jackson had married a Scot and they had one child,

THE FAMILIES OF JASPER TRAVERS WOLFE AND HIS BROTHER WILLIE WOOD WOLFE

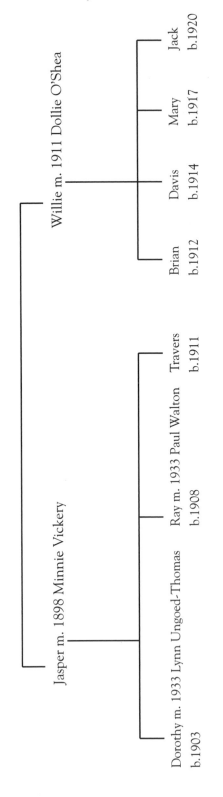

Jack, who grew up to be an even more dedicated sailor than his father and just as friendly with the Wood Wolfes, both on the water and off. The husband of one of his Catholic cousins was even best man at his marriage (the Bishop of Cork having been more or less bamboozled into allowing official permission to be given for a Catholic to feature in a Protestant service). May had no children, but Winnie married a brother of Minnie Wolfe's, a doctor who settled in Wales. They had two daughters, who were brought up to avoid the Catholic Wolfes at all costs. The younger daughter, Margaret, remembers her mother suddenly hauling her away from playing with some other children on the beach at Tragumna – they were Wood Wolfes. Margaret, however, did not inherit her mother's prejudice.

Around the time of the Second World War, Jasper's grandchildren, offspring of Dorothy and Ray, started to arrive. None of us was ever told by anyone, least of all by our mothers, that we had Catholic cousins living not just in County Cork, but actually in Skibbereen. It was only by complete fluke that we learned the truth. One of my sons, by chance, was on holiday with friends near Baltimore. He came across two young brothers with the surname Wolfe, who were renowned locally for their fearless sailing. My son, who was not averse to a bit of risk-taking himself, was much interested in the possibility of a family connection. Very shortly, he found himself in a house overlooking the bay and, astonishingly, gazing at portraits of his great-great-grandparents, Willie John and Rachel Wolfe. He had discovered some of his Catholic third cousins. After a break of eighty years, the descendants of Jasper and Willie Wood Wolfe were at last able to mend their bridges and set about rebuilding relationships.

PART THREE

THE TROUBLES,
1916–1922

14

CROWN SOLICITOR

In June 1916 Jasper was appointed Crown Solicitor for Cork City and County West Riding. This office, peculiar to Ireland, had originally been established at the beginning of the nineteenth century. The holder was responsible for conducting Crown prosecutions at the assizes, quarter sessions and occasionally petty sessions. He could also be required to appear for the Crown at inquests and military courts martial. Usually, particularly at assizes and in major cases, he would brief barristers. Sometimes, however, he would himself appear for the prosecution.[1]

In normal times a Crown Solicitorship was a highly desirable post. It carried the lucrative annual salary of just over £850 a year, was pensionable and allowed the holder to carry on his private practice. It was seldom particularly onerous, because, while many Irish participated enthusiastically in the sort of behaviour that the authorities considered illegal, their activities, except at times of high political tension, rarely erupted into serious criminality. In Munster, in the early years of the twentieth century, assize judges regularly commented on the peaceable condition of the country. As late as the winter assizes of 1916, the first Jasper attended in his new capacity, the presiding justice congratulated southern Ireland on its generally peaceable condition, the only exception being County Clare.

Along with its other advantages, a Crown Solicitorship brought with it considerable prestige. Appointment to Cork city, the 'Capital of the South' as it was often called, was particularly significant. Jasper's immediate predecessor, Henry Wynne, had been promoted to Chief Crown Solicitor in Dublin, was subsequently knighted and became a member of the Privy Council.

Skibbereen was delighted by Jasper's success. Congratulations poured in. The local magistrates were particularly complimentary. This body, which thanks to the appointments policy of the Liberal government was no longer dominated by Protestant landowners, included in its number Jasper's old sparring partners Timothy Sheehy and Jim Burke. The bench of the petty sessions passed a motion unanimously recording its 'appreciation'.

The comments of those who spoke in favour of his appointment reflect the general opinion of Jasper at the time:

Mr Wolfe is a great favourite with all classes. This is not to be wondered at for we all remember how he went through England and showed the masses of the English people that the Catholics of Ireland are not so intolerant as certain people wanted to make them out. It is a great honour to our town to see that this and other important positions have been lately given to gentlemen in this part of the country.

Mr Wolfe has worked his way up by sheer merit, by his ability, his courtesy, and by the care and attention which he has paid in any case entrusted to him by his clients. He has taken as much pains with the most trivial case as with one involving thousands of pounds. In that way he has endeared himself not only to his clients but has extended that practice which he established in this town not only to the surrounding villages but to the towns and petty sessions districts throughout the county of Cork. Throughout the province of Munster his name is practically a household word as an able solicitor.

One final tribute was offered by District Inspector Foster of the Royal Irish Constabulary:

I also beg to be associated with the congratulatory remarks to Mr Wolfe. We often had 'tiffs' in this court. In a way I am glad to say that this is finished and that he cannot oppose me any more.' (Laughter.) (*Eagle*, 10 June 1916)

In the early months of 1916 it was still possible for Jasper, and others like him, to hope that all would turn out well for Ireland and those who desired that it should achieve self-rule within the United Kingdom and Empire. It appeared, for instance, that many Irish, including their leaders, were ready to support Britain in its fight against Germany. In the opening months of the Great War, Redmond had spoken strongly in favour of Irishmen volunteering to fight in the British forces. His own brother, Captain William H. K. Redmond MP, was to be killed in action.

In Skibbereen Jasper, together with his brother Willie, was an active member of the Recruiting Committee, giving talks, lending his car for meetings and contributing money. While Anglo-Irish ascendancy figures were well to the fore (Lady Coghill and Mrs Chavasse were both committee members), Catholic Irish were also represented (Dr Timothy O'Meara, the distinguished local GP, was an active supporter). Military bands played, British soldiers stationed in the Town Hall paraded in their military best and good numbers of Protestants and Catholics joined up. All in all, the local regiment, the Royal Munster Fusiliers, did very well in Skibbereen. As for opposition, there appear to have been few, if any, open signs of hostility.

Constitutional Nationalism, which had just succeeded in getting Home Rule on to the statute book, seemed to remain strong. In West Cork it was able to demonstrate this even as late as the autumn of 1916. Following the death of James Gilhooly, the veteran O'Brienite MP for West Cork, a by-election was held. Willie Wood Wolfe, still loyal to the All for Ireland League, campaigned hard for the O'Brienite candidate. Jasper, sidelined by his new role as a goverment law officer, acted as deputy returning officer. The vote ended in a narrow victory for the Redmondite. While the result finally finished the O'Brienites as an effective political body, it appeared, if only momentarily, to give hope to the Irish Parliamentary Party. An unofficial Sinn Féin candidate trailed in a poor third. (Sinn Féin, not yet formally Republican, had been founded in 1905 as a voice for militant Nationalism.)

In the first years of the war, Home Rule did not appear to be in imminent danger from a Republican challenge. In reaction to Ulster's systematic preparations for armed rebellion, the Irish Volunteers had been founded in late 1913. Although the setting up of a Nationalist private army had the potential to threaten rebellion against the British, its immediate aim was not so much the foundation of a Republic as the prevention of partition, by force if necessary. In this sense it could be seen simply as a militant wing of the sort of all-Ireland political programme endorsed by the O'Brienites and the more Nationalist Redmondites.

The initial response throughout southern Ireland was enthusiastic. In Skibbereen, recruits, including numbers of Protestants, signed up by the dozen, and photographs survive of men drilling and of splendid parades of mounted Volunteers, the leaders sporting sashes in the national colours. However, there were no arms or uniforms available and the initial momentum was lost. As Jasper's cousin Willie Kingston recorded in his memoirs, 'there was very little local interest, and the movement died away'.

Easter was late in 1916. Just over a month before his appointment as Crown Solicitor, Jasper read in his copy of the *Eagle* of a 'Terrible Occurrence in Dublin'. A week later came headlines announcing 'Collapse of Rising in Dublin. Leaders shot' and 'Full Account of Fighting in Streets'. It was not obvious at the time that an historic event in Irish history had just occurred. In Skibbereen, the initial reaction was calm. Willie Kingston recorded that 'the rebellion . . . had few sympathisers . . . and in fact there was a sense of relief when it collapsed'. When, a fortnight after the Rising, the army sent a contingent of 400 men into Skibbereen, the *Eagle* was scathing, talking of 'this military steam-hammer brought solemnly along to crush the little harmless butterfly of sedition in this town'. In the absence of anything more serious to do, the military marched up and down, their bands played and numerous recruiting meetings were held, Jasper and Willie both doing their bit. To all appearances, it was business as usual.

However, concern grew as it became clear that the authorities in Dublin were intent on pursuing a policy of executions. The *Eagle*, British supporter though it was, proved not only forgiving, but prescient. In a leader headed 'The Quality of Mercy', it argued that 'there never was a time or occasion more fitting for the exercise of the divine attribute of mercy than now and here in

Ireland. The refusal of it may have consequences for our country's future that no man can foresee.' Willie Kingston described how opinion in Skibbereen rapidly changed. 'The brutalities of the British forces during the fighting, and particularly the shooting of the prisoners afterwards, caused a great revulsion of feeling, and paved the way for the Sinn Féin rising.'

Further massive resentment against Westminster rule arose when Asquith's government, driven predominantly by jingoist pressures, proposed to introduce conscription. While the Irish in their thousands had proved ready to join up voluntarily, to be forced to do so was quite a different matter. Nationalist opinion felt it was being treated with contempt. Nor were the Irish alone in their opposition. In Britain, the radical wing of Liberalism, which included many Nonconformists, deeply resented their party flouting its sustaining principles of liberty of conscience and freedom of the individual. As for Irish Dissenters, such as Jasper, while they mostly accepted conscription, it made them deeply uneasy, both on religious and political grounds. A few, like Willie Kingston, actively opposed it. In 1916, when conscription was first introduced, Irish and radical campaigning ensured that Ireland and conscientious objectors were exempted. But the issue remained alive and by 1918 Irish conscription was again being debated. While once again the idea was eventually shelved, the proposal drove many, particularly young men, into the ranks of the Republicans. And it further dismayed numbers of radically minded Protestants. When in Skibbereen a public petition against conscription was organised, Willie Kingston was among those who signed. 'To compel a man to fight against his will seems to me a negation of all religion and humanity', wrote Willie.

In September 1916 Yeats composed his poem 'Easter, 1916'. It included these lines:

> Was it needless death after all?
> For England may keep faith
> For all that is done and said.
> We know their dream

But England did not keep faith. It could look, from where Jasper and other Southern Protestant Home Rulers stood, as if the Liberal government and its leaders were acting in bad faith. In one move, or refusal to move, after another, Asquith, and later, when he became Prime Minister, David Lloyd George, failed to stand up for the radical principles which had underpinned the campaign to return self-government to Dublin. As early as 1914, when Unionist forces in Ireland had threatened armed revolt and when British officers at the Curragh appeared to be involved in plans to mutiny on behalf of Ulster, the British government had remained supine. When the Home Rule Bill finally became law, in a piece of unscrupulous parliamentary *legerdemain*, the fulfilment of the act was shelved, not merely for the duration of the war, but until after its formal conclusion. When Asquith resigned and Lloyd George formed a coalition, Edward (later Lord) Carson, Ulster Unionist leader; Andrew Bonar Law, leader of the Conservative and Unionist party; and Walter Long, a strong Unionist, all joined the government. Not an Irish Home Rule supporter was to be seen. (Redmond had, in fact, been offered a post by Asquith in his coalition of eighteen months earlier but had refused it. So the Nationalists had to carry some of the blame for their political impotence. Nevertheless, Lloyd George's tilting of the scales in the Unionists' favour was, at best, unstatesmanlike.) Finally, and perhaps most damagingly of all, Lloyd George, who many years previously had written to his wife-to-be that his career would come before all else, proved true to his word. The man who, as a pro-Boer, had stood up for 'the little five foot nine nations' and as a Welsh Baptist had defended liberty of conscience, now not only pressed for conscription, but harried conscientious objectors and, in act after act, whether covert or public, displayed an uncaring disdain for the one small and unfree nation whose fate he was placed to influence directly for the better. There were many moderate-minded Irish, whether Protestant or Catholic, whose previous belief in at least the underlying goodwill of the British government, and indeed of the British people more generally, did not survive the political happenings of the war years. Willie Kingston spoke for many more than himself when he wrote, 'I realised that . . . all I had been taught of the justice and kindness of mankind, and especially of the British, was merely propaganda and that all virtues disappeared under the slightest strain'.

The democratic, middle way of Irish politics began to crumble. Many Protestant Home Rulers were forced, reluctantly, onto the Unionist side of the road, while numbers of their Catholic colleagues, equally reluctantly, found themselves being pressured towards the Republicans. Yeats had written 'Things fall apart; the centre cannot hold / Mere anarchy is loosed upon the world'. But a minority of Irishmen, including Jasper, whatever their religious beliefs, remained true to their vision of an Irish state, one which would be in some way related to, but not dependent on, the United Kingdom. Such men and women did not surrender in their fight to hold the centre, and never accepted defeat in their efforts to contain 'mere anarchy'.

15

'YOUR GRANDAD PUT MY DAD IN GAOL!'

Jasper, as things were turning out, could hardly have been appointed Crown Solicitor at a less propitious moment. He was to be public prosecutor for a government that was fast losing authority and respect, in a nation on the edge of revolt. He might, however, have found some comfort and hope in a strange quarter. Not long after the Easter Rising there appeared, inconspicuously, on an inner page of the *Eagle*, a headline of 'Text of the Rebels' Manifesto'. This, given in full, was a 'Proclamation' of 'the Irish Republic as a Sovereign Independent State'. It was seen by a few at the time, and by many since, above all as an inspirational summons by Ireland to her children, 'in arms in the face of the world', to rally to her flag and strike for her freedom.

Written in the great tradition of eighteenth-century libertarianism, the Proclamation outlined a generous vision of a free and self-governing Irish nation.

The Republic guarantees religious and civil liberty, equal rights and equal opportunities to all its citizens, and declares its resolve to pursue the happiness and prosperity of the whole nation and of all its parts, cherishing the children of the nation equally.

For a Protestant like Jasper, for members of any minority and for free-thinkers of whatever persuasion, here there was little to fear: no announcement of a theocratic state, no narrow, rigid sectarianism, no hint of any racist dogma, no elevation of the rights of the state above the needs of its people. This was a wholly liberal vision of civic order.

The Proclamation also spelled out how the Provisional Government, now in theory established, expected its adherents to conduct themselves in the coming struggle.

We pray that no one who serves the cause will dishonour it by cowardice, inhumanity, or rapine. In this supreme hour the Irish Nation must, by its valour and discipline, and by the readiness of its children to sacrifice themselves for the common good, prove itself worthy of the august destiny to which it is called.

If it did come to a shooting match, the Republicans at least intended to fight according to rules. Which, for anyone likely to be in the line of fire, such as Jasper, at least offered a flicker of hope.

In the summer of 1916, while Jasper was starting his new duties, many Irish families were worrying, not so much about their homeland, as about events in France. In the Battle of the Somme, day after day, young men were dying in numbers never before imagined: on 1 July, the first day of hostilities, 20,000 men were killed and almost twice that number wounded. Thousands of Irishmen, Protestant and Catholic, were at the Front. Families, relations, friends and neighbours, when they met, asked of war news and when they opened the newspapers they looked first at casualty lists and obituaries. Jasper was fortunate. He and his brothers were too old to volunteer and too young to have sons of an age to fight. However, Jasper knew many of those who had joined up, having helped to recruit a considerable number of them.

As Jasper prepared Crown briefs for barristers in major cases at the assizes, and himself prosecuted in lesser trials at the quarter sessions, prospects for peace in Ireland darkened. In May 1916 the British imprisoned 800 Nationalists at Frongoch in North Wales, releasing them six months later. In the summer of 1917 an Irish Convention was called by Lloyd George to reach agreement on the future of the country. Within a year, it had disintegrated in failure.

The Republicans were, while all this was going on, proceeding to lay the foundations of a new Irish state. In the autumn of 1916 a split took place in the Irish Volunteers. John Redmond called for the Volunteers to fight, not just in defence of Ireland, which had been his previous policy, but 'wherever the firing line extends'. In other words, he summoned them to take up arms for imperial Britain in Europe, or wherever else the conflicts of the Great War might occur. While many southern Irish (approaching 160,000) had voluntarily joined the British forces, and were at the time fighting on the Somme in the 16th Irish Division, leading Republicans strongly resented any attempt by the Nationalist Irish leadership to offer official support to the struggles of the British war machine. Consequently the active Republicans, retaining the title 'Irish Volunteers', set up their own paramilitary movement and before long this morphed into the Irish Republican Army (IRA). Redmond's sympathisers, who for the moment encompassed the great majority, reformed as the 'National Volunteers'.

While in Ireland Republican leaders who were still free were beginning to lay the foundations of an organisation capable of effective armed resistance to the British, the internees at Frongoch, under the leadership of Michael Collins, were turning their gaol into what became, to all intents and purposes, a residential school on how to achieve Irish independence. Once freed, these leaders of the Republican movement, now much better informed and prepared, spent 1917 planning for action. In July, Éamon de Valera won a by-election at East Clare (caused by the death in action of William Redmond, brother of the

Irish Nationalist leader John Redmond). In October, the Republicans engineered some significant changes to their organisation and leadership. At its Ard Fheis (annual convention), Sinn Féin agreed a detailed constitution for itself, which enshrined as its primary aim to secure 'international recognition of Ireland as an independent Irish Republic'. At the same time, the party elected de Valera its president, and, when de Valera was also chosen as president of the Irish Volunteers, the prospect improved of more effective co-ordination between the political and military wings of Republicanism.

In 1918, on the Western Front, the allies seemed to be on the verge of defeat and then rebounded from retreat to advance – and victory. In Ireland, the British authorities and the Republicans squared up to each other in ever more menacing fashion. Sinn Féin mounted a fierce campaign against conscription. The recently appointed Lord Lieutenant, Earl French of Ypres, a gung-ho military leader whose incompetence was exceeded only by his ignorance of Ireland, riposted by arresting virtually the entire Sinn Féin leadership for plotting with the Germans against the British, a charge for which neither at the time nor since has any significant evidence been produced. Two months later, as civil unrest grew, Sinn Féin, the Irish Volunteers, Cumann na mBan and the Gaelic League were all declared dangerous organisations, although not yet actually banned. Simultaneously, under the Defence of the Realm Act and the 1887 Criminal Law and Procedure Act, a series of official initiatives increased military, police and legal powers. John Dillon, the new Irish National Party leader (John Redmond having just died), declared that Ireland was 'lying under the unfettered tyranny of a military government'.

The British in Ireland were now about to suffer a crucial defeat, inflicted not by armed revolutionaries, but by the ballot box. After the armistice had been signed in November 1918, Lloyd George called a general election. He chose not to rejoin the Liberal Party, but to go to the country at the head of a coalition. This now consisted of the Conservative and Unionist Party, as it had become known, and a minority of pro-war, mostly Unionist, Liberals. In effect, Lloyd George was now the prisoner, albeit out on bail, of the Unionists. Their power, and momentarily his, was confirmed by comprehensive electoral victory on mainland Britain. However, in Ireland, it was a different story. The parliamentary Home Rule Irish Nationalists went down to total defeat, and Sinn Féin won 73 out of 105 seats. Republicans now indisputably held both the political and, even more significantly, the moral high ground. Their claim for Irish freedom could henceforth be grounded not only in appeals to myth, history, natural justice and romantic idealism, but in democratic right and will. They held a potentially winning hand.

In Cork, life was not standing still. After Jasper's first few months of mundane activity as Crown Solicitor, his work soon became rather more challenging. Exactly what he was doing becomes increasingly difficult to follow. As outbreaks of conflict spread, cases could be moved from one court to another at short notice, reporting restrictions became more common and courts martial, where the army usually led prosecutions, dealt with charges which fell within the ever-widening net of military law. Some years later when applying to the British government for compensation, Jasper wrote of his responsibilities at this time, 'During 1916, 1917, and 1918 I prosecuted civilians at Military Courts Martial for the entire Southern Command and also conducted prosecutions of a large number of cases under the Crimes Act, and appeared for the Crown at Inquests'. Specifically, he prepared Crown cases in military and civil courts, briefing either a barrister or a legally qualfied military officer or appearing himself.

Jasper owed much of his workload, and its changing nature, to the activities of the Irish Volunteers. Immediately on the release of Republicans from Frongoch, the secret Irish Republican Brotherhood group started organising in Cork. Amongst the most active leaders were Tomás MacCurtain and Liam Deasy, both men whom Jasper would shortly encounter. One of their first priorities was to recruit and train Irish Volunteers. So successful were they that special legal arrangements were introduced to curb their activities and before long the Volunteers were declared an illegal organisation. Numerous prosecutions resulted, all of which in Cork city and the West Riding were the responsibility of Jasper.

In later years, when passions had settled down somewhat, those whom Jasper had successfully prosecuted were often ready to forgive, although very seldom to forget. But this was not always the case. Some time after the Second World War, a cousin of mine was a student at Trinity College Dublin. In the early hours of the morning, after a formal ball, he went with his girlfriend down to a quay where one could get something to eat and drink. There he started talking with a middle-aged man. To begin with, all was friendly.

'You're English, so?'

'Well, not exactly,' answered my cousin, 'My mother is Irish.'

'So where would she be from?'

'County Cork.'

'Well, for Heaven's sake, just like myself. And what did your people do?'

'My grandfather was a solicitor, and a member of the Dáil.'

'Oh, is that so now. And who might your grandad have been?'

'Jasper Wolfe.'

A terrible change came over the Irishman. 'Jasper Wolfe, did you say?'

'Well, yes.'

The man approached my cousin, seized him by the lapels of his dinner jacket and yanked him off his feet. 'Your grandad,' he shouted, 'put my dad in gaol!' The encounter ended then and there, but not amicably, as can be imagined.[1]

One of Jasper's best-known court appearances occurred in April 1920, when he acted for the Crown at the inquest into the murder of a leading Republican. As one lawyer put it at the time, this was widely regarded as 'the most important, and solemn investigation which has occupied the attention of any court in the annals of crime in this country for a very long time'. In January 1920 municipal elections had been held throughout Ireland, including Cork city. At the time, Tomás MacCurtain, the leading Repubican activist in Cork, was on the run from the authorities. Nevertheless, he stood for office as a Sinn Féin councillor and was successful. He was proposed by the Republicans, now the largest party on Cork City Council, as Lord Mayor. Since a warrant was out for his arrest, he had to be smuggled at dawn into City Hall, where the election was to take place. At noon, in the council chamber, MacCurtain was unanimously elected. He was now the local Brigade Commander of a recently proscribed military organisation, and legally appointed head of the civic administration of southern Ireland's second city.

In the early months of 1920 tension escalated and tempers shortened in Cork city. The Royal Irish Constabulary, which was under constant threat from the Republicans and was afflicted by increasing numbers of resignations and falling morale, was finding it difficult to police the city effectively, particularly at night. On 10 March a district inspector was shot and wounded while guarding ballot boxes at a local by-election and the police went on the rampage, hunting out Sinn Féiners. No disciplinary action was taken against them, and tit-for-tat attacks followed. On 19 March an experienced off-duty constable, unarmed, was fired at seven times and killed. Early the next morning, Tomás MacCurtain was shot dead in his home.

The facts were indisputable. The area around MacCurtain's house, in Blackpool, an area just to the north of the city centre, had been sealed off by considerable numbers of armed men, most with blackened faces. At about a quarter past one MacCurtain's wife answered the door in response to loud knocks and shouts. Two disguised men rushed upstairs and shot the Lord Mayor, while companions of the killers held Mrs MacCurtain at the door. Also in the house were the couple's five young children and eight other members of the family. Hardly an hour later, a contingent of British soldiers arrived with orders to arrest MacCurtain. On learning that he had been killed, the accompanying police refused to enter the house, but the military went ahead anyway and searched the premises, including the bed on which lay the corpse of the Lord Mayor.[2]

In the inquest which followed, the coroner told the jury that it was their duty to establish 'the immediate cause of death'. He also added that 'if on the evidence you can find out who are the parties who inflicted those wounds it is open to you to do so'. In Dublin, while the inquest was in progress, Lord French gave an interview to the *Daily Express* in which he accused Sinn Féin supporters of the crime. Invited to send his evidence to the court, he declined. He was not, said a message from the Chief Crown Solicitor, 'in a position to give any evidence to the enquiry'. To most people other than the Lord Lieutenant, it seemed more than likely that the killing had been carried out, not by Sinn Féin, but by the police, possibly with the assistance of the military.

The inquest, in effect, turned into a trial of the Royal Irish Constabulary. Jasper, as Crown Solicitor acting for the government, had the task, not so much of identifying the guilty men, as of defending the police. Since he had always excelled in acting for the accused, he was more than qualified for the job. But it was a tough challenge. He used most tricks in the book, and a few that were not.

He began, as was his custom, with flattery (*Eagle*, 24 April 1920): 'I would like sincerely to thank the jury for the very great kindness and courtesy you have extended to me, and also for the very great skill and ability which you have brought to bear on the very troublesome and unusual task on which you are engaged.' He then flattered the coroner himself, commenting on the high reputation which he rightly enjoyed in the city of Cork, and thanking him for his exemplary conduct of the enquiry. Jasper then proceeded to open his defence of the police. The constabulary, he claimed, had the most excellent relationship with the Lord Mayor, whom they esteemed, and rightly. Why, almost the last act of the late Tomás MacCurtain had been to telephone his sympathy to the family of the officer who had been killed the evening before his own assassination. The last thing on police minds would have been a desire to kill Cork's first citizen.

The police, argued Jasper, were honourable upholders of law and order. The charge made against them 'is outrageous . . . It would be a scandal if the charge is persevered with to the end'. So how, asked Jasper, did the rumour that they were somehow responsible get started?

> When policeman after policeman throughout the country is being murdered it is true that the man in the street is found saying – people who ought to know better the patience of the police – 'a day will come when they will get their own back'. And so, gossip started, and found listeners. The originators of the story which was circulated should feel ashamed of their conduct.

Then Jasper claimed that the police, and indeed he himself, were true Irishmen, with nothing but the best interests of their own country at heart. He himself had become 'solicitor of the people, sometimes called Crown Solicitor'. As for the constabulary, they are 'as fine a body of men as ever Ireland produced. They are sprung from the people, kith and kin of the people, and friendly towards the people. It is in the interest of every Irishman, no matter what his politics, instead of acts of murder and brutality, to preserve and enhance those friendly relations.'

Jasper next dealt with the substance of his case. It appeared that Cork on the night of the murder had been well populated with shadowy figures, of allegedly murderous intent, half glimpsed by some witnesses, not noticed or perceived in a different light by other witnesses. Jasper proceeded to use one of his favourite tactics. As once he had deeply confused a bench of magistrates over the whereabouts of naval and alleged smuggling vessels off the west coast, he now tried to make it impossible for the jury to conclude with any certainty who it might have been that was on the loose, and where. To further exonerate the police, he put numbers of them on the witness stand to swear that, with the exception of small duty patrols who undoubtedly were too few to have carried out the murder operation alone, all local members of the constabulary had been in barracks or lodgings. Furthermore, records showed that at the relevant time no police car had been out of its barracks, no police weaponry had been issued and no ammunition was unaccounted for.

Unfortunately for Jasper and the RIC, there was the question of the police rampage of 10 March. Despite his earlier praise of the police, Jasper admitted that the events were 'a regrettable occurrence'. He hoped that they would be 'a lesson to everybody – a lesson to the police, in the first instance, that they may never again so far forget themselves, and forget their duty to the force, to their country, and to their best traditions'. But, he added, 'I hope also that it will be a lesson to the people, because they should remember that the police, like everyone else, are human, and were driven to desperation by foul and brutal murders.' Jasper went on to say, and this was his main point, that, although the police had admittedly behaved reprehensibly, they had nevertheless caused no serious harm. No one had been injured, let alone killed. 'The jury should remember that not a hair on the head of one person was injured that night.'

However, as the barrister acting for the MacCurtain family, a distinguished King's Counsel, had little difficulty in pointing out, events on the evening of 10 March had not been exactly as Jasper had described them. For a start, while no hairs might have been hurt, some fairly serious bruises were inflicted. Far more significantly, it was proved that the constabulary had falsified their records to show that policemen were in the barracks when in fact they were not. If this had happened during the night of 10 March, it could also have happened less than two weeks later in the early hours of 20 March. The Crown case did not stand up against this argument.

The jury considered its verdict for two and a half hours. It emphatically did not accept Jasper's 'eloquent plea', as the press described it. It found that 'the late Lord Mayor . . . was wilfully murdered . . . and that the murder was organised and carried out by the Royal Irish Constabulary' (loud applause) 'officially directed by the British government and we return a verdict of wilful murder against Mr David Lloyd George, Prime Minister of England; Lord French, Lord Lieutenant of Ireland . . . district inspector Swanzy' ('hear, hear' and applause) 'and some unknown members of the Royal Irish Constabulary'.

The jury had, in some sense, spoken for Ireland, but not as Jasper had argued it should.

16

'I HAD THE HONOUR AND PRIVILEGE OF BEING THREE TIMES SENTENCED TO DEATH'

Nearly two decades after the Troubles, by which time Jasper was a distinguished citizen of the Irish Free State, he made a speech on being presented with an inscribed silver salver by his fellow lawyers in West Cork. The presentation ceremony was held to honour the appointment of Jasper as president of the Incorporated Law Society of Ireland. Looking back over his career, he recalled of his time as Crown Solicitor that 'I had the honour and privilege of being three times sentenced to death. The most peculiar aspect of that was that all three of my would-be executioners afterwards became my warmest friends' (*Southern Star*, 18 January 1941).

Jasper knew there was nothing personal in the attempts to kill him. He understood very well that the Republicans were putting their major efforts into state building, not vengeful assassinations. They had a national parliament (the Dáil), they had a national government, they controlled most local councils, they had an army and they had a legal system. Unfortunately, at least from the Sinn Féin perspective, not only were most of these institutions embryonic, but, local councils excepted, they were deemed illegal by the British government.

It was the Republican policy on the administration of justice which most immediately, and gravely, affected Jasper. Sinn Féin developed its own courts and simultaneously worked to undermine those of the United Kingdom. Justices of the Peace were threatened, many resigning, and most courts of petty sessions ceased to function. In higher courts, juries were either intimidated or chose of their own free will not to appear, so county and assize courts, in their turn, began to disappear. However, certain key officials, including Jasper, continued to work. As a result, a skeleton system of British justice went on functioning, which the Republicans were absolutely determined to wipe out entirely. Agents of British government law enforcement who remained active became prime targets. Top of the Republican hit list in Cork county and city was Jasper Wolfe.

17

MICHAEL COLLINS

In West Cork, one man above all others inspired Republican opposition to the forces of the British state. It was his leadership as much as anything else which was to make life so dangerous for Jasper, and many others.

Jasper knew a good deal about Michael Collins. To begin with, there was a family connection. Just below Seaview farm, where Jasper's mother Rachel Wood had spent her girlhood, lived the Collins family. Here Michael Collins had been brought up on a ninety-acre farm at Woodfield. Amongst the close neighbours of Collins' parents were the Deanes, themselves great friends of the Woods. Protestant Woods and Deanes knew the Catholic, Nationalist Collinses. What is more, they got on well together, not least because Michael's mother, a remarkable, generous-minded woman, believed in being a good neighbour to everyone, whatever their religion and background. A member of the Deane family had attended her funeral when she died of cancer ten years or so before the Troubles.

Jasper also knew of Michael Collins through his local activities. In the 1918 general election Collins had been elected to parliament, unopposed, as a Sinn Féin candidate for Skibbereen's constituency of South Cork. When Sinn Féin refused to take up their seats in the House of Commons and set up Dáil Éireann, Michael Collins, besides emerging as a national leader of Republicanism, retained a hands-on interest in his South Cork constituency.

Collins, as Jasper was well aware, was a military as well as a political actor. He played a crucial role in establishing the IRA throughout County Cork, and in West Cork in particular. It was he who presided, as a representative of Republican General Headquarters in Dublin, at a meeting in January 1919 near Dunmanway, when the West Cork Volunteers were reorganised into the third Cork Brigade, with six battalions. By the end of the year this formed part of what was becoming known, not as the Irish Volunteers, but rather as the Irish Republican Army. In August 1920, after a successful training camp in Glandore, a meeting of the West Cork Brigade Council was held just outside Skibbereen at Caheragh, and a comprehensive scheme for the reorganisation of personnel was drawn up and immediately implemented. Again, Michael Collins presided.

It was not long before attacks on Jasper began in earnest. Michael Collins was on the run in Dublin for much of the time, and so not personally involved. However, although he himself was not present when Jasper was sentenced to death, as a member of the Republican high command he may well, though probably on not more than one occasion, have approved the death sentence.

18

GUNRUNNING

The Republicans may have enjoyed popular support and a coherent military organisation, but these alone were not sufficient. If the Republican writ was to have effect in West Cork, and elsewhere in Ireland, it had to be enforced. This task fell to the IRA. However, the organisation was desperately short of arms so, while life could be made very difficult for the British authorities, there was little chance of securing real control over the courts, or anything else.

Of the various ways of getting hold of arms, one was to import them by boat. In the autumn of 1920, Jasper's brother Willie was tricked into providing cover for an illegal shipment. Willie was on good terms with Barney O'Driscoll, a farmer from Union Hall, and also a fellow member of the Skibbereen Urban Council. A larger than life character, Barney was also, as it happened, a known and ardent Republican and had been the first commandant of the Skibbereen Volunteers when they were founded in 1917.

Willie was also friendly with Joe O'Regan, whose family owned a successful creamery business at Aughadown, a few miles to the west of Skibbereen. The O'Regans were strong Nationalists and Joe, like Barney O'Driscoll, was an active Republican. Between them, Barney and Joe dreamed up a plan to import a cargo of ammunition and rifles. Joe was very well placed to do just this. As part of its normal business, the Aughadown creameries regularly exported butter to Cardiff and loaded up with coal for the return trip. If armaments were purchased, they could be hidden in the hold.[1]

Having managed to find a supply of weaponry, Barney and Joe were left with one serious difficulty. The boat would have to be checked by the authorities on its return. How was officialdom to be hoodwinked? This was where Willie came in. He was a Protestant, a Justice of the Peace (one of the few who had not been intimidated into resigning) and, although a known Home Ruler, an equally well-known opponent of Republicanism. If Willie could be persuaded to come along, the authorities would be unlikely to feel suspicious. So when Barney O'Driscoll next met Willie Wood Wolfe, no doubt at a council meeting, he casually asked him if he would fancy a boat trip.

'We're away to Cardiff in a few days. Would you fancy a ride with us?'

It turned out Willie was game. 'Sure, that's a grand idea, altogether.'

Willie had no one except himself to blame for failing to smell a particularly putrid outsize rat. He knew perfectly well that in West Cork anything was fair in war and most other human goings on – with the possible exception of love. So he let himself become the victim of what was at one and the same time an IRA action, and a huge practical joke.

Once docked in Wales, with the butter safely unloaded, Joe took Willie on an extended tour of the local public houses. By the time of the return trip, with Willie at least in a particularly happy condition, the ship's hold had been filled with good Welsh coal, and, as far as anyone could see, nothing but coal. On its way back to Ireland, the boat had to report to the customs in Cork city's Queenstown harbour (Cobh) for official checking of the cargo. When Joe O'Regan and his men signed in with the authorities, one of the customs officers immediately recognised Willie.

'How you doing, Willie? Been away for the craic? Was it a grand trip you've had? Come in and take some tea.'

So, Willie, Joe, Barney and one or two others settled down for a chat in the office. The customs hardly glanced at the cargo. Eventually, with good wishes all round, the sailors returned to their boat and set sail for home. Having docked at a Reenadhuna pier (which still exists) at the mouth of the river Ilen, Willie was helped on shore and made his way back to Skibbereen less than four miles distant.

Mission nearly accomplished. Once night had fallen, and with Willie safely off the scene, the coal, together with the cargo of 160 rifles and 20,000 rounds of ammunition, was unloaded and transported to the creamery at nearby Aughadown. Here, the coal was piled up for sale locally. As for the huge stacks of weaponry, they were laboriously packed into butter boxes, which were then distributed without difficulty. The British authorities were aware that creameries were frequently nerve centres of Republican activity, visited as they were every day by farmers, many of whom were strong Sinn Féiners. Transported by cart and loaded onto trains, the haul was despatched to Barney O'Driscoll's and Joe O'Regan's good friend Tom Barry, head of the recently founded Flying Column. He was duly grateful.

In the immediate aftermath of this adventure, little gratitude was shown to Willie for his admittedly inadvertent contribution to the Republican war effort. He continued to perform his duties as a Justice of the Peace and was rewarded with threats of boycott to his business, a stone through his front window and warning notes pinned to his premises. However, once the Troubles were over, all concerned were ready to carry on as normal. Barney, who was now emerging as a very successful businessman and was still on the Urban Council with Willie, took to referring to him as 'my former Unionist friend', a phrase which, while amiable, was also provocative, since, as Barney well knew, Willie was not and never had been a Unionist. As for Joe O'Regan, he and Willie would often go up to Norton together for Jasper's card parties.

19

'SLOUCHING THROUGH LIFE MEEK AND TAME'

By the New Year of 1921 West Cork's Republican war machine, if still somewhat ramshackle, was cranking into action. It had already engaged in various more or less successful actions and was now preparing to move into top gear. On Sunday 6 and Monday 7 February a Brigade Council meeting was held at Kilmeen, inland from Clonakilty. It was decided to improve intelligence gathering, to deal severely with anyone found passing information about IRA activities to the British authorities and to escalate harassment of the opposition.

Among the immediate targets were Skibbereen – and Jasper Wolfe. Skibbereen was a particular irritant to the Republicans. The major town in West Cork and a very significant strategic centre, its citizens, with rare exceptions, resolutely refused to answer the Nationalist call to arms. Amongst the nearly 3,000 inhabitants there were only a handful of Republican Volunteers, a mere four according to Tom Barry, although I have been told that those who should know estimate that there were a few more than that; certainly there was one who worked for Willie Wood Wolfe in a garage business he had set up.

Skibbereen was garrisoned by a battalion of the King's Liverpool regiment, commanded by Colonel Hudson. The plan was to attack the British military and, following a successful engagement, to sweep westwards towards Bantry, routing whatever opposition was found and bringing all West Cork under Republican control.

The Republican operation was planned for Tuesday 8 February, the day after the Kilmeen meeting. It was to be carried out by the Flying Column, whose young commandant, Tom Barry, was a remarkable and charismatic figure. Like nearly all the West Cork Brigade, he was local, coming from Rosscarbery. However, he was hardly typical. His father was a former member of the Royal Irish Constabulary and he had few relations locally. His clothing and modest domestic needs were mostly looked after by members of the very active Republican women's organisation, Cumman na mBan. He had fought for three years in the British army, mainly in the Near East. As a man, he was upright, both physically and morally. He was also, above all, a born soldier and leader. However, like many military men he was no politician. Throughout his long life he remained immovably and inflexibly committed to his Republican principles.

Tom Barry had a famously low opinion of the inhabitants of Skibbereen. He could not begin to understand why they were not, like him, white-hot Republicans. He castigated them as 'spineless, slouching through life meek and tame, prepared to accept ruling and domination from any clique or country, provided they were left to vegetate in peace'.

It was with considerable enthusiasm, not to mention optimism, that the Flying Column of fifty-five riflemen departed from the Republican stronghold of Caheragh, a couple of miles northwest of Skibbereen, and approached the town via the Ilen bridge and the railway station. As dusk was falling, having posted the majority of his men in ambush positions, Tom Barry himself and a dozen men crossed the river. Shooting out the street lamps as they went, the shadowy fighters moved towards the army positions in the centre of town.

It was now that the Flying Column started to fall victim to the Skibbereen effect. Tom Barry's idea had been to provoke the King's Liverpool men into a fight, but the British refused to play. They simply stayed behind their defences and, like Brer Rabbit, lay low and said nuffin'. The Republicans fired a few volleys, but there was still no response.

Tom Barry probably had too few men to risk a full-scale assault on defended buildings. He could, no doubt, have tried a few low tricks, but here he faced a problem. The British commander, Colonel Hudson, was not only tactically astute, he was also, unlike his opposite number in charge of the Essex regiment in Bandon, an honourable soldier. He obeyed the rules of war and he regarded the IRA as worthy opponents. Consequently, he was well respected by the Volunteers. Barry, accordingly, was not prepared to abandon the ethics of fair combat.

There were, nevertheless, some consolations for the Flying Column commandant. By a stroke of good fortune, two unarmed off-duty British privates were found and taken captive. Instead of being shot, used as hostages or otherwise ill-treated, they were taken back to Caheragh for the night, where, at least according to Barry, they were fed, given more than enough to drink and taught a couple of Republican songs. Towards dawn, they were put into a horse and trap and returned to their unit, possibly still singing a few of the refrains they had learned.

Another who fell into Republican hands that night was none other than Jim Burke. He was not a favourite of Tom Barry's. While being a staunch Catholic and a native Irishman, he remained a constitutional Home Ruler. Even worse, as a leading figure in the town he exerted considerable influence. He was the most culpable of what Tom Barry recalled in his memoirs as a 'despicable group of local native politicians who, invoking the name of Parnell, Redmond . . . and Mother Ireland, degraded the public life of this unfortunate town'.

Jim Burke was summoned to the presence of Tom Barry and given a very serious talking to. Above all he was castigated for the District Council's continued compliance with the British adminstration's requirement that all council minutes be sent to Dublin Castle. According to Barry, Jim Burke 'snivelled quite a lot' but promised to raise the matter at the next meeting.

However, that was not the end of Jim Burke's troubles. The Volunteers may have been heroes in the eyes of many, but they were not necessarily saints. To use Michael Collins' words, they were 'bloody country fellas'. As a glance at the newspapers of the pre-war period makes clear, rural life was frequently tough, rough and very short-tempered. It could also be liberally laced with very black humour. The Volunteers were nearly all very young men from small farming communities. One or two of the Flying Column now decided that, while the citadel of Skibbereen had failed to fall to the blast of their trumpets, one of its first citizens should at least pay a price. Jim Burke was selected to be humiliated. While the local inhabitants stood around (having been prevented from returning home in case they got inadvertently shot), Councillor Burke was invited to mount an empty porter barrel in Ilen Street, not far from the bridge over which Tom Barry and his men had arrived, and give the assembled crowd a song. As everyone knew, owing to his squeaky voice Jim Burke was not a particularly distinguished vocalist. It was also suggested that, to demonstrate his loyalty to the Irish Republic, the District Councillor should give a rendering of 'The Soldier's Song'. This piece, already the signature tune of the IRA and before long to be the Irish national anthem, would not have been a favourite of Jim Burke's. However, he could hardly refuse the request of the Volunteers, so he squawked forth:

> I'll sing you a song, a soldier's song,
> With a cheering, rousing chorus
> As round our blazing camp-fires we throng
> The starry heavens o'er us.
> Impatient for the coming fight . . .
> Soldiers are we, whose lives are pledged to Ireland . . .

Leaving Jim Burke on his barrel and letting loose a few more provocative volleys, the men of the Flying Column finally withdrew. Tom Barry still hoped the British would pursue him as he retreated and so fall into ambushes he had prepared, but it was not to be.[1]

As a result of the Skibbereen raid both sides emerged with increased respect for each other. Colonel Hudson let it be known that he appreciated the way his captured soldiers had been treated. The Republican leadership admired the canny and safety-first tactics of their foe. And so it went on. Some months later, Tom Barry and others were attending a meeting of the Skibbereen battalion a few miles outside Skibbereen. At that time, the King's Liverpool appeared to have eased up on raids, but, to the dismay of the Republicans, a squad of soldiers unexpectedly arrived at the house where they were staying that night. With seconds to spare, the Volunteers managed to escape out the back. However, Tom Barry left behind a much-valued trench coat and this was taken away by the soldiers. Barry was furious. In the words of the brigade commandant, Liam Deasy, who was also there that night, Barry 'worked himself up into a state of righteous indignation, though the remarks he used to express his feelings were more forceful than righteous'. Anyway, when he had cooled off slightly, Barry sat down and wrote to Colonel Hudson complaining that his (and another man's) trench coat had been removed after the raid, but that, since these could not be regarded as contraband of war, they had in effect been stolen and he demanded their return. When the colonel received the letter, he called on the editor of the *Southern Star*, trench coats in hand, and, explaining the circumstances, asked if the newspaper would be so good as to ensure that the garments were returned to their rightful owners – which they were.

A couple of months earlier, the Skibbereen garrison and the IRA had been involved in another exchange of courtesies over the mining of Derrinard bridge, near Ballydehob. This key strategic point, together with a good many others, had been destroyed by the local Volunteers following the Brigade Council meeting at Kilmeen. In April, the King's Liverpool regiment decided to get the damage repaired. Some of the local labourers who had been employed on the job strongly suspected that the soldiers had hidden a mine in the stonework, so the local IRA commandant was informed. Once the military had safely departed, the Republicans arrived and began cautiously dismantling the bridge. Sure enough, two small wooden boxes were discovered, each containing a Mills bomb primed to explode. These were successfully made safe and kept for future use. One of the boxes was subsequently returned to Colonel Hudson containing a note which expressed gratitude for the contents and requesting a further supply.

The good working relationship which existed in Cork's wild west between the freedom fighters and their imperial foe did much to ensure that there was no grisly escalation of mutual hostilities and atrocities. This is not to say that both sides did not go flat out to win, nor that there were no vicious incidents, but Colonel Hudson for his part not only played fair, but did his utmost to ensure that others on his side did too. The IRA was convinced that, but for his interventions, the eighty or so Black and Tans stationed in Skibbereen (maverick ex-soldiers recruited in England to augment the RIC) would have caused far greater havoc. As for the Republicans, while effectively securing control over much of the countryside and certainly resorting to violence every now and then, they carried out relatively few of the sort of brutal acts that took place further east, especially in and around Bandon. Skibbereen itself, despite various provocations, was able to carry on with its own idiosyncratic way of doing things. No doubt Tom Barry was not pleased, but he had done his own bit to ensure that a minimum of decency was observed.

Meanwhile, what of Jasper Wolfe? It seems more than likely that ways of dealing with him were considered at the pivotal Kilmeen Brigade Council meeting. The offence of which he would have stood accused was passing information to the enemy. Actually, in his favour, it was well known that, like Colonel Hudson, he on occasion used inside information to neutralise the activities of the Black and Tans. Many years later, one of the De La Salle Brothers (a Catholic order which bought Norton after Jasper's death) wrote: 'It is doubtful if Jasper Wolfe had any evil intent, as he was known to have timely word passed on to the Republicans when one of the local leaders was in imminent danger of arrest.' Likewise, it was common knowledge that Jasper had intervened to prevent the burning of a house belonging to a Republican member of the District Council (very possibly none other than Barney O'Driscoll). However, as Crown Solicitor there is no question that Jasper was regularly collecting evidence against Republicans and presenting it to army prosecutors so that it could be used in courts martial. Mitigating circumstances there may have been, but, to the Republicans, guilty he certainly was.

Accordingly, plans were made to deal with Jasper. An attempt to apprehend him took place a week or so after the Kilmeen meeting and the attack on Skibbereen. It was undertaken, not by the Skibbereen fourth battalion, but by the Bantry fifth. It is possible the intended attack was initiated by the Bantry commandant, Tom Ward of Durrus, but it is more likely that it originated at a higher level, with Liam Deasy and Charlie Hurley (who was killed a few weeks later), respectively adjutant and commandant of the West Cork brigade.

One morning in mid-February Jasper set off by car, driven as usual by a chauffeur, for Durrus and Bantry. He was accompanied by Willie Kingston, now employed as a solicitor in Jasper's office, and Miss Browne, a trainee solicitor also working for Wolfe & Co. Willie was appearing in the Durrus Petty Sessions (still just functioning), but he finished early. Jasper disappeared on business of his own and he only met up with the others as it was getting dark, in Vickery's hotel in Bantry. Here he learned from Willie that there were men in the town on the look-out for him. In the square at Bantry Willie had encountered two characters, one of whom, staring at him, said to the other, 'There he is.' The unfortunate Willie, not unnaturally, had the feeling he was 'in a fix', even though, as he wrote in his memoir, he felt it was 'a case of mistaken identity'. He walked nonchalantly past the men and that was that. However, as he went to the hotel to meet Jasper, there was another incident. 'A man sprang out of a shadow of a house and peered into my face, and then vanished without saying anything; but it was obvious that something was on foot, and somebody was being looked for.'

Jasper had met an acquaintance in Bantry, T. T. McCarthy, and whether through luck or cunning had offered him a lift back to Skibbereen. Bawnie McCarthy, as he was known, was settled in the front beside the driver, while Willie and Miss Browne sat themselves in the back. Jasper was slumped down beside them, 'sleepy from drink' in Willie's view, but evidently not seriously the worse for wear, since the whole crew had stopped on the return journey for tea with Miss Browne's mother, hardly an occasion for drunken behaviour.

The ambush had been set up in Caheragh, where the IRA were thick on the ground and well organised. The intention, almost certainly, was not to shoot Jasper at that point but to capture and court-martial him. At a corner with projecting stones, by a side road, the chauffeur had to slow down and a loud whistle sounded near the car. Willie and Miss Browne ducked down, expecting to be fired on, but Jasper did not move. The car accelerated away and nothing further happened. The look-out, seeing, in Willie's words, 'the profile of McCarthy, including bowler hat and large stomach [which] clearly proclaimed a cattle dealer' and not catching a glimpse of Jasper, evidently concluded that this was not the car being sought and signalled to let it pass. On his return to Skibbereen, Jasper heard that word was out that an ambush was being laid for him.

20

NEILUS

The incident at Caheragh proved to be no more than a curtain raiser. Two agenda items at the Kilmeen IRA brigade meeting were to have very serious consequences for Jasper. First, extended powers were given to battalion commanders to obtain evidence of guilt of those suspected of passing information to the British authorities. They were not given the authority to execute, which is why the aborted ambush at Caheragh was almost certainly an attempted arrest rather than an effort at assassination. However, as Tom Barry made clear in *Guerilla Days in Ireland*, local commanders, under pressure of circumstances, very soon did authorise executions.

The second Kilmeen decision that seriously affected Jasper was an agreement to change the commandant of the Skibbereen battalion. Previously, Sam Kingston (very distantly related to Willie) had been in charge. Kingston, together with his wife and daughters, was a dedicated Republican, but, although a number of intimidatory attacks occurred while he was in command, he was perhaps too humane a man for the merciless phase of the conflict that was now beginning to unfold. His new post of brigade police officer probably suited him better than a front-line position.

Sam Kingston's deputy, and now his successor, was Neilus Connolly. Neilus was an altogether different proposition. He was an experienced man in his mid-thirties, a good deal older than many of the Volunteers. He came from a small tenant farm at Coolnagrane, a couple of miles northeast of Skibbereen. His father, Con, had been a strong Nationalist, a member of the Irish Party and a great admirer of Davitt and Parnell. Con Connolly took the *Southern Star* and the *Freeman's Journal* and every Saturday Neilus, his brothers and sisters would sit and listen as their father read out the news to neighbours, 'perched on the hob or in front of the fire'. As the company talked about matters such as Home Rule and the Land Acts, the children were allowed to ask questions. Otherwise they had to keep very quiet. As Neilus recalled, 'While the readings and explanations were on God help any of us that uttered a tittle, except when my father was cross-examined about so and so and what it meant.'[1]

It was not a childhood, as Neilus put it, 'pampered with too many luxuries in food or clothes'. Nevertheless, he was not short of things to do. Apart from receiving a sound education in the basics at the local country National School, he went swimming in the river and he learned to dance and to play the penny whistle, the Jew's harp, mouth organ, melodeon and fiddle. There was as well plenty of sport; he enjoyed football, went bowling and spent time at athletics and race meetings. He recalled that he had 'a really good time' in his youth.

By the time he was twenty-five, Neilus, together with his mother and sister Katie, was managing the farm (which the family now owned, thanks to the 1903 Wyndham Act). In fact, Neilus was the only man in the family left in Ireland. His father had died after falling from a horse, one brother had emigrated to Australia and the other had joined the British civil service and was working in London.

As the Troubles gathered momentum, Neilus took up the Republican cause. He had some good connections. His brother Dick in London had got to know Michael Collins, where both officially worked for the General Post Office. However, unofficially, the two were active as members of the secret Irish Republican Brotherhood. Eventually, while Michael departed for Dublin to join the Easter Rising, Dick had to flee England when he was suspected of providing passports to the USA for wanted Republicans.

Neilus met Michael Collins on a couple of occasions quite early on. The first was during Christmas 1916, when Collins, shortly after his release from Frongoch prison, stayed at a local farm. In the summer of 1917 Neilus once again encountered Michael Collins. In June, he had started drilling in secret on Sunday evenings with the Skibbereen Sinn Féin club. In August, he was on parade when Collins and Count Plunkett came to Skibbereen for a great meeting of around 500 Sinn Féin Volunteers. Neilus was very impressed by Collins: 'He was a fine, athletic type, without any brag. I felt very much at home with him on the spot.'

Neilus' other contact with the leadership of the Republican movement was his next-door neighbour. Gearóid O'Sullivan, who was still in his twenties, had been in Frongoch with Michael O'Collins and it was at the O'Sullivan farm that Neilus had first met Collins. Gearóid had been a brilliant scholarship boy and was a fluent Irish speaker. He was renowned as the man who had hoisted the Republican colours over the General Post Office in Dublin during the Easter 1916 Rising. It was he who had initiated Neilus into the Volunteers (and also into the secret Irish Republican Brotherhood). Later, he succeeded Michael Collins as adjutant-general of the IRA, a position he also held in the Free State Army. Apart from giving Neilus a vivid account of the Rising, Gearóid also provided him with a rifle (though there was no ammunition) in order that he could teach other Volunteers how to shoot. Unfortunately for Neilus, the constabulary had a good idea of what he was up to and put a watch on his house. In summer 1918 the police and a company of soldiers sur-rounded the Connolly farm and immediately went to where the off-ending weapon was hidden in a box under a stone wall.

Gearóid O'Sullivan.

Neilus was arrested and sentenced to two years' hard labour. For the authorities, he proved to be a difficult prisoner. In Belfast gaol, he was one of the leaders when Republicans captured a warder, barricaded themselves in and stripped the roof (unfortunately, it was Christmas time and it rained). Transferred to another gaol, in county Meath, he was kept in his cell for 24 hours a day but still managed to take part in another riot. This time he was permanently handcuffed and watched. From January until April, when with some others he was transferred to Strangeways in Manchester, he had neither wash, shave, nor haircut. The authorities, commented Neilus, 'were delighted to be rid of us, as we were as desperate a crowd as ever entered any prison'.

Neilus was very impressed by the conditions at Strangeways. He found it immaculately clean, a great contrast to the filth and cockroaches which had greeted him in Belfast. Moreover, after a side-show in which he and his friends confused the warders by answering each other's names, the governor was persuaded to give them status as political prisoners. None of this, however, softened Neilus. He and his fellow prisoners managed to contact Michael Collins, who made arrangements for their escape. In the autumn Neilus was one of a group of six who managed to get out of the prison by climbing a rope over the perimeter wall. A bike was waiting for him, but not unfortunately the contact who was meant to organise his getaway. He cycled through the traffic, with difficulty avoiding getting stuck in the tramlines, until he eventually asked a passing workman the way to the nearest Catholic church. Here he met an Irish priest, who hid him in a boiler room, where he spent a night or two closely observed by some strange-looking rats: 'there was scarcely any hair on any of them from running over and under the hot pipes; they were in a ring about me staring with their green eyes and long tails'. Eventually, although the priest wanted to get him to America, he insisted on returning to Ireland.

In Dublin, Neilus was conducted to a safe house, where there were more than a dozen others who were also on the run. They slept fully armed and were looked after by Michael Collins, himself a wanted man, though very relaxed about it: 'for a man with a price on his head', observed Neilus, 'he was as unbothered as if he was minding the cows on the side of a hill at Sam's Cross'. Collins warned Neilus against returning home, but without success. Later in life Neilus became a great

Neilus Connolly (extreme left) in family group.

reader, and in his memoirs he reflected that 'there is something in the saying "the savage loves his native shore", or Goldsmith's lines, "The hunted hare that hounds and horn pursue / Flies back towards the spot from whence it flew"'.

Before long, Neilus was on the train from Cork to Skibbereen. Unfortunately for him, some policemen who had been attending the quarter sessions in Cork were also travelling. At Dunmanway junction the train carried on to Bantry, so everyone going to Skibbereen had to change. As Neilus made his way to the Skibbereen platform, he passed a group of constables who were standing and chatting with P. J. Cullinane. This man, a coachbuilder from Townshend Street in Skibbereen, was a very active Republican. Unfortunately, on this occasion, as frequently happened, he was 'raving drunk'.

Recognising Neilus, and forgetting that he was on the run, he called out to him, 'Would that be you, Neilus? How you doing?'

'Great altogether,' replied Neilus.

As Cullinane and the police got into the train, Neilus was seriously worried: 'I was afraid that he [Cullinane] would explain who Neilus was.' When the train slowed down for Madore, the next station, Neilus jumped from his compartment – and straight into a dyke of water. However, despite the splashing, his departure went unnoticed.

After being given refuge with a teacher and his family for a week, Neilus visited his family for an hour, where he discovered that since his escape the police had called every week, ransacking each 'hole and corner, even scattering the potato pit with their bayonets'. Nevertheless, after a very uncomfortable few days hiding out with another family ('I was a prisoner under petticoat rule'), Neilus decided to return home and sleep rough. His sister brought him two meals a day, always leaving the food in a different spot. And this was the life Neilus led until the amnesty which accompanied the Treaty.

By the time Neilus took over command of the Skibbereen battalion, he was an authentic, and blooded, Republican hero. Whether or not he had originally been a tough character, his encounters with the British authorities had hardened him. While he was deeply principled, he could also be ruthless.

21

'THE PURSUIT BECAME SO HOT'

Such was the man that Jasper now faced. No sooner was Neilus commandant than he raised the temperature. His top priority was dealing with those whom Republicans saw as spies or informers. In his sights were two local Protestant farmers, William Connell and Matt Sweetnam, and Jasper. The three of them were sentenced to death, in their absence, by IRA court martial. First to be dealt with were Connell and Sweetnam.

Since the previous September the IRA, desperately short of funds, had been levying contributions from local farmers and professional and business people. Catholic Home Rulers and Republicans paid up. Protestants were in a more difficult position. Virtually all were loyalists, although some of these were Home Rulers and others Unionists. A handful may have paid. Unionists mostly refused outright and did whatever they could to oppose the tax. Home Rulers often tried both to salve their loyalist consciences and to avoid unnecessarily provoking the IRA. One such Home Rule loyalist was one of Jasper's cousins, Harry Wolfe of Ilen House (son of William, the corn merchant, who had helped Jasper's father set up in business). A group of local Volunteers called on Harry and demanded a contribution to their arms fund.

'I am very sorry, but I cannot in conscience pay you,' said Harry.

Nothing deterred, the visitors removed a fat cow. One of the young lads involved boasted of his heroic exploit, or 'blathered', and as usual in no time everybody, including the Royal Irish Constabulary, knew what had happened. The police could not themselves bring a charge, as this was a civil and not a criminal matter, so they went to call on Harry.

'We hear you might be missing a cow,' said an officer.

'Well now,' replied Harry, 'I can't rightly say that at this minute I've lost any animals.'

'So you won't be wanting to take any action? Give us any information? Lay any charges?'

'I think not,' said Harry.[1]

Sweetnam and Connell were a very different proposition from Harry Wolfe. They were strong Unionists, totally unprepared to compromise with those whom they saw as dangerous rebels. Not only, like Harry Wolfe, had they refused to contribute and so lost cattle, but, a far worse crime in IRA eyes, they had officially reported the matter to the police. Connell received a letter warning him that he was in danger. He asked advice from Willie Kingston, Wolfe & Co. being his solicitors. Willie advised him to take the letter seriously and leave the country. William Connell decided to stay. He did, however, ask Willie to make out a will for him. A few days later a neighbour of Sweetnam and Connell came to Willie to tell him that some IRA men were on his land and the two were at risk of their lives. Willie immmediately told Eddie Swanton, a Justice of the Peace and close friend of Jasper. Eddie, however, laughed the matter off. In fact, up to that time there had been no local killings. That night, Sweetnam and Connell were shot dead in their homes.

Just over two weeks later, a party of Black and Tans raided Neilus Connolly's family farm at Coolnagrane and burned down the house and the outbuildings. Katie Connolly and her mother moved in with neighbours, but they continued to milk the cows every morning and evening and to look after the farm as best they could. It was not to be rebuilt for several years.

Neilus was now seeing red, misting into crimson. He was absolutely determined to get Jasper and so a potentially lethal game of hide-and-seek began, which was to last up to and beyond the 1921 July truce. Common sense would suggest that Jasper stood little chance. Every day he had to travel about performing his duties, and many of his movements were known in advance. His opponents, on the other hand, were free to plan and attack when and where they chose.

However, things were not quite as straightforward as they seemed. Jasper had a good deal going in his favour. He was remarkably well informed, as much information came to him both as Crown Solicitor and as a local lawyer. He also, as Willie Kingston commented, 'was fortunate enough to have friends in both camps'. In other words, besides being told of what the police and military knew, there were also Republicans who were tipping him off. Then there were all those friends and acquaintances who wished him well. John O'Shea, to whom he had been close for years, was not only the town clerk but also kept a public house in North Street, and a good deal of helpful gossip was passed on from there.

The Catholic Church too contributed greatly to Jasper's survival. In Skibbereen, Bishop Kelly of Ross, in the mould of many a Catholic prelate, was an able, authoritarian and intransigent man. Like various other members of the Irish Catholic hierarchy, he was deeply suspicious of Republicanism, which he regarded as infected by Godless Socialism, not to mention Communism, and as unjustifiably violent.

The Bishop's appointment had long been regarded by more ardent Sinn Féiners in West Cork as a 'catastrophe'. While Republican sympathisers were quite happy to see clergy intervening politically, provided it was on their side, much of what Bishop Kelly did, which was often hostile to Sinn Féin, was not approved of. He preached passionately against the Easter Rising, calling it

Dr Kelly, Bishop of Ross.

Father Florence McCarthy.

'murder pure and simple, with all its dreadful consequences', and up to his death in 1924 he championed Home Rule so strongly that he became known, to his opponents at least, as the 'Imperialistic Bishop of Ross'. He was not prepared to offer any religious succour to Republicans. When Sinn Féin in Skibbereen requested that a Tipperary Volunteer who had died in prison be mentioned in the prayers for the dead, the bishop, who had already instructed that dead Volunteers were not to be prayed for in the cathedral, stuck to his policy. During the service, when the prayers for the dead failed, as expected, to include the Tipperary man, a lady stood up and asked that a prayer be said. Bishop Kelly responded by quoting from St Paul that 'women should not speak in church'.[2] The next day the lady, a teacher, was dismissed from her post.

Technically, the bishop was also the parish priest of Skibbereen. In practice, such duties were taken on by an 'administrator'. Throughout the Troubles this office was occupied by none other than Jasper's good friend since their schooldays, Father Florence McCarthy. This was a man who stood in great contrast to his bishop. 'Father Mac', as he was fondly known, was, as someone who remembered him well told me, 'a great pourer of oil on troubled waters'. And much oil was needed. He was also, it was generally agreed, a very strong personality, greatly respected throughout the parish and wielding considerable influence. People of very different views, and not only Catholics, listened to what he said and frequently followed his advice. His influence did much to keep Jasper safe.

Sinn Féin needed to keep the support of the people, and this also helped to protect Jasper. The Republican leadership had to pick its way through very tricky terrain. The great majority of the inhabitants of West Cork wanted the British out, and they had eventually turned to Sinn Féin as the party most likely to achieve this. However, quite significant numbers, whether or not influenced by their religion, were unwilling to support – and indeed were likely to be horrified by – any killing of ordinary people, particularly those they knew or knew of. Neilus Connolly probably got a serious fright from the reaction to the shootings of Connell and Sweetnam. It was widely felt, as someone told me, that the IRA had 'gone too far'. Support appears to have wavered. After that it seemed unlikely, although given some of the wild characters involved still not impossible, that the fourth battalion would have tried to gun down Jasper in full public view.

Ultimately, it seemed as if Jasper had been born under a lucky star. Willie Kingston thought that Jasper was simply fortunate. 'He had', remembered Willie, 'many narrow escapes, more often by accident than otherwise'. Willie no doubt had a point, but there was more to it than simple good fortune. Jasper was blessed with a quality the ancient Greeks called *metis*, which translates roughly as 'cunning intelligence'. More often than not he could see trouble coming and, if it caught up with him, he invariably found a way to outwit his opponents.

So Jasper and Neilus proved to be very evenly matched. Jasper would hardly have been surprised when the IRA started to go after him in earnest. Rumours of kidnappings and killings were heard almost every day. Every now and then a stray shot might be heard. Jasper, writing to his younger daughter, Ray, aged fourteen at the time and away at school, described one incident which gives a good idea of the prevailing atmosphere:

> The Courthouse is now occupied by the soldiers and they are too fond of losing their heads to make their stay pleasant. Last evening when leaving for the office about 9 p.m., as I stepped outside the dining-room door' [a side exit], bang went four rifle shots and I retreated to find Travers [aged ten] rushing down in his nightie, terrified and believing that the shots were fired at the top of the house. I went down a few minutes later and spoke to a soldier and discovered it was a sentry whose 'wind had got up'. I hope he won't make the same mistake when I am passing.

Because he was away so often during the day, Jasper had to do much of his office work in the evening. Sometimes he called at Norton first, but on other occasions he went directly to the office from the station. At about this time, he began to spend occasional nights in his office rather than risk returning home late. Situated as it was in Market Street, just in front of the RIC barracks, the premises of Wolfe & Co. were well placed to offer protection. Jasper's own room, occupying the whole of the first floor, provided plenty of space for a bed. If he did decide to risk walking back to Norton, there was always the possibility of running for cover with either his friend John O'Shea at his pub in North Street, the military at the courthouse or Father McCarthy, whose presbytery was in the complex of Catholic buildings at the top end of North Street. On at least one occasion he did have to take refuge in the priest's house.

Jasper may have been the IRA's prime target in West Cork, but there were others. The *Eagle* (26 June 1920) reported how, one night well after eleven o'clock, Jasper was in his office with his friend Eddie Swanton, who, as a Justice of the Peace and managing director of the pro-government *Eagle*, was also in danger and sometimes, like Jasper, slept at the Wolfe & Co. office. Suddenly a man outside shouted, 'Are you there?' When the door was opened, he staggered into the office and collapsed into a chair. He had been daubed all over with tar and feathers, so at first no one recognised him, but it turned out to be Mr Sheehy, editor of the *Eagle*, a gentleman well known for his lively attacks on Republicans and consequently not popular with them. The GP Dr O'Meara was sent for and Eddie Swanton and Jasper went to the police barracks, but it was deserted. They then walked to Sheehy's house, where they found a tin of hot tar and a rope.

A great many stories are told of Jasper's adventures at this time. He himself, knowing that for some Irish people a private conversation is a contradiction in terms, wisely kept fairly quiet about what happened to him. Nevertheless, plenty of others who for one reason or another had a shrewd idea of what was going on were less reticent. As far as I can tell, what follows is a fairly accurate account of events, although sometimes I have had to balance what appear to be rather different versions of the same incident.

Throughout the Troubles, Minnie, as far as possible, kept the normal routine going at Norton. Once the Volunteers came looking for Jasper and they were met at the front door by the housekeeper, Mollie O'Donovan. A relation of hers now lives in Norton Lodge, the former home of John Cadogan and his family, and it was he who told me this story.

'And what,' enquired Mollie, 'might you be wanting?'

'Would Mr Wolfe be in the house?'

Mollie launched straight into 'You should be ashamed of yourselves . . .', and a great deal more in similar style. The Republicans retreated and it was some time before they ventured up to the Wolfe home again. Mollie subsequently married a Free Stater and emigrated to New York, where, by pure chance, she again encountered the man she had last seen waving a gun on the doorstep of Norton.

Jasper and Minnie assumed, as did most other people, that Sunday was a day of rest, for Protestants, Catholics, IRA, police and military alike. However, on one particular Sabbath the Volunteers, possibly even more than usually irritated with Bishop Kelly, decided to ignore the day of peace and take to the warpath. Minnie always played the organ at the Methodist church and she left an hour or so early to practise the hymns. On this occasion, before she reached North Street she noticed a couple of gunmen who, according to my mother, were hiding behind a hedge. However, the route Minnie would have taken was bounded by high walls, so it is probably more likely, as I was told by the daughter of someone who also remembered seeing them, that the Volunteers had stayed behind after mass and set themselves up on the convent wall, which conveniently overlooked the narrow lane separating the nuns from Norton. Having observed the gunmen and reached the foot of the lane, Minnie, instead of turning left down North Street towards the centre of town, shrewdly turned right and returned to Norton via the main entrance. Jasper thus warned, instead of going to church as usual, stayed put. Minnie set off again, this time along the boreen at the back of the house.

The pursuit of Jasper by the IRA continued. On at least one occasion, Bishop Kelly himself came over to Norton to deliver an urgent warning. On another, Jasper was with ten-year-old Travers and the Volunteers held fire for fear of hurting the boy.

Eventually matters came to a climax. It was May, and Jasper had gone to Baltimore, probably to deal with some dispute over the ownership of a property. He was either chased into Baltimore or spotted when he was there. Either way, he fled to the quay and hid under a large pile of netting. A passing fisherman was surprised to see a well-dressed, middle-aged balding man lying tangled up in trawling tackle, but he decided it was none of his business. After all, it was as good a place as any to sleep off a bout of heavy drinking. Failing to see Jasper, the gunmen returned to the town to pursue their search. Some time later, feeling cramped in his hiding place and tiring of the smell of dead fish, Jasper noticed a trawler moored by the quay that appeared to be deserted, so he decided to seek refuge there. Once in the cabin, he felt a lot safer, as well as more comfortable. However, before long he observed his pursuers returning for one last look around the quay. Finally giving up, they too saw the tied up boat and likewise decided it would be a good resting place. Jasper just had time to hide under a bench before the Volunteers came aboard and seated themselves above their quarry.

Some time later the frustrated search party went their way, but Jasper realised it would be wise to make himself scarce for a while.[3] As he later wrote, 'the pursuit became so hot that I was compelled to leave the country and remain away for some weeks'. He decided to make for England. He may have sailed directly from Baltimore, on a privately owned vessel, as he had very good contacts there – until quite recently his brother Willie had been chairman of the Baltimore and Skibbereen Harbour Board – or he may have arranged to sail with a Royal Navy ship, either from Baltimore or from some other port. Whichever, he remained out of the country for some time.

'The IRA offered the services of the parish priest'

Jasper returned to Ireland around late June 1921. At that time serious negotiations were beginning between Sinn Féin and the British government with a view to establishing a truce. This was finally agreed on Saturday 9 July and came into force on Monday 11 July.

The truce might have been seen by Neilus and the fourth battalion as a chance to go easy and take a much needed rest. Far from it. Very possibly fearing, and perhaps justi-fiably, that the British might use the pause in hostilities to re-establish their authority, Neilus decided to try and deal with what remained locally of the United Kingdom's justice system.

Amongst the first Republican targets were two of the still-operating Justices of the Peace, Willie Wood Wolfe and Eddie Swanton. On the day the truce was agreed, the Saturday, Neilus wrote to Willie, in his own hand, the following letter.

> Headquarters
> 1V Batt
> 3rd Cork Brig
>
> 9.7-21
>
> Sir
>
> You being a justice of the peace and having sworn your allegiance to a government hostile to the people of this country, you are hereby warned to withdraw your allegiance within seven days from above date, and give full publicity to the fact that you have done so. Otherwise you are to be treated as one of the enemy forces.
>
> Signed
> o/c 4th Batt
> 3rd Cork Brigade

This letter, posted late on Saturday evening or on Sunday, was post-marked, and probably delivered, on the Monday. Willie ignored the threat, and in the event suffered no more than a ratcheting up of attempts to damage his business. However, by the time he read Neilus' letter, he can have been in no doubt that he was in very real danger, for he would already have heard of the events which had occurred on that very morning, and on the previous day.

Early in the evening of Sunday 10 July, Eddie Swanton, together with various friends and others, was returning from a day's bathing at Tragumna when he passed a few young chaps who greeted him. A little further on he encountered a larger group, which was stopping vehicles and rounding up everyone returning from the beach. Eddie Swanton himself was put in a car and driven off. It rapidly became clear that he would not be returning home for some time, if at all. He was moved from house to house, occasionally having to spend nights in the open, and was allowed to send home for clothes. He also followed the golden rule of those targeted by the Republicans: he never complained or criticised. Shortly after his capture, he wrote home to say he was being well treated and later, when claiming compensation from the courts, he said that he was 'treated most kindly'. This, however, was not the story some of his close friends remember. It appears he was even held for some time in a cellar. His magnificent, upward-sweeping brown hair turned white over that period.

After ten weeks in captivity, Eddie found himself alone on the upper floor of a house where he was being held. While his gaolers were in another room, he jumped from the window and succeeded in getting away. He went in search of Jasper, who arranged for his escape to England. Eddie's father, Richard, who ran a successful shop in Skibbereen, was then targeted by the disgruntled Republicans. His business was boycotted, debts were unpaid and display goods cut and damaged.[1]

By far the most serious of the assaults mounted by Neilus occurred on the Monday within the first few hours of the truce coming into force. This time Neilus was intent on destroying the morale of the RIC which, like the Justices of the Peace, was still functioning more or less effectively in Skibbereen. What happened attracted local and national outrage. The *Eagle* (16 July 1921) reported how, on that morning, Constable Clerke, a middle-aged family man originally from Tipperary, was returning home from the barracks when he was attacked in Townshend Street, where two men approached him and without warning fired at him, wounding him in the face. When he tried to escape, they followed him into a house and shot him dead on the stairs. His body was taken to the mortuary in the Pro-Cathedral. Father McCarthy officiated at the funeral service. Alexander Clerke was the last person in Ireland to be shot during the conflict between the British government and the Republicans, which officially ended with the truce.

After the truce, the Volunteers emerged from the undergrowth – literally, in the case of Neilus and various others. Although no official amnesty had yet been declared, IRA men wanted by the British authorities were, in practice, fairly safe from arrest. In Skibbereen as elsewhere the Republicans waved their flags, cocked their triggers, and made their presence known. On 1 October a great parade of Republican troops was held in the Skibbereen town park. Reviewing the Volunteers was Commandant Tom Barry. According to one estimate, there were over 3,000 cheering onlookers. The *Southern Star*, which was staunchly Republican, was ecstatic. 'There is', it reported, 'something solemn and soul-stirring in the well-ordered and measured tread of marching men, and there was a resurgent ring in the steady swinging step of these well-trained young men as they tramped boldly on'.

Meanwhile, what of Jasper? He had escaped the initial Republican assault on representatives of the British justice system. Very possibly, after the furore caused by Constable Clerke's killing, the IRA felt it could not afford another serious violation of the truce, and moreover, one involving a high profile figure. However, within a week of the parade in Skibbereen, the Republicans finally did decide to deal with Jasper. Quite apart from his position as Crown Solicitor, Jasper had managed to annoy the Volunteers through various other of his activities. His capture no doubt had something to do with the Skibbereen battalion's anger at the help he had recently given Eddie Swanton in evading their justice. However, it was his success in getting compensation for clients who had suffered at the hands of the Volunteers that finally broke whatever restraint or patience the IRA, in light of the truce, might have been exercising.

What was going on can only be fully understood when viewed against the background of the utterly bizarre way in which justice had come to be administered – or not – in West Cork. For over a year, local cases had almost entirely been dealt with in Sinn Féin courts. Originating in courts of arbitration, mainly handling land cases and initially accepted by the British, these Republican courts had been taken over by the proscribed Dáil. Now illegal in the eyes of the authorities, they nevertheless thrived.[2] In the summer of 1920 the Irish bar council declared it was professional misconduct for any of its members (barristers) to attend Sinn Féin courts. At about the same time, the Incorporated Law Society (representing solicitors) took no such stand. The fact was, barristers were seldom required in the Republican legal system, whose higher courts hardly really got going, while solicitors were almost essential in the local courts. And anyway, they needed the fees.

From the start, Wolfe & Co. represented its clients in local Sinn Féin courts. Jasper did not actually appear himself (as Crown Solicitor that might have raised a few eyebrows), but Willie Kingston was a regular attender. Indeed, he acted for a plaintiff in the first Sinn Féin court in Skibbereen, which was held in Bridge Street at the now demolished Land and Labour Hall. The defendant was accused of having dishonestly inflated the sale value of a tailless cow by attaching to it the tail of another animal. Willie won his case. He subsequently represented Wolfe & Co. at various further hearings, which were held, more discreetly, out in the countryside and protected by look-outs, on one occasion a small boy. Willie described the position succinctly: 'all the local solicitors attended these courts, as we could not desert our clients whatever happened. In fact, Jasper knew and approved of my attendances, though I expect he would have had to prosecute me if I was caught!'

Meanwhile, the British legal system, although greatly weakened, was taking a long time to die. Despite the best efforts of the IRA, a few courts succeeded in staying open, including those of the quarter sessions circuit of West Cork. These remained in business for two reasons. The first was the circuit judge, Mr Justice Hynes KC. He was no Unionist, in fact he was a patriotic Irishman and a staunch Home Ruler. However, politics had little or no influence, one way or another, on his determination to remain sitting as a judge. Like many in his profession over the years, his first loyalty was to the rule, not of this state or that, but of justice. As long as he was able, he was determined, as a matter of conscience and of principle, to uphold and administer the law of the land as officially established.

The courts of the West Cork quarter sessions also stayed open because they were very popular. This was mainly on account of the power they had to award damages for material or physical injuries. In practice, claimants were almost exclusively public bodies, Crown employees or loyalist individuals who had been attacked by Volunteers.

Republicans, quite apart from their opposition in principle to the very existence of the circuit courts, were further angered by the effects on themselves of the multitudinous claims for damage which were not only being made, but frequently being endorsed, by the judge. As the law stood, damages awarded for malicious personal injuries, which could be substantial, had to be paid by local councils. Nearly all of these were controlled by supporters of Sinn Féin. Understandably, they did not appreciate having to pay compensation awarded by British courts to those attacked by the military wing of the

Republican movement of which they were the elected political representatives. There was also the question of whether councils could afford to pay, and for one reason or another they frequently refused to settle up.

Enter Jasper. A well-established procedure existed in the law of the United Kingdom for dealing with those who declined to disburse money which courts judged they owed. It was known as a garnishee order.[3] A complainant could go back to the court which had awarded compensation, apply for a garnishee order and, once obtained and provided certain safeguard procedures were followed, go to a bank or any other body or individual taking care of funds belonging to the party refusing to pay and get hold of the sum awarded.

Jasper obtained, on behalf of claimants who had received awards for malicious personal injuries, garnishee orders against a number of West Cork rural and district councils, mostly Sinn Féin strongholds. Banks were more or less immune from Republican pressure. If they held council funds and were presented with a garnishee order, they would almost invariably pay out. The Republicans were livid. Jasper was warned that his actions would have severe consequences. As usual, he ignored the threats and carried on regardless.

Wednesday 5 October was a long day at the Bandon quarter sessions. Dealing with compensation claims dominated the business, as described in the *Eagle* (8 October 1921). His Honour County Court Judge Hynes doled out payment and garnishee orders as if there were no tomorrow – and indeed his court was to enjoy only a brief future.

Jasper acted for various claimants. There were a number of petitions for compensation for malicious personal injury. Four constables, a sergeant and a district inspector were awarded sums ranging from £60 to £2,000 for injuries received, mainly gunshot wounds, resulting from Republican attacks, including the burning of Castle Barnard and the kidnapping of Lord Bandon. Altogether, the day's work resulted in awards of over £51,000 being made. Awards for malicious personal injury accounted for somewhere approaching £3,000 of the total. The IRA was not prepared to put up with this sort of thing any longer, and severe action was planned.

Jasper returned that evening by train to Skibbereen, arriving just after eight o'clock. He was making his way back home to Norton, Minnie and a late supper when, outside the Eldon hotel in Bridge Street, he was apprehended by three men. He tried to fight them off but failed and was shoved into a waiting car, which drove off westwards. He was carrying a revolver but managed, unobserved, to drop this onto the road. Republicans themselves carried arms almost as a matter of course (Tom Barry, attending the London Peace Conference, was photographed, holster on hip, when the wind blew his coat aside), but the IRA regarded the possession of guns by civilian state officials as close to a hostile act. Many years later, a senior partner of Wolfe & Co., Jim O'Keeffe, found another revolver in the back of Jasper's old desk. This may have been Willie Kingston's, given to Jasper for safe-keeping, although Willie thought Jasper may have handed that over to Father McCarthy.

I have never read, nor been told in so many words, who carried out Jasper's kidnapping. It seems to me, however, inconceivable that Neilus was not directly in charge of an operation that was both very high profile and which took place entirely on the Skibbereen battalion's territory. I assume, therefore, that he was present from start to finish.

The Republican car with its captive made its way, beyond Ballydehob, to some quiet spot on the shore of Roaringwater Bay and from there a boat departed for Cape Clear. According to Seán Ó Faoláin's account of the incident in *An Irish Journey*, Jasper was tried by court martial for offences 'against the Republic' and sentenced to be shot. In this extremity, Jasper asked to see the Bishop of Ross. 'His captors', wrote Ó Faoláin, 'whether he intended to suggest it or not, were impressed by the idea that he wished to become a Catholic'. The request would have put Neilus and his comrades in some difficulty. Hostile though they might be to Bishop Kelly, they were at heart good Catholics. Could they have it on their consciences that they refused the chance of conversion, confession and absolution to a man whose execution they were contemplating? Eventually, since Dr Kelly was away, 'the IRA offered the services of the parish priest, Father McCarthy. These were accepted by the prisoner.'

When Father McCarthy arrived, he seems to have spent rather more time with Neilus than with his captive. Father Mac had high-value cards to play in his efforts to save Jasper. First, the execution of a government official would break the terms of the truce and, secondly, an IRA shooting of a Crown Solicitor could seriously undermine the Republican delegates in the negotiations for a peace treaty that were just about to open in London. However, as so often is the case, it was probably local considerations which counted most. Father McCarthy not only exercised great personal authority, but it is also more than likely that the Republicans owed him favours. For them, this was probably payback time. Whatever was discussed, the outcome was clear. As Seán Ó Faoláin put it, 'The Catholic priest did not leave without the Methodist lawyer'. It was Friday evening, just two days since Jasper had been abducted.

In Skibbereen, news of the kidnapping was rushed to Minnie at Norton. She had been planning to visit Dorothy and Ray, who were now away at school in North Wales, but had to send a telegram cancelling that arrangement. She spent the next forty-eight hours, as efforts were made to locate Jasper, in a flurry of activity, as exhilarated as she was anxious. Eventually, Jasper turned up in the early hours of Saturday morning. On the Sunday, she and Jasper having attended church as usual, Minnie settled down to write to her daughters. She opened with an apology for cancelling her visit: 'I am sure it was a great disappointment when you got my wire. But as you now know the reason you won't blame me for not turning up.' She then gave an understandably breathless account of events:

We had such an exciting time from Wednesday night until Saturday morning at 3a.m. when Daddy threw gravel at my window and called out,

'Mignon.' I knew on the Friday night he would be likely to be released soon, but I didn't believe it until I saw him. Everyone was so kind and did what they could. London, Dublin and Cork were all busy. I had so many visitors I didn't know what to do. He hadn't a pleasant time and was quite ill one day and couldn't eat anything – sodden bastable cake and smoky butter and tea was what he got in one house for breakfast and dinner. Oh, it is such a relief to have him home again. Just fancy, he was in seven houses for the short time he was 'out'. His hat fell off in the tussle and he lost his glasses. He had to drive to Ballydehob without his hat and they got a cap for him there. From 1 o'clock in Bandon when he had lunch, until 9.30. next morning he had nothing to eat.

On the following Monday, to make sure that no one had overlooked Republican anger over garnishee orders, Neilus arranged for two officers responsible for serving legal documents, including garnishee orders, to be kidnapped. Point made, they were released before long.

23

'THEY WANT TO TERRORISE THE LANDLORDS'

In December 1921 the Anglo-Irish Treaty was finally signed. At first it seemed as if real peace might finally be on its way and in much of Ireland the agreement was widely welcomed. On New Year's Eve, Skibbereen Town Council voted unanimously in favour of the Treaty. Less than three months

Michael Collins addressing a meeting in Skibbereen.

later, Michael Collins visited the town. By now he was the dominant personality in Irish politics, chairman of the Provisional Government established under the Treaty and Minister of Defence. He gave a speech from a platform erected in front of the Town Hall and it was estimated that 5,000 people were present. 'They came along', reported the *Southern Star*, 'to cheer Mr Collins and by their presence endorse the policy . . . he stands for'.

However, yet again the centre could not hold and things began to fall apart. Many members of Sinn Féin and the IRA opposed the agreement, because, although it offered a significant degree of political independence, it did not provide for a Republic. A particular sticking point, of huge symbolic if little practical significance, was that the Treaty required all 'Members of the Parliament of the Irish Free State' to take an oath of allegiance to the British monarch (Article 4). Pro- and anti-Treaty forces soon emerged, while the British military and police forces began a rapid withdrawal.

The inhabitants of West Cork soon began to see the practical effects of these historic events. As the British disappeared, and as the IRA started quarrelling amongst themselves, public order, such as it had been, began to break down. Willie Kingston, having left the country after the shooting of Connell and Sweetnam, came back after the signing of the Treaty expecting Cork to have returned to 'its usual peaceful condition'. He rapidly discovered that he had made a bad mistake. 'The country', he wrote, 'was more upset and dangerous than when I left . . . There was no real authority . . . and any man with a gun was a law unto himself'.

With the signing of the Treaty, rural disorders started to increase. Some tenants, whether in pursuit of what they saw as fair rents or to force owners to sell, resorted to withholding rents. Others began to help themselves to livestock and movable agricultural goods belonging to landlords. There were also occasional outbreaks of violence. Many Republicans, no longer being attacked by the British and with time on their hands, now turned their spare energies to dealing with what for many of them had been the key issue all along: land ownership. The IRA both supported and stimulated agitation over land issues. The Volunteers were getting into the business of controlling the land market.

In Skibbereen, from as early as the autumn of 1921, Sinn Féin initiated various tactically astute manoeuvres which, while attacking landowners, had the added benefit of simultaneously targeting other buttresses of British rule, specifically local government and the legal system. The first steps of the Sinn Féin land reform campaign were taken through the Town Tenants' League (Sinn Féin strength in this innocuous-sounding organisation provides further evidence that there was a rather more solid and active core of Republican support in Skibbereen than Tom Barry was prepared to acknowledge).

The opening gambit of the League was to put the Skibbereen Town Council, which was not noted for its Republican sympathies, on the defensive. It passed, and forwarded to the town clerk, the following motion:

RESOLVED; That we the Skibbereen branch of the Town Tenants' Association of all Ireland call upon the DAIL EIREANN to bring forward a bill at the earliest opportunity compelling all ground landlords to sell to their tenants in town and country the property which they state belongs to them – but which we maintain is the purely confiscated property of the Irish Nation and to have these sales take place on just and equitable terms, as we think that every tenant should be the owner of his or her own house or farm. We call upon the County Council and various District Councils . . . to join us in this request.[1]

This request was embarrassing for the council because it required it to carry out business with the still-proscribed Dáil. A year previously it had, it is true, passed a resolution of allegiance to Dáil Éireann, but the Dáil minister for local government had not been prepared to accept this. Their action, he wrote to the town clerk, 'is not sufficient'. The problem, from a Republican perspective, was that Skibbereen, unlike many other local councils where Sinn Féin's influence was stronger, had failed to introduce a policy of non-cooperation with the British Local Government Board. For the council of Skibbereen this had tangible benefits. The British Board had not, as it had with rebel councils, refused it grants or permission to collect rates. However, this was perceived by Sinn Féin as working, not with the Dáil, but with the imperial authority.

Faced with the tricky dilemma posed by the League's letter, the council, chaired by Timothy Sheehy, decided on a tactical retreat. Aware that the Dáil was likely to be officially recognised in the near future (that is, if the Treaty negotiations in London were successful), it graciously changed sides. A proposal, seconded by Jim Burke and with Willie Wood Wolfe among its supporters, was unanimously passed 'that all communication with the English Local Government Board cease from henceforward'. Accordingly, the League's letter was endorsed and forwarded to the Dáil minister for local government. One up to the Republicans.

Alongside their political manoeuvrings, key members of the League also initiated direct action. Their prime target was a major local landlord, Sir Eustace Becher. To begin with, four leading members of the League, Skibbereen tenants of Sir Eustace's, withheld payment of rent. The landlord, refusing to be intimidated, arranged for John O'Connor, Michael Harrington and Ben Hill, all of North Street, together with John Sheehy of Bridge Street, to be summoned to appear at the Skibbereen quarter sessions.

The real hot spot, however, had been not in Skibbereen itself but a few miles to the north, around Caheragh. Here, in the week before they were due to appear in court, the Skibbereen refuseniks had encouraged other tenants of Sir Eustace to withhold payment. One thing led to another and it was not long before fighting erupted. The following Sunday, delegates from the Skibbereen Unpurchased Tenants Association held meetings at Dromore and Caheragh. They were, as their chairman later put it, 'accorded a hearty welcome. The country members unanimously decided to act as brothers and will pay no rent until Becher sells.'

It was on Monday 23 January, the very next day after the meetings at Dromore and Caheragh, that the four ringleaders had been summoned to appear in court. Despite everything, but in accordance with the terms of the recently signed Treaty, Mr Justice Hynes was still holding his quarter sessions. He was doing so in a spirit of optimism and goodwill. Like so many others, he welcomed the Treaty. 'I am absolutely convinced', he declared, 'that a great future is in store for our beloved land'. As the court assembled, Republican leaders must have been well pleased with their progress. They had forced the Town Council to come off the fence and declare full recognition of the Dáil's authority, they had ignited an anti-landlord campaign in town and country and now they were more than likely going to create local martyrs for their cause (if only minor ones), while at the same time stoking up local feeling against the British court system.

At this moment, Jasper emerged from the sidelines. Local Republicans may momentarily, as the truce and Treaty negotiations went ahead, have taken their eyes off him, but the land campaign was about to remind them of his existence. He was solicitor to the Town Council, something of which Sinn Féiners had long disapproved. They certainly suspected, no doubt correctly, that his legal advice had done much to ensure that the council had continued to cooperate with the British authorities. Now Jasper was to appear once more acting in opposition to their activities. He was Sir Eustace Becher's solicitor, and as such it was he who would appear in court arguing for the payment of the withheld rents.

Jasper, as usual, pulled no punches. 'These men', he charged, 'not merely insisted on not paying rent themselves, but entered a criminal conspiracy to prevent others from doing so by a series of threats. They want to terrorise the landlords and all people who wish to pay their rents'. The case was duly proven, and His Honour awarded decrees against the defendants for the amounts due.

That, however, was by no means the end of the matter. Pro-Treatyites, such as Jasper, Sir Eustace and Mr Justice Hynes, may have been loyal to British justice, but Republican anti-Treatyites most certainly were not. The very next day after the court decision, a packed meeting was held of the Skibbereen Town Tenants' League, of which those found guilty were leading members. The chairman made his attitude, and that of the convicted men, very clear: 'I tell this land-lord and his agent that these men regard those decrees as so much waste-paper, and are willing to present them to Becher and his agent to light their pipes, and have a comfortable smoke.'

After the court case, the Unpurchased Tenants' Association, a nationwide body, rapidly arranged meetings in the area of the original disturbances at Dromore and Caheragh, as well as at Drimoleague, Drinagh and elsewhere. The enthusiasm was great, and large numbers joined. Unrest and ill-feeling over the question of land now began to escalate throughout West Cork. (The *Eagle*, 28 January 1922, reported on the quarter sessions and on the meetings of the Skibbereen Town Tenants' League and Unpurchased Tenants' Association.)

After these events, the IRA once more had Jasper firmly in its sights, and within a few weeks it again set about hunting him down. Towards the end of February Jasper was attending the Schull district court (part of the Republican justice system). This was in the IRA fifth battalion area, where the conflict between Becher and his tenants had broken out. Sean O'Driscoll of Ballydehob, commandant of the local battalion, together with some of his men, came looking for Jasper. By luck, or forewarned – as usual it was not clear which – he had gone before the IRA arrived. However, Willie Kingston was still in court and the IRA had to content themselves with questioning him. Another solicitor, Charlie Kennedy, a Catholic and a friend of Willie's, saw that he was in trouble and came over and persuaded his interrogators to let him go.

24

LANDLORDS OF CASTLEFREKE

Jasper did not only, on occasion, act for clients who also happened to be landlords, he had somehow found time to become a landlord himself. In the entrepreneurial spirit of the Wolfes, and like his father Willie John, he was more than ready to risk his hand at investing in real estate. Just as the Troubles were approaching boiling point he had, most unwisely as it turned out, got involved in the purchase of a very substantial property.

Late in 1919, the sale was announced of one of the best-known ascendancy estates in West Cork. The castle and thousand-acre demesne of Castlefreke were very familiar to Jasper. The estate overlooked Rosscarbery Bay and on its eastern flanks it bordered Kilkeran, the farm where Jasper's maternal grandparents, William and Mary Wood, had lived towards the end of their lives. The vendor, the tenth Baron Carbery, was about as good a representative of decadent ascendancy aristocracy as one could hope to find. The land had been owned by the Evans Freke family since the time of Cromwell and John had inherited the title in 1898, aged six, when his father, Algy, died of tuberculosis.

The young John, Lord Carbery, and his brothers grew up surrounded by grandeur. The castle itself was massive, with a vast vestibule, inner hall (containing, amongst other hunting trophies, a full-sized stuffed elephant), dining-room and smoking room, thirty bedrooms, plus various nurseries, bathrooms and dressing rooms, and extensive 'culinary offices'. Outside were various gardens, lawns, walks, tennis courts, stabling for fourteen horses, trout fishing in Kilkeran lake, shooting in the woodland and yacht anchorage. The estate also included agricultural land and woodland, together with various cottages.

To keep the whole show on the road, there were innumerable staff. In the castle itself, the children alone had a small platoon to look after them – a nanny, a governess, a nursemaid and a tutor. There were also a Scottish maid, ten or so other maids, a housekeeper, a butler, two footmen and an odd-job man. In the grounds were a head gardener, 'her ladyship's own gardening man', three under-gardeners, a carpenter, two married couples and various small boys. At the stables worked a coachman, a groom and four other men, one of whom became the chauffeur. Finally, on the land itself were a steward, a cowman, a carter, a labourer, a married couple who acted as lodge-keepers, three roadmen, a fisherman, a fisherwoman and a 'watcher of the strand'.

All this sustained a very agreeable way of life for the Carberies. In the summer the children, in a dog-cart pulled by a Shetland pony, would be taken down to the beach. If there was a breeze the younger ones would be swathed in ermine and placed on a large plaid blanket. Meanwhile, the hunt met in the grounds, balls and dinners were held for the local gentry and guests came from all over Ireland and England to attend house parties.

As the young lord grew up he proved to be a big hit with the locals. A handsome, charismatic daredevil, his exploits provoked much interest and admiration. At the age of fourteen, after a secret visit to Cork, he returned driving his first motor car. Not long after, he took up flying, once landing on the strand at Castlefreke. In the summer of 1914 he gave displays in Cork city, Bandon and Clonakilty, which frequently caused some alarm, one newspaper reporting that there were 'shrieks and gasps of terror' when 'the noble lord looped the loop over the crowd'. There was also a good deal of consternation when, on the opening day of the war, he landed at Blackrock, near Cork, as some in the neighbourhood assumed he was spearheading a German invasion. While all this was going on, he was also competing in the Schneider Trophy (a prestigious competition for the fastest plane on earth), setting speed records on the Cresta Toboggan Run and becoming an expert skier.

From early on, however, there was trouble behind the scenes. Four years after Algy's death in 1898 his widow remarried. Mary Carbery's second husband, 'Kit' Sandford, appeared ideal. He had been the ninth Lord Carbery's closest friend, he was said to be 'the best-looking man in Cork', he was descended from an impeccably lineaged ascendancy family and, to cap it all, he was, as a renowned professor at University College Cork, a 'famous and attractive figure in Irish medicine'. However, while his mother and stepfather may have been happy, John most certainly was not. Beside his parents, he had one brother and before long two half-brothers. He took against the lot. He was not simply upset, which would have been natural in the circumstances, but his behaviour was extremely disturbing.

Once John's mother reminded him that, it being the anniversary of a particular saint (possibly St Francis), it was the duty of all Christians to be especially kind to animals on that day. That afternoon John said to his mother, 'I was kind to animals. Very kind.'

'Oh good, John. What did you do?' asked his mother.

'I gave the canary to the cat.'

On another occasion, alerted by yells, Mary Carbery found her oldest son using a stone to hit the hands of his younger brother, Ralfe, who was clinging onto the ledge of an upstairs window. However, the most serious trouble in the family came from John's relationship with his mother. He called her 'Bloody Mary' and all his life he hated her with a visceral, unrelenting hatred.

An apparent moment of mutual goodwill came with the celebration of John's coming of age. In 1913 a huge ball, complete with 'horse-loads of beer and porter', was thrown for the quality and gentry to celebrate the coming of age of the tenth baron. However, John was now in legal control of what had been his mother's house. Almost immediately, hostilities erupted. The immediate *casus belli* was John's choice of a bride. José was an Australian commoner and the daughter of Major Jumbo Metcalfe, a member of White's club in London who was a very heavy gambler. She was spectacularly attractive and deeply disproved of by Mary Carbery, who considered the girl to be socially inferior. When the new Lady Carbery visited Castlefreke, her mother-in-law hid the family heirlooms and refused to invite anyone to meet her.

The tenth baron hit back in style. He moved into Castlefreke, turned his mother out and told the lodge-keepers to forbid her entry. He rejected the ascendancy world in which he had been brought up and declared himself a Nationalist. 'In politics', he declared, 'I am personally a supporter of the Irish Party, and absolutely dissociate myself from the Unionists'. In July 1914 he presided at a meeting in Clonakilty when it was decided to set up a branch of the Irish National Volunteers. By a unanimous vote it was named the Lord Carbery Branch of the Irish Volunteers. For the next few years, the Irish tricolour flew over Castlefreke, and the sight of this banner may well have helped save the castle from the destruction which was suffered by many other great houses. Finally he discarded the title, added an 'r' to his surname and now called himself simply John Carberry.

However, the ex-lord did not prove to be a patriot in the mould of other great Protestant Irishmen. He was hardly a Robert Emmet, a Charles Stewart Parnell or a W. B. Yeats. Having volunteered for the Royal Naval Air Service, he fought throughout the war and on its conclusion emigrated to colonial Kenya, where he joined the famously dissolute Happy Valley society of aristocratic white supremacists. Here he took to beating his wife (who promptly divorced him) with a sjambok cattle-whip, spent a year in gaol (for currency offences) and was described by one author as 'an unpleasant character with a cruel sadistic streak, particularly towards animals'.[1]

On departing for Africa, John Carberry decided to dispose of his estate. In July 1919 Castlefreke was put on the market in London by Knight, Frank and Rutley, and it was the announcement of this sale which had caught the attention of Jasper. A syndicate was formed to make a bid, consisting of Jasper, William Wood and Francis FitzMaurice. The three men were friends and did a good deal of business together. William Wood, a neighbour and cousin of Jasper's, was the leading estate agent in West Cork, while Francis FitzMaurice was an established elderly solicitor and land agent in Dunmanway. The bid proved successful and so, for the first time in centuries, Castlefreke had new owners. The initial plan was to sell the whole demesne to the famous Irish tenor, John McCormack, but the deal fell through. All was far from lost, however. Castlefreke remained a particularly attractive investment. It was untenanted, so the land could be split up and sold on. It also had extensive woods. Due to wartime shortages, timber was in great demand and selling for a good price. It was obvious that substantial profits were there for the taking, provided the Troubles did not deteriorate into social chaos.

That was the gamble. But it did not pay off. Jasper, William Wood and Francis FitzMaurice, one by one, found themselves in deep and ever deeper trouble with the IRA over the fate of Castlefreke. The Castlefreke demesne was in an officially designated 'Congested District', which is to say that too many families were having to scratch a precarious living from a severely limited supply of impoverished soil. Many local people felt strongly that they should have had an opportunity to buy lots of, or otherwise benefit from, the estate, but there were no provisions in existing land laws to assist small farmers or agricultural workers purchase untenanted land and standing timber.

Michael Collins had been born, brought up and educated in the neighbourhood of Castlefreke. He was also the local TD. In no time at all he was hearing of local anxiety about the fate of the demesne. By July 1920 he was asking Art O'Connor, his ministerial colleague responsible for agriculture in the Republican government, to investigate the problem. O'Connor travelled to Clonakilty and commissioned a detailed report on the estate, concluding that there were approaching 500 acres of land suitable for farming, but that one of the principal assets of the estate was standing timber of various kinds. This was valued at about £3,000.

Meanwhile, Jasper and his friends, unable to offload their purchase quickly, started to make what profit they could from it. Their initial decision to lay off casual labour failed when the Republicans issued them with an order to keep all workers employed. If the order was ignored, then the IRA threatened that there would be a walkout. Next, the syndicate decided to sell off some of its assets. Jasper took the lead by marketing timber, which was becoming a particularly controversial activity, since the high price of wood had attracted speculators. Locals were resentful and Sinn Féin in West Cork issued public statements attacking such profiteering and the desecration of the Irish heritage. Jasper, with his legal and local knowledge, was well placed to negotiate these political rapids. Moreover, he could get advice from his brother Willie, who had invested in woodland at Cononagh, a few miles to the west of Castlefreke.

If from no one else, Jasper rapidly learned from Willie that selling off timber in the Rosscarbery region was likely to be unpopular. From the start Willie's enterprise had been opposed, and indeed was long remembered. As late as the years after the Second World War, one of his sons happened to stop for a drink near Cononagh and got into conversation with an elderly local.

'Now,' said the man, 'You'd be a Wolfe, I'd say.'

'Right enough. But how would you know?'

'I'd recognise a Wolfe anywhere. Sure, you all look the same.' After some further chat, the man asked, 'And you wouldn't be related to Willie Wood Wolfe, would you?'

'He's my father,' replied Willie's son.

There followed a tirade about Willie's iniquity in buying, desecrating and obscenely profiting from Cononagh wood. What was not mentioned was that, at least according to Willie, much of the cutting down of trees was carried out by locals who, as policing more or less ceased following the truce, helped themselves to free fuel.[2]

By the New Year of 1921, Jasper had arranged to start the cutting and sale of standing timber at Castlefreke. Absolutely predictably, the locals were angry. Once again they complained to Collins, who again got in touch with O'Connor. The result was that official letters were sent to each member of the syndicate enclosing an order to cease tree-felling. So as to ensure that the order would be enforced, a copy of the correspondence was sent to the Dáil's minister of defence and the IRA.

Jasper hit back, writing a letter of vociferous complaint to Tim Healy (from West Cork, and formerly a leading Nationalist politician, but currently supporting Sinn Féin, and shortly to accept office as the first governor general of the Irish Free State). He stated that he only started felling to provide work for the men he had been forbidden to dismiss and explained that, in any case, only useless timber on the outskirts of the demesne was being cut. If the prohibition order was official, he enquired, was he 'to dismiss the men' doing the logging 'and send them adrift'. He added that, in the event of giving the men notice, 'I take it we will be permitted to state that they have been dismissed by order of the Dáil Éireann'. In a final riposte, Jasper added: 'it does seem strange to me that in a Republic, people who are trying to do some good by keeping labour on should be sentenced first and apparently tried afterwards . . . I must say I prefer the old-fashioned method of trial before sentence'.

Tim Healy forwarded the correspondence to Michael Collins, who took the complaint seriously and asked Art O'Connor to look into it. Collins, who of course knew exactly who Jasper was, was not impressed by his attitude. The tone of the letter, commented Collins to O'Connor, 'is rather dictatorial and somewhat impertinent'. Local enquiries revealed that Jasper had given rather less than the full picture. In July Michael Collins received a letter from an Albert Scully, who seems to have been the leading complainant about the situation in Castlefreke, which read as follows: 'When I was in the district last Easter . . . I was informed that the policy of the owners . . . was to get as much out of the place as possible before they would sell it.' Back in Cork city, Mr Scully had had a word with Jasper, who apparently agreed that substantial tree-felling was indeed taking place.[3]

This brouhaha over timber illustrates exceptionally well the insouciant approach that was becoming characteristic of Jasper's relationship with Republicans. First, just as in the conduct of his solicitor's practice, he was perfectly prepared to deal with the Dáil, its bodies and representatives, and even implicitly to acknowledge its claim to sovereignty, even though it was currently viewed as an illegal and rebellious organisation by the very British government of which Jasper himself was an official. Secondly, he was not above slyly provoking Republicans. Finally, like many lawyers, he does not seem to have regarded truth as holy light that reveals the real nature of things, but rather as a piece in the game of life to be moved around as necessary to help secure a winning position, or at least to defend a vulnerable one.

While Jasper was getting into difficulties with the Republicans over the felling and sale of timber, William Wood, as the estate agent in the syndicate, should have been arranging for disposal of the farmland. However, he had been unavoidably delayed in this. Like Jasper, he was perennially out of favour with the IRA, mainly on account of his involvement in property dealings, which were not necessarily always in the interests of small tenant farmers and the untenanted. However, unlike his cousin Jasper but like various other members of his family, William Wood was not only a resolute Unionist but an abrasive and combative character. Staunch, tough, inflexible, he was not prepared to give an inch to Nationalists of any stripe, let alone Republicans. As he himself put it, 'I was always loyal to, and an open and pronounced supporter of the British government. I never countenanced or submitted to any illegal or rebel organisation.'

As the Troubles intensified, William Wood was regarded with ever greater suspicion and hostility by Republicans. In April 1921, he was arrested by the IRA, ostensibly for spying. 'I was accused of giving information to the British army and the government, and was told several times during my detention that I was about to be shot, and a revolver was constantly being clicked at my ears, whilst blindfolded.' After his release, he left the country for six weeks.

Shortly after his return, in June 1921, William Wood began preparing for the sale of Castlefreke agricultural property. Like Jasper in his efforts to unload the timber, he almost immediately ran into local opposition, particularly from the IRA. In April 1921, Liam Deasy, as commandant of the West Cork Brigade, had issued an order that no exchange of property would be legal or permitted without his sanction. All auctioneers in the region, including William Wood, were informed of this decision. Permission for sale would usually only be given if the asking price was significantly lowered – and various pressures could be exerted to achieve this. When a sale was completed, agents had to hand over ten per cent of their fees to the IRA and any attempt to avoid this would be summarily dealt with. The second battalion area of Clonakilty, in which the Castlefreke demesne was situated, seems to have been particularly active in its efforts to manage the sale and purchase of land. A note survives in Jasper's papers to a fellow solicitor in Clonakilty from Jim Hurley, the second battalion commandant.

It has come to my knowledge that certain changes have taken place, or are about to take place in this area by PRIVATE TREATY. Such changes will not be allowed unless with permission of BRIGADE COMMANDANT, with whom you can communicate through me.

The sale of Castlefreke land became ever more contentious – and bogged down. The castle itself, now uninhabited, was damaged, with locals helping themselves to anything they needed. In the January 1922 quarter sessions at Bandon, Jasper, William Wood and Francis FitzMaurice applied for compensation and were awarded £8.10s in damages.

Meanwhile, William Wood's problems continued. Neilus Connolly was angry with him. Nothing new there. For some considerable time the estate agent, with his obdurate loyalism, seems to have been a particular bête noire of his local IRA battalion commandant. This time, amongst other offences, Wood had made himself unpopular by conducting a sale of British army surplus goods at Lissard, just outside Skibbereen (this was one consequence of the British military withdrawal following the Treaty). Not only did Neilus consider that this material should have been handed over to him, but he was angry about the profits being made. William Wood received a letter, unsigned, but recognisably in Connolly's handwriting:

> Look here – your action in seeking and obtaining damages in a very frivolous case recently was shady [no doubt another successful claim for malicious personal injury or loss]. I was very near giving you a very serious rejoinder. But patience prevailed and the affair was let slide.
>
> You know your record is not a good one – bigoted Masonic and anti-Irish, you have fattened and battened on the kindliness of your countrymen. But like an insatiable parasite, the more liberty you get, the more you try and squeeze the life-blood of your less fortunate countrymen.
>
> At the auction you are at present conducting at Lissard, you are exceeding your previous efforts at Shylockism. It is no longer a secret that you bought up the whole lock, stock and barrel at a mere bagatelle. Now there are hundreds of poor creatures who gave their all in the big war, and who are entitled to any little bargains that may be going from the outgoing army of occupation. But you with your fiendish greed are trying to extort a profit of from 500% to 800% from the most deserving and neediest of the community.
>
> Beware. Forewarned is forearmed. Don't overdo it. If you do, take the consequences.
> By Order
> IRA

This communication was less threatening than its belligerent tone suggested. Neilus was one of only two battalion commandants in the West Cork brigade who had come out in favour of the Treaty. It was fairly unlikely that he would risk upsetting his comrades in the new Provisional Government, in particular

Michael Collins and Gearóid O'Sullivan, by breaking the agreed terms through arbitrary kidnapping or killing.

Far more worrying would have been a note that William Wood received some time in March or early April. This was from Jim Hurley, commandant of the Clonakilty battalion. While brief, it was very much to the point. It read: 'Having transgressed the IRA laws already, I now remind you if you repeat your actions you can do so at your own risk.' Hurley was an anti-Treatyite. Moreover, the Castlefreke estate came within his territory. It is highly probable that the transgressions mentioned, together with other, lesser, land transactions, involved William Wood's continuing and persistent efforts to sell off the Castlefreke demesne. Hurley, well aware of the strength of local feeling, was wholly resolved that any disposal of Castlefreke properties should benefit the landless or the unpurchased tenants of the neighbourhood.[4]

25

'A LEADING PROFESSIONAL MAN IS MISSING'

As the spring of 1922 approached, much of West Cork, particularly in the more rural areas, appeared on the verge of anarchy. It seemed almost inevitable that sooner or later, and probably sooner, the smouldering lawlessness would flare into uncontrollable outrages.

An early warning sign came one day when there came a knock on the door at Norton. Minnie answered it. Outside were two or three young men.

'Very sorry to trouble you, ma'am, but we've orders to burn the house.'

'Oh My! Oh My! Oh My! Mr Wolfe's inside. I'll just give him a call. JASPER!!! JASPER!!! COME QUICK!!!'

Jasper emerged from his study and came down the hall. Minnie explained the situation, then rushed back towards the kitchen.

'Well, well,' said Jasper. 'Don't just stand there, lads. Come on in. I'm just having a drink. Why don't you join me? I expect the women will want to get a few things out. We can give them a few minutes, can't we?'

'That would be fine, I'd say,' replied the leader.

The young men disappeared with Jasper into his study. Two or three hours later the bold Fenian men re-emerged, but by that time they were incapable of lighting a cigarette, let alone a house. They all lurched back down the drive and Jasper, himself not too steady, waved them a friendly farewell.[1]

The feared eruption of violence finally exploded in the last week of April. In Dunmanway, in the early hours of Thursday 27 April, Francis FitzMaurice answered a hammering on the door of his house in Main Street. Outside were a group of armed men. With his wife watching, the solicitor was shot twelve times. His murderers went on to kill two more Main Street residents, a retired draper and a chemist. The three men were all Protestants.

Late on the evening of the same day, armed men turned up in Skibbereen and called on William Wood and Jasper. As far as I can discover, they targeted no one else. William Wood managed to flee, in his slippers, through the back door and found refuge with a friend out in the country. The next day, he left for England, to be joined by his wife a week later. The two finally returned in July 1923.

At Norton, the gunmen also failed to get their quarry. As luck would have it, Jasper was away on business in Cork. By way of compensation, the

Republicans drove off with Jasper's motor car, an American 1920 model Maxwell.

Early on the morning of Friday 28 April, a message reached Minnie telling her of the attack on William Wood. She had already heard of the murders in Dunmanway. Within a few hours news also reached her of further shootings in the neighbourhood of Dunmanway and near Clonakilty. It was rumoured that the bloodshed had started when the acting commandant of the IRA Bandon battalion, Mick O'Neill, had been shot dead when raiding the farm of staunch Unionist landowners. His killer and two others had disappeared, presumed dead, and the murders ricocheted westwards from there.

As everyone now recognised, these events were unprecedented. They had few, if any, of the signs of a planned IRA operation. Apart from anything else, the killings had occurred in three different battalion areas, Dunmanway, Bandon and Clonakilty; if the attempts on Jasper and William Wood were included, then a fourth battalion, Skibbereen, was also involved. Republican commandants, alpha males that they were, did not expect members of other prides to go marauding across their territories, although sometimes leaders might get together and plan a joint operation. This did not appear to be such an operation, but rather it seemed that some Volunteers had slipped the leash of Republican discipline and were running wild. What would happen next was anybody's guess.

Meanwhile, what of Jasper? It was obvious that if he came home, as he was due to do for the weekend, he would be in serious danger. Minnie, knowing her husband's willingness to take chances, and fearing that he would be more than likely to return to the danger zone, determined to warn him off. She set off without delay by train for Cork. At Bandon, she alighted and searched the westbound trains as they stopped there. When she eventually spotted him, she was able to persuade him to turn back. With many others who had also decided to seek safety, he crossed that night to Fishguard via Rosslare. A newspaper reporting on the drama added, in the enigmatic fashion so popular with the Irish press, 'a leading professional man is missing since Friday night and fears are entertained for his safety'. Minnie cut out the piece, underlined the relevant passage and added a couple of exclamation marks. Jasper was back home within a few weeks.

Throughout West Cork, near panic persisted for several days. In Skibbereen, as elsewhere, there were rumours of further attacks. Willie Kingston was amongst those who took precautions. Not long before, Francis FitzMaurice had offered him a half share in his legal business, so he had good reason to think he too might be at risk. Having got the idea from a Wild West story, he planned to immerse himself in a large water tank above the lavatory in order to hide from any attacker that might come to call. He put on his oldest clothes and provided himself with a tube for breathing. Come the evening, came a knock. He made for his tank, but first had a quick look out the front, only to discover that it was a just neighbour calling to seek safety advice. Willie spent the rest of the night sitting on his bed, jumping at every sound, but there were no more visitors. He left for Dublin in the morning, where he stayed with his sister Sarah and her husband. Later in the year he emigrated to South Africa but returned to Skibbereen in spring 1924.

While Willie Kingston was in hiding, there was one more shooting, not far from Bandon. This brought the number of men killed to ten. Many Protestants now began to fear a bloodbath. The exodus that had begun after the first killings continued for a couple of weeks, but there were no more outrages. For this the senior command of the IRA in West Cork must take at least some credit. The leadership of uniformed or armed organisations is always notoriously reluctant to admit wrongdoing by its members. While no one is known to have been disciplined for the killings, the commandant of the 3rd West Brigade (Bandon, Clonakilty, Dunmanway), on Friday 28 April, even before the rampage had ended, issued a 'Definite Military Order' to all his battalion commandants that no 'soldier in the area was . . . to interfere with or insult any person . . . even capital punishment will be meted out' to those 'not upholding the rigid discipline of a military force'.

In Skibbereen, which since reorganisation following the truce belonged to a separate South West Brigade, Neilus Connolly issued a public notice, which was published in various places including the *Eagle*, stating that the IRA would do all in its power to 'protect the lives and property of all citizens irrespective of creed' and would 'faithfully observe the amnesty proclaimed by Mr M. Collins'. A system of guards was set up, in Skibbereen and other threatened towns. That the IRA leadership was sincere is hardly open to doubt. Neilus Connolly, for instance, however tough an operator he may have been, was certainly not two-faced. What he said, he meant, and he had the courage to stick by his decisions. Previously, loyalists in his area may have suffered, and died, at the hands of his men, but his actions in April 1922 almost certainly saved lives.

One question remains. At the time, and since, many considered that the massacre was motivated by sectarianism. The danger of religious differences growing into hatred and spilling over into violence was something community leaders in southern Ireland had been grappling with for decades. Religious and political figures of all shades of belief had almost without exception consistently done their best to promote at least mutual acceptance by Catholics and Protestants of one another (although this did little to prevent at times outrageously unscrupulous competition between the churches for converts).

The experience of Jasper Wolfe, not only at the time of the April killings but throughout his life, does not suggest that, for him and his relations and acquaintances, animosities fuelled by sectarianism ever reached a crisis point, and in April 1922 quite different matters seem to have been occupying Republican minds: hostility to 'Free Staters', fear of possible loyalist counter-revolutionary moves and lingering resentments against those who were suspected, rightly or wrongly, of having actively worked for the British during the struggle for independence.

Finally, there was the ever inflammatory question of land. Of the syndicate who had controversially purchased the demesne of Castlefreke – all of whom, in one way or another, were also otherwise actively involved in agricultural affairs – Francis FitzMaurice had been shot dead, while Jasper and William Wood had both been targeted. In their case, at least, it seems plausible that it was their involvement with land, and particularly with Castlefreke, that had got them onto the hit list.[2]

'I WAS INFORMED I WOULD BE SHOT'

In early June 1922 Jasper returned home. Later that month a general election (held according to the proportional representation system) was held. This was, in effect, a plebiscite on whether the electorate of southern Ireland was prepared to accept the Treaty and the Free State constitution, which had just been finalised. In Skibbereen, Neilus, now an active Free State supporter, proposed Michael Collins, the sitting member, as candidate for West Cork. Despite a confused and complicated political situation the result, declared on 24 June, showed that in Cork, as almost everywhere else in the country, there was a very substantial pro-Treaty majority.

As feared, opponents of the Treaty, and particularly hard-core Republicans, were not prepared to accept the election result. As early as mid-April an IRA group, now becoming known as 'Irregulars', had, without authority, occupied certain buildings in Dublin, including the Four Courts, the national centre for the administration of justice. Almost immediately after the election hostilities broke out between Free State troops and the Irregulars.

At this time, Willie Kingston, having fled Skibbereen after the April killings, was still staying in Dublin at his sister's house. He witnessed the crisis which now erupted:

About 4.30 a.m. on 28th June . . . we were awakened by cannon fire, and afterwards we learned the Free State Army was attacking the Four Courts . . . Later, sister Sarah and myself decided to walk to Merrion Street . . . We saw some young men dressed in trench coats and leggings. They must have been waiting in ambush because when we returned some twenty minutes later, we saw a motor car . . . with the back riddled with bullets, and large pools of blood and oil. Some of the bystanders told us that the car, which was carrying Free State Officers had been bombed and shot up, and two of the occupants had been killed and three others wounded.

On the evening of 30th June there was a tremendous explosion when the Record Office [next to the Four Courts] was blown up and, though some miles away from us, we could see a huge cloud of smoke rising into the air, and I picked up some of the papers which had gone up in the explosion.

Even before the siege of the Four Courts had ended (on 5 July), civil war was flaring up across the country. In County Cork, Skibbereen was the only urban centre in government hands. Here, on the withdrawal earlier in the year of the British army and the Royal Irish Constabulary, the IRA fourth battalion had occupied the police barracks and the adjacent inspector's house. This battalion, alone of the IRA forces in West Cork, now remained loyal to the Free State.

The Sunday before the Four Courts were attacked, Neilus had resigned as commandant. In two days' time he was planning to get married to his childhood sweetheart, Kathy Walsh. He told his men of the decision and asked them to elect a replacement. Jer McCarthy was the obvious candidate. He had been a medical student at Cork when the Troubles broke out and soon joined Tom Barry's Flying Column, fighting in most of its main engagements. He was, wrote Neilus, who thought highly of his potential successor, 'a young athletic man of 24, who did not know what fear was'. Jer McCarthy was chosen unanimously. The new commandant was, like Neilus, a strong supporter of the Free State, but his abilities, determination and leadership were very shortly to be severely tested.

For the Irregulars, it was an insult to the honour of Republicans, not to mention a serious tactical disadvantage, that the key town in West Cork should be in the hands of forces loyal to the government. A major operation was very soon launched to rectify the situation.

The inhabitants of Skibbereen soon discovered that something serious was afoot. In the early hours of Sunday 2 July, the Wolfes in Norton, together with their neighbours, were awoken by the sound of motors. By breakfast time it was obvious that the town had been occupied by Irregulars; these troops, it turned out, were drawn mainly from the South West and West Cork brigades, under the joint command of their respective commandants, Gibbs Ross and Tom Hales. During the day, they were joined by Liam Deasy, formerly commandant of the West Cork brigade and now a general with the southern command.

Throughout Sunday, Deasy negotiated with Jer McCarthy and the Free State troops to try to achieve a peaceful surrender. From the first, Father McCarthy was active in the situation, as the *Cork Examiner* put it, 'moving amongst the people freely, and in consultation with the leaders of both sides'. Meanwhile, the rank-and-file Volunteers were settling themselves in for a long stay. They took over the Town Hall and looked around for suitable accommodation in which to billet themselves.

The townspeople, seeing that there appeared to be no imminent danger of hostilities breaking out, continued with their usual Sunday routines. In Norton, Jasper, realising that he was personally in danger, briefly considered making a run for it, but it soon became obvious that he had little hope of escaping undetected, so he stayed put. In the afternoon, having attended church as usual, he and Minnie went out visiting.

Left alone at home was Dorothy, who was now eighteen. In the last few years she had enjoyed her own share of excitement. She had been attending the High School for Girls in Cork city when confrontations between the police, the British army and Republicans began to get serious. In the autumn of 1919 she and her sister Ray were sent to a school in North Wales, Penrhos College, a Methodist foundation that had been recommended by Jasper's sister May. After some difficulties settling in, Dorothy thrived. Garnering various exam successes and prizes, she eventually gained entrance to Oxford. She was now at home waiting to go up to university. She was being congratulated by one and all and feeling pretty pleased with herself. She was also seeing a good deal of Frank O'Meara, a medical student and son of the local GP, who lived just round the corner in North Street.

That Sunday afternoon there was a knock at the door and Dorothy opened it. Outside was an officer of the Irregulars, together with a squad of his men. She, like her father, was up for any crisis.

'Excuse me, miss,' said the officer, 'but I have an order to quarter troops in this house.'

'I see,' said Dorothy. 'I'm afraid you'll have to wait a while, because my parents are out. But they'll be back soon.' Suitable arrangements were agreed in due course. When Jasper heard of this incident, he was impressed by his daughter's coolness. Writing to Ray a few weeks later, he commented, 'Dorothy behaved like a brick, and appears to enjoy it.'

By Monday, the phoney war was over. The previous day, as the official Republican army report put it, 'every avenue for an amicable settlement [had been] explored'. There is no doubt that everyone wanted to avoid a showdown. Liam Deasy, a reasonable person and a superb organiser and manager of men, was no firebrand. Until recently, he had been in command of all the Volunteers now confronting each other and the last thing he or they wanted was fighting amongst former comrades. But the result was total deadlock. Even Father McCarthy failed to engineer a breakthrough. Jer McCarthy, commandant of the Free State forces, was adamant that he and his men were 'appointed custodians of the barracks by the Provisional Government and would hold them for that body'. The Irregulars were equally determined to secure Skibbereen for the Republicans. So that was that.

Preparations for a siege were made. Buildings surrounding the barracks and the district inspector's house were taken over and occupied by snipers. An ancient cannon was brought over from a nearby house of one of the gentry (where for years it had seen service as an ornament) and mounted on the roof of the Bank of Ireland. A field dressing station was set up and arrangements agreed for temporary cessation of hostilities if casualties needed to be removed.

Throughout Monday and Tuesday, all businesses remained shut and most people stayed at home. The unfortunate inhabitants of the area surrounding the barracks, however, wisely decamped to stay with relations or friends in the country. Heavy firing continued all day. The cannon, which was in line of sight of the barracks, was primed to make its contribution. However, the Irregulars, who realised it might be less than reliable, fired it via a long fuse.

The gun blew up, ripping the top off the bank, but otherwise causing little damage. This was fortunate, not only for the defenders of the barracks, but also for the offices of Jasper Travers Wolfe & Co., which stood almost directly below the line of fire. Despite this mishap, by Monday night the Republican army was gaining control. It had cut off water and gas supplies to the government troops and was starting to dig a tunnel under the barracks, so as to blow it up. In their own words, the Irregulars had 'completely enveloped' the positions of the pro-Treatyites.

On the Sunday evening the Irregulars had begun to move into Norton. Early on the Monday morning the family were preparing to leave for Snugville, where there was plenty of spare room. However, they were without Jasper. He had been arrested and marched down to the Town Hall, where, as he put it, 'I was informed that I would be shot'.

The Wolfes were also without a horse to draw the trap. The Volunteers had commandeered the animal, which, up until then, had been grazing in its paddock. When Minnie had heard of their plans to take her horse, she had confronted the soldiers with tears in her eyes, declaring that she could not bear to be parted from her beloved companion. This was a tricky one for the Volunteers, who were usually both frightened of and respectful towards women. They eventually agreed that Minnie could at least say farewell to the animal.

This animal led an enviable existence. It spent most of its time in a lush pasture, it had its own stable, was lovingly tended by Jerry, and in return all it had to do was make occasional outings pulling the trap. It was therefore hardly surprising that it liked getting its own way. A disinterested observer might well have thought it wilful and bad-tempered. Amongst the idiosyncrasies of this creature was a total refusal to respond to a normal bit (that is, one in its mouth). It would only work with a 'clean bit', which pulled at the throat.

When Minnie was making her way out to say goodbye to her horse via the hall and the kitchen, she looked out of the window onto the yard and saw that Jerry, watched by Irregulars, had already started the harnessing and had the clean bit in place. She quickly summoned Mollie O'Donovan, the housekeeper, and provided her with a large bag containing tit-bits for Dolly. The two, apparently most upset, approached the horse. Minnie hugged and stroked the creature at length and succeeded in removing the bit, which she surreptitiously passed to Mollie, who hid it in the bag. Jerry was quietly told to put on a normal bit, which he did, and the Republicans took the horse and trap away, albeit with some difficulty. That evening, in a fury, they returned alone without the horse. The Wolfes, they said, were more than welcome to have their 'crature back – the divil was in it'. At present it was running wild on the Cork road.[1]

The next day, Tuesday, proved critical for almost everyone. Even Neilus was sucked into the crisis. He had found it a great deal more difficult than he had anticipated to get away from Skibbereen. Married the previous week, on Tuesday 27 June, Mr and Mrs Connolly had set off for their honeymoon in

Dublin the next day. Unfortunately for them, it was on that Wednesday that the Four Courts were attacked, and so they soon learned that all trains into the capital had been cancelled.

Neilus now ran into even greater difficulties. He found himself assailed by serious woman troubles. He and Kathy decided, since they could not reach Dublin, to visit a sister of Neilus who was a nun in Enniscorthy, in Wexford. It turned out that Sister Mary Kevin was far from pleased with her brother. Whether from a commitment to universal peace or, much more likely, from a white-hot belief in the Republican cause, she was extremely upset about the Provisional Government attack on the Four Courts. Since her brother was a Free Stater, she felt he could not escape blame for what was going on. As Neilus remembered it, 'Sister Mary was furious with me. One would imagine by the way she spoke that I was responsible for the civil war.'

Retreating from the convent, and on the way back towards Cork, Neilus and Kathy heard about the attack on Skibbereen. It was now that Neilus ran into his first marital confrontation. It was clear to him from newspaper reports that the garrison in Skibbereen could only hold out for a day or two at most, so there was little point in trying to return. Kathy, however, was implacably determined that he should go back and help with the defence.

'You were responsible for recruiting the men,' Kathy told him, 'and I know you'll not be deserting them now.'

Neilus found himself retreating again. 'I will join up,' said he.

However, when the couple reached Cork city on Monday evening, they could not get any further. A friend, who in fact was anti-Treaty, tried to get Neilus a car but road travel to West Cork was impossible. As for trains, although they were still running it was known that the Republicans were screening all passengers at Skibbereen. Neilus was told most emphatically that if he turned up in the battle zone he would undoubtedly be arrested. So, throughout Tuesday Neilus and Kathy were stuck fast.

In Skibbereen, as Neilus had suspected, the endgame was approaching. In the early hours of Tuesday morning the RIC district inspector's house, a formidable building next door to the barracks, was taken. The defenders managed to escape through a deep ditch to the barracks, but this in itself, now exposed, opened up a new line of assault. Throughout the day, Irregulars attacked the barracks with rifles, grenades and heavy round-shot: 'a terrible fire', said one report, was 'poured upon the building, which was responded to with equal vigour by the defendants'. Much damage was done, not only to the barracks itself but to surrounding buildings. Windows were smashed, their frames torn out, and walls were pitted with bullet marks. Surprisingly, however, there were relatively few casualties. Although not all reports agree, it seems the Free Staters survived unscathed, while the Republicans had one man fatally wounded and a few less seriously injured. No civilians were injured. By evening the Free State garrison was ready to surrender and within an hour acceptable terms were agreed, and honoured.

At about the same time, Jasper was released. The Irregulars, buoyed up by their success and in a forgiving mood, were reluctant to take their first life, not least since the execution of a respected local civilian would have been seen by many as a callous murder. Father McCarthy had also been arguing for mercy. It was a short walk for Jasper from imprisonment at the Town Hall to his family, who were now settling into Snugville. He and Minnie decided that, yet again, he had better get out of the country, and as fast as possible. Since the Norton car had been requisitioned by Republicans a couple of months previously, the Wolfes no longer had a vehicle of their own. However, they managed to borrow one.[2]

A chauffeur, too, was available: Dorothy. She had recently started learning to drive. No driving tests existed at the time, but she could just about manage. Cadogan, in particular, had been generous in his advice. 'Nice an' steady in the middle of the road, Miss Dorothy', had been his exhortation. These words were a great deal more sensible than they might at first appear. In those days, the roadside could be a very lively place: poultry, stray animals, children, chatting adults, horse and traps momentarily pulled up, and much else, could all be found by the verges, pursuing their various interests, more or less oblivious to their surroundings. In contrast, the centre of the highway, with its infrequent traffic, was relatively calm and predictable.

Flight by car would certainly be very risky, but the gamble seemed worth taking. Jasper packed a bag with a few clothes and settled himself under the back seat, concealed beneath a rug. The hope was that, even if Irregulars saw the car, they would be unlikely to challenge a vehicle driven by a lone young woman. In any case, the attention of the Republicans would be focused on celebrating their victory and taking over the barracks. Father and daughter made off towards Cork. Eventually, and without any scares, either from Irregulars or Dorothy's inexperienced driving, they arrived safely and Jasper boarded a ferry and found his way to England. Dorothy returned to Snugville.

The following day, Wednesday, Neilus and Kathy finally made it back to Skibbereen. They found the townspeople resuming their usual way of life and the Republican troops on a high of brotherly love. They had only walked a few hundred yards from the station when they met, as Neilus recalled, 'several groups of Regulars and Irregulars chatting with each other'. One of the Irregulars, seeing Neilus and Kathy, congratulated them on their marriage and asked them to go for a drink. They spent a couple of convivial hours with pro- and anti-Treatyites in a pub, and one of the Irregulars even gave Kathy a lift home in his car.

Neilus meanwhile stayed on in Skibbereen to attend the funeral of the dead Republican. Patrick McCarthy came from Kilcoe, near Ballydehob. His home was only a few hundred yards from the Aughadown graveyard, the resting place mainly of Protestants, but it was here, in a far corner overlooking the estuary of the river Ilen, that the twenty-two-year-old was buried. Neilius and the others at the funeral would have walked past the fresh graves of the two farmers, William Sweetnam and Matt Connell, who had been shot by the IRA just eighteen months previously. After the service, Neilus had a drink with several Irregulars and four of their leaders gave him a lift home. As he commented, "tis more like fiction than facts'.

All this, however, was too good to last. A week after the fall of the barracks, Jer McCarthy and one of his men set out for Dublin. They travelled on foot, since cars and trains were too dangerous for them and in any case were not getting through. On their arrival in Dublin, they met Michael Collins, who promised to try and organise the recapture of Skibbereen. The Republicans in Skibbereen soon scented danger, however, and looked to strengthen their defences. It was felt that Norton was dangerously vulnerable to attack, so they abandoned it, taking with them a camera of Minnie's and virtually all of Jasper's clothes. Since these mostly consisted of sober three-piece suits, some of the Irregulars must have appeared rather oddly dressed for military men. As soon as Norton was empty, Minnie and Dorothy, joined by Ray and Travers, who were now both back from school, returned home.

Early in August, a contingent of the Free State army attacked Cork city from the sea and captured it. At about the same time another detachment, under the command of Jer McCarthy, sailed for Union Hall, a few miles from Skibbereen. When they disembarked they were joined by Neilus and other Volunteers, so that they numbered in all well over 200 men. The defending Republicans, realising that they were outnumbered, made plans to withdraw, but not before they had made life as difficult as possible for their enemy. They burned down the barracks and the district inspector's residence. They intended to treat the Town Hall in similar fashion, only refraining when Tim Sheehy, Jim Burke and, at the last minute, Father McCarthy succeeded in persuading them that it was of no military value. Finally, the Irregulars gave warning that they would torch any private residences that could be of use to the Free Staters. On this occasion, no attempt was made to burn Norton. Perhaps it was spared because, as the Republicans had discovered for themselves, it was of less than no use strategically. The fact that it was a Protestant house, and the home of a man seen for some years as an enemy of the Republic, did not, for these properly disciplined Irregular forces, necessarily mark it out for destruction.

On the other hand, two fine Catholic mansions were targeted. The Irregulars feared that they could prove helpful to the Free State forces. Glencurragh House and Clover Hill both belonged to 'Miss May'; a devout and respected single lady, she was the only remaining direct heir of the powerful and influential McCarthy family. The torching of Glencurragh proved quite a social occasion. There was time to remove most of the contents and many of Skibbereen's inhabitants assembled to watch the fun. One girl who was musically gifted remembered all her life being seated at a piano and playing on the lawn as the splendid edifice went up in flames. What with destroying Catholic property and leaving Protestant Norton standing, no one could have accused the Irregulars, on this occasion at least, of sectarianism, vengefulness or indiscipline.[3]

They were, however, militarily ruthless. On Tuesday 8 August, after a brief gun battle on the outskirts of Skibbereen, the Free State Army marched in unopposed. The retreating Irregulars blocked roads, destroyed bridges and cut the railway line. For a few days Skibbereen was effectively cut off from the rest of the country.

The Free Staters, like the Irregulars before them, decided that Norton would do very nicely as a billet for their troops, but, like the Irregulars before them, it was not long before they realised that Norton would leave them open to attack. As he handed the house back to Minnie, the commandant remarked that not only was the dwelling of no military importance, but that it was in fact 'a veritable death trap'.

On Tuesday 22 August General Michael Collins, President of the Free State Executive Council and commander-in-chief of the army, visited Skibbereen. Neilus, who had recently been appointed a brigade commandant, was amongst those who held meetings with him in the Eldon hotel. Later that day, not far from the Woodfield farm on which he had been brought up, Collins' convoy was ambushed by Irregular forces and he was shot dead.

Exactly a week later, Jasper boarded a schooner at Cardiff and returned home, this time for good.

27

'My warmest friends'

So, who were the men that Jasper in later life publicly referred to as three would-be executioners who afterwards became his warmest friends? And what happened to them when peace returned?

Neilus, without doubt, was one. After the Civil War, he stood as a candidate for the Free State party, Cumann na nGaedheal, and came top of the poll in West Cork. However, he did not take to politics. He found 'the talking shop at Leinster House' boring and staying in Dublin expensive. At the next election, in 1927, he did not stand again and devoted himself to farming and raising a family. 'I could', he concluded, 'be as well off and more contented with a pair of long reins behind two horses'.

A few years later, when a daughter of Neilus fell seriously ill, he was in Cork visiting her in hospital. There, he and Jasper came across each other on the steps of the courthouse. Jasper asked after the sick child. The two shook hands. After that they often had a drink together in Jasper's favourite pub in North Street.[1]

Liam Deasy was almost certainly another of those who, having condemned Jasper to death, afterwards made his peace with him. As adjutant of the West Cork brigade, he had been at the Kilmeen meeting that decided on the first attempt to capture Jasper, in the ambush at Caheragh. He had also been, as a general in the Republican Southern Command, in charge of operations when Jasper was apprehended during the Irregulars' taking of Skibbereen from the Free State troops. Towards the end of the Civil War, when Deasy was already thinking of advocating 'a termination of present hostilities', he was captured by Free State forces. He escaped execution by signing a document calling for an immediate unconditional surrender. This action, which caused a rift with some more hard-line Republicans such as Tom Barry, he justified both at the time and afterwards. Following the Civil War he established, after an initial struggle, a very successful business, the Dunloe Men's Clothing Company. As a leading industrialist in the young Free State he played a prominent part in the business life of Cork. Deasy and Jasper, both active and influential local figures, would certainly have met on innumerable occasions.

The identity of the person Jasper had in mind as the third of his 'best friends' is less certain. As far as I can tell, nobody fits the known facts exactly.

However, he was probably thinking of the man who had tried to arrest him at Schull some weeks after the signing of the Anglo-Irish Treaty. Sean O'Driscoll originally came from Ballydehob, where his father ran a small building business not far from the shop of Jasper's grandfather, Sean Og Wolfe. During the Troubles, most members of the O'Driscoll family became active Republicans. Sean's young sister, who belonged to the Republican women's movement, Cumann na mBan, used to carry messages for the IRA, sometimes concealed in the ringlets of her hair. Towards the end of the Civil War, Sean was captured and condemned to death. However, peace and an amnesty came just in time to save his life.

After the war, O'Driscoll became an inspector with the Board of Works. A studious, stern, conscientious man of great integrity, he bore no grudges from the time of the Troubles. Nor was he a bigot. He used to tell his children that some of the best friends he ever had were Protestants. He lived in Skibbereen, at first near Snugville and later a little beyond Norton on the Cork road.[2] I could uncover no stories of him and Jasper spending time together – and they would not have met for a 'jar', since Sean never drank – however, when I was talking to someone who had been a neighbour of the O'Driscolls and who remembered the 1920s and 1930s well, she was in no doubt that the two would have been friendly. 'Sure,' she said, 'all the men knew each other.'

PART FOUR

TOP OF THE POLL
1922–1932

28

RATSVILLE

Jasper returned home on Tuesday 29 August 1922, three weeks after the Free State forces reoccupied Skibbereen. He sailed from Cardiff in what he referred to as a 'schooner', no doubt landing at Baltimore or Union Hall. He found Minnie, Dorothy, Ray and Travers all installed once again at Norton. But not for long. On the Wednesday, the day after his return, the Free State troops, deciding that the danger of a major full-scale assault by the Irregulars was now unlikely, again commandeered Norton. Once again the family had to decamp to Snugville. Father McCarthy offered to look after a few of the household belongings, so Minnie managed to transfer some of the more precious household furnishings to the nearby Catholic presbytery. Meanwhile, Ray, going up to her room to collect her things, was surprised to find three soldiers, booted and armed, stretched out on her single bed. ''Tis very nice and comfortable here, miss,' said one appreciatively.

It would be more than two years before the Wolfes could return. Snugville was spacious, and Rachel, who sometimes felt lonely, welcomed the company. Nevertheless, there were tensions. Jasper was not particulary affected, since he was well used to keeping his head down in domestic situations, and in any case he had other things on his mind. However, with the women, it was rather a different matter. Minnie and her mother-in-law were both extremely strong willed and used to running their own shows, so sharing accommodation was far from easy for either of them.

For the children, things were more or less bearable, not least because none of them had to stay in Skibbereen all the time. Dorothy was about to leave for Oxford, Ray was still at school in North Wales, while Travers was being sent to the Protestant Portora Royal School, at Enniskillen in the north of Ireland, which his uncle Robert Vickery had attended before him. Travers, who was still only eleven, was probably the most upset by the move. He particularly disliked the way that rats, thriving as never before, regularly visited Sugville from the Caol at the bottom of the garden and helped themselves to soap and any food left lying around. He soon dubbed his grandmother's house 'Ratsville'.

To make matters worse, with the Civil War growing in ferocity, daily life, while it suited the vermin, was distinctly less easy for humans. One sign of how bad things were can be seen in the takings of Protestant shopkeepers. Even though these were no longer suffering from the boycotts that some had endured during the Troubles, the turnover of many was down by as much as half. Rachel Wolfe, writing in the autumn to her granddaughter Dorothy at Lady Margaret Hall in Oxford, gave a picture of what their existence was like. Referred to the Irregulars, she described how 'The Rebs are outside the town watching for an opportunity to come in'. She also wrote about how the government troops (the Free State Army) had now not only 'settled down at each end of town' but had also occupied, in addition to Norton, a good many other buildings: 'The Corner House and the Bridge House [home and shop premises of, respectively, cousin William Wolfe and Willie Wood Wolfe] and nearly all the large business houses are occupied by the Free Staters.' She reported that at the Corner House 'troops are posted on the flat roof' (overlooking the main square and post office). Despite all this, Rachel describes how at least some degree of normal life carried on:

I am glad to say we have had no more murders here, and we feel free to go about. The posts are fairly regular now, only it is still fairly risky to send any parcels. The sale of work at the Manse was held last week and was very successful. It realised £40, which is very good considering the few little odds and ends we had – we had a lot of people at it considering the very small Protestant population of this place.

The most serious problem was the disruption to travel. In September, Dorothy, Ray and Travers all just managed to leave for college and school, but by October things were deteriorating badly. On 26 October Rachel wrote to Dorothy, 'there are no trains coming or going to this place'. Exactly a month later she was reporting that road transport too was now at a standstill: 'even the motors between here and Cork have been stopped today'.

As for Jasper, he was all but marooned in Skibbereen. Twice since his return in August he had been called to Cork on essential Crown business. On both those occasions he had been obliged to travel by sea, courtesy of the British navy, on board a destroyer. With Christmas approaching, Jasper and Minnie faced a real dilemma: what to do about their children? It seemed that it would be virtually impossible to get Dorothy and Ray back home. One option would be for them to stay with their Aunt Lillie, Minnie's younger sister, who lived in Wimbledon with her husband Tom Holroyd, an English civil servant, and two children, Nancy and Patrick. Jasper, however, who had official business in both London and Dublin, hoped it might just be possible for him to travel to both cities and give his daughters Christmas in an English hotel. As the December days passed, it became clear that he would have to give up this always dubious plan.

On 3 December he was writing to Dorothy, 'all passenger motor traffic is forbidden by the Irregulars, and motors are threatened to be fired on; this I think will not happen, but they may burn the cars, and if they burn one no other car will be induced to go'. A fortnight later, having failed to get to Dublin, the situation seemed much as before. 'All motor passenger traffic between here and Cork is still forbidden, and getting through is quite risky. There is only a bare chance that I may get away. There is only one motor passenger car going to Cork, and that only occasionally as it was stopped and warned a few days ago. I am afraid you will have a rough Xmas.'

There was also a problem over Travers, who seemed hopelessly stuck: 'How Travers will return is a mystery, but things may improve, or anything may happen in this dear, delightful country.' In the event, things did not improve, or at least not in time for Christmas. Travers probably spent his holidays in Dublin with Jasper's cousin Sarah, a sister of Willlie Kingston. She was the wife of a Bank of Ireland official and the mother of three children who were more or less the same age as Travers.

29

Money matters

Jasper may have been having a rough ride domestically, but it was nothing to the uphill struggles he faced professionally. There was a very real chance that he would end up with little work, less money and his status in the community gone. After all, active Home Rule supporter though he may once have been, he was not only a faithful member of the Protestant Anglo-Irish community but now was seen as a man who had been a key figure in the British struggle to maintain control of Ireland – a struggle in which he had emerged on the losing side.

For Jasper, joining, indeed working to make a success of, the new civic order in Ireland was not a problem. In fact, the Free State embodied the sort of generous measure of Home Rule that he had advocated all his life. Here now was a new Irish nation, which was in principle non-sectarian, a member of the British Empire, loyal to the British Crown (yet not subject to Westminster) and in control of its own policies, both domestic and foreign. More he could not have hoped for.

What was a mighty problem for Jasper was persuading others, particularly those who held power, to accept that he would be loyal to the new Ireland. His first priority, however, was simply survival, and this required funds. Financially, the losses which Jasper faced were potentially catastrophic. Before his appointment as Crown Solicitor, his income had been sensationally high and, although it declined during the Troubles, it remained very substantial. In 1920–1 his gross earnings were nearly £100,000, and probably more. The next year they had almost halved, while in 1922–3, the year of the Civil War, they stabilised at just under £50,000. Of course, there were expenses to pay out of these sums, but these were modest. Salaries and wages, for example, were very low. Willie Kingston, the only solicitor employed by Jasper until the 1930s, was on £250 a year in 1911 and reached a maximum of £720 by the late 1920s. And he was the highest paid employee at Wolfe & Co.

To put these sums in context, a successful shopkeeper in Skibbereen, or 'merchant', as such traders liked to call themselves, virtually never earned more than £20,000 and could live very comfortably indeed on that (detached private residence, children at boarding school, and so on). So, for example,

Jasper's brother Willie in ordinary times usually had an annual turnover averaging around £15,000, with a maximum of about £19,000 in 1920–1, while the business that Jasper's great friend Eddie Swanton ran with his father Richard usually took rather less than £10,000. In the light of these figures, one can see that, while successful shopkeepers were definitely doing well, a top professional man like Jasper was seriously wealthy.

In early 1923, with the Civil War not yet over but the Free Staters beginning to look like the eventual winners, Jasper was contemplating a bank balance which, while it had fallen dramatically, momentarily appeared to be stabilising. That he still had some income was probably due to fees being paid by the many Anglo-Irish who were disposing of their Irish property or otherwise making arrangements to deal with life under, or away from, the new regime. However, even this modest flow of funds seemed unlikely to last for long.

Also due to diminish, though not to disappear, was his remuneration as Crown Solicitor. This position, under the Anglo-Irish Treaty, was abolished as from 1 January 1923. After questions in the British parliament, and various toings and froings, Crown Solicitors received generous compensation. Jasper was awarded a lump sump of £1,730, together with a lifetime pension of £800 a year.

Finally, like many others, Jasper could claim for losses suffered as a result of the Troubles and the Civil War. Up to the ending of British rule, he could have applied to quarter session courts for personal injury compensation. This, however, he had decided against. As he put it: 'I would probably have received compensation from the County Court Judge amounting to at least £1500 if I had applied for compensation for injuries arising from my first arrest. As a Crown Solicitor I did not think it right to do so, and it would have appreciably increased the dangers through which I lived.'

There were, though, other sources of compensation and these Jasper did try to tap, with some success. His main hope for significant compensation lay with the Irish Office in London, where the British government had set up a Grants Committee to deal with claims for losses arising from the truce of July 1921 until the time when the Irish Free State took over the running of the country (the committee seems to have interpreted the latter deadline rather vaguely). An ex-military man, Major Jamieson, acted as secretary to this body and he and Jasper saw a good deal of each other. As well as dealing with his own claim, Jasper was frequently in London appearing before the committee on behalf of various clients who, like him, were hoping to recoup some of their losses. (For a short while, these clients included Jasper's brother Willie. However, Willie soon fired Jasper and hired in his place their old family friend Herbert Z. Deane, who obligingly more than doubled the original claim. But the English civil servants, hardly a gullible breed, were less than impressed. One commented: 'The original Form of Application was for £2,766. The revised claim is for £7,115. Generally speaking I would have thought that Mr Travers Wolfe was in the best position to judge the extent of his brother's losses.')

Major Jamieson had a lot of time for Jasper. He admired his resilience as Crown Solicitor and he was grateful for his helpful and reasonable attitude towards claims, both those of clients and his own. However, even though, unlike others, Jasper was not required to provide witnesses for all his claims, this did not mean that all he asked for was nodded through without question. Jasper claimed for loss of business, personal expenses arising from his flights to England, incidental losses arising from his dismissal as Crown Solicitor, and injuries to health. The major had his suspicions (almost certainly justified) about Jasper's claim of £3,000 for 'injury to personal health', mainly in connection with his arrest and kidnapping during the truce. 'His health', commented the major sceptically, 'may have been affected, though he does not give that appearance. I have asked for medical certificates.' In due course, Dr O'Meara obliged with the required statements. Eventually, Jasper received, from a claim for £7,670, a total of £2,200, the final instalment not being received until 1928.

Jasper could also hope for compensation from the new Irish Free State. When he applied to the Office of Public Works in Dublin for £2,240 for losses arising from the occupation of Norton both by the Irregulars and by the Free State troops, he received £950. Finally, under one of the first acts of the new state, he could also apply to the recently established circuit courts for damage done to property. The judges concerned awarded him £468 for goods taken from Norton by the Irregulars and a further £102, to be shared with W. G. Wood, for property removed from Castlefreke. So, when money from all the claims had come in, he banked a total of rather more than £5,000. (Considerable variations in prices, together with rapid inflation at the time, make it very difficult to translate post-World War Irish prices into modern equivalents. Very roughly, £1 probably equals around €25–30).

30

'WE SHOULD NOT KEEP HIM HERE'

The various payments, whether one-off or continuing, which came Jasper's way as recompense for the losses he had incurred, while welcome, were little more than dry biscuits when compared with the fare to which he was accustomed. If Jasper was to restock his finances, he now had to find ways of getting in further supplies.

He rapidly achieved a remarkable turnaround in his fortunes. By the end of 1924, less than two years after the end of the Civil War, he was writing to Major Jamieson that he had 'entirely regained his business'. Of course, this retrieval of his professional career may not have immediately brought the sort of income that he had previously commanded. Even so, things had certainly stabilised and, by the end of the 1920s, he was undoubtedly once again a wealthy man.

How had Jasper restored his credit? His first concern had been to make sure he was not excluded from public employment, as any loss of status would have lost him respect and professional standing, ultimately resulting in loss of financial and social security.

Typical of the one or two lesser harassments that he had to address was an incident which occurred in the summer of 1923, just after the ending of the Civil War. A Mr McCarthy, official rate collector for the Skibbereen District Council, took it upon himself to launch a mini-vendetta against Jasper when he issued him with a rate assessment for Norton. Jasper refused to pay for the period from the previous August, on the very reasonable grounds that, since then, the house had been requisitioned by Free State forces. 'I wish', wrote Jasper to Mr McCarthy, 'to pay for the entire time during which my family was in occupation, but unless compelled to do so I do not feel called to pay for the period during which the National Army were in occupation'. Mr McCarthy, refusing to withdraw the rate demand, now issued Jasper with a summons for non-payment.

At this point the dispute went public and was reported in the *Southern Star* (14 July 1923). The District Council was embarrassed because two of its officers (Jasper was still solicitor to the council) were at each other's throats. It then emerged that not only had Mr McCarthy failed to clear his action with the council, but that he had not issued any rate assessments to the various Catholic householders whose premises had also been taken over by the army. This made it look as if the council was in the business of discriminating against Protestants, whereas sectarian action was something the majority of its members had always done its best to avoid. Then, unexpectedly, they were all offered a surprise solution. Jasper realised that the writ against him for non-payment of rates had been delivered, not to Norton, as it should have been, but to his office. It was therefore invalid. For whatever reason, no further writ was issued. End of story.

Potentially far more worrying for Jasper than such minor incidents were efforts to have him dismissed, at the instigation of the IRA and Sinn Féin, from various of the official posts that he held. These had begun well before the truce and the Treaty, but at that point such sallies, while politically motivated, were quite legitimate, being little more than minor forays in the overall, predominantly violent, Republican campaign against the British.

The first attempt to dismiss Jasper from a public office had occurred early 1920, at Bantry. Here a proposal was made to replace him as solicitor to the Bantry Rural District Council. A vigorous debate followed, the chairman putting the Republican viewpoint very succinctly: 'We have heard of the objection that he is a Protestant. We don't object to him for that or for being a milk-and-water Home Ruler; but as Crown Prosecutor we should not keep him here.'

Jasper had just one solitary supporter, but he spoke up loudly. One of his most potent points was that privately many Irish people continued to employ Mr Wolfe: 'If you go to the quarter sessions you will find he is employed by every Sinn Féiner and Nationalist in the country.' Nevertheless, Jasper was dismissed. He was also voted off as solicitor to the Bantry Board of Guardians, as well as being replaced, without being formally dismissed, as solicitor to the Castletownbere Rural District Council and Board of Guardians.

Since this all took place during the Troubles, it was probably fair enough. However, once the Anglo-Irish Treaty had been signed and ratified by the Dáil, similar less easily defensible efforts were made to smear Jasper's name in Skibbereen and keep him out of local life. The attacks on him came, not only from paid-up Republicans or other longstanding opponents, but also from chancers who, emerging from the shadows, were now rushing to put the boot into the defeated British loyalists.

In February 1922, with the new Free State already at risk from growing anarchy and the threat of civil war, a major assault was mounted on Jasper. In the Skibbereen Urban Council, a motion was proposed that Mr J. T. Wolfe be dismissed as its solicitor. There were three main charges against him. The proposers of the motion, Mr O'Connell and Mr Duggan, said that their main aim in seeking the dismissal of the council's solicitor was to protect the people of the district. Mr Wolfe, they argued, had, as Crown Solicitor, pledged his allegiance to the enemy and had 'prosecuted and persecuted' the people for years.

The second charge dealt with Jasper's appearing at quarter session courts on behalf of clients claiming compensation for malicious injuries. This, of course, was the very issue which had led to Jasper's being kidnapped and condemned to death by the IRA the previous October, and it was still very much a live and sensitive matter. Only two weeks previously, Mr Justice Hynes had held the quarter sessions in Skibbereen. There, 76 claims for malicious injuries had been heard, Jasper either appearing personally or instructing counsel (Jim Burke) on behalf of several of the litigants. Amongst those who made successful claims were Eddie Swanton, for his kidnapping (£1,500). In total, approaching £10,000 had been awarded. The councillors seeking Jasper's dismissal were incensed, both because the districts in which successful claimants lived (and these included Skibbereen) had to pay a proportion of the damages awarded and because Jasper himself, as solicitor to the council, was instrumental, through his successful representation of those claiming for malicious injuries, in costing it money. As Jasper's accusers expressed it, 'Mr Wolfe acted against the Council in appearing for applicants for malicious injuries, a portion of the money awarded having to be paid by the people of Skibbereen . . . he was instrumental in getting a lot of money from the bogeyman Hynes.' Messrs O'Connell and Duggan refrained from adding, a fact neverthess well known to all present, that their own sympathies, as Republicans, were not with the victims, who were predominantly Protestant and British government supporters, but with their attackers, who were IRA members or supporters.

The third charge against Jasper was that, during his prosecution of a leading Republican, Alderman Tadgh Barry of Cork city, he had compared the Gaelic tongue to the language of the Hottentot. All in all, the proposers of the motion for dismissal considered that, 'as honourable and straightforward men we should not retain Mr Wolfe one hour longer in our service'.

If Messrs O'Connell and Duggan thought they would easily secure support for their motion, they were much mistaken. The charges they had made ignited a sulphurous debate about the very nature of the new Irish state that was now being created. The first to speak in Jasper's defence was a fellow solicitor, Mr P. Sheehy. He charged O'Connell with undermining the spirit and the letter of the new Anglo-Irish Treaty:

> We are now all subjects of the Irish Free State, entitled to all its privileges as we are bound by its laws. I refuse to admit anybody has a right to make a 'corner,' as they say on the Stock Exchange, in the new free constitution of Ireland. It is the common heritage of us all, of every religion and class . . . Mr Michael Collins and his colleagues were big enough to sit at the same table in Downing Street with Sir Hamar Greenwood [Chief Secretary of Ireland], and with him and his Prime Minister arrange an Irish settlement. They agreed, by a fine gesture of friendliness, and for the great cause of Irish peace, to forgive and forget here at home. Are we to disregard such an

example; and by the dismissal of Mr Wolfe brand ourselves with a stigma of bigotry unworthy of the narrowest bigots of the land? Are we going to allow it to be said that here in the extreme south of Ireland the first public act of a Nationalist Council will be to hurl from office a man competent and loyal to our interests, because some of us disagree with him? Are we going to sink to the level of the resolution submitted by Mr Duggan, charged as it is with venom and spite; subversive of tolerance for the past, and without hope for the future? Why, if the poisonous spirit of the resolution we have heard to-night is to be taken as a promise of the new time in Ireland, then our old country will be a dwelling place and a home fit only for the reptiles we were told St Patrick had banished. No man of honour would consent to live in such an atmosphere of hate, but would hasten to shake from his shoes the dust of a country so befouled.

More specifically, Mr P. Sheehy defended Jasper's right to appear for anyone claiming compensation for malicious injuries. Since Skibbereen Urban Council, along with all other councils in West Cork, refused on principle to be represented at the quarter sessions (a court of British justice), it was not possible for Jasper to appear on its behalf. Moreover, he was not salaried but only paid for the work he did, and he had a living to earn. Despite all this, he had asked the council for guidance and had been advised that he could do as he wished. Clearly, he had not betrayed the council by representing clients at the courts.

Timothy Sheehy, Jasper's old adversary, also spoke up in his defence:

Timothy Sheehy.

No one might consider himself better entitled than I to vote against Mr Wolfe, and in a measure give blow for blow. On two occasions when I stood at the County Council elections, Mr Wolfe devoted all his energy and ability – unsuccessfully – to have me rejected. But Mr Wolfe was entitled to support whom he wished, and no action he has taken will induce me to be a party to his wrongful dismissal. We are now entering a new era in Ireland. I ask that the proposers drop the motion, and act in a spirit of harmony and peace in order to engage the many questions engaging our town. That would be acting in the best spirit of the Irish settlement.

At this point James Duggan intervened, boasting of his Nationalist credentials. This was an unwise move, as it was well known that this particular councillor had always kept well away from any danger zones during the Troubles. As the *Eagle*, albeit admittedly not entirely impartial, expressed it: 'We have seen him day by day during the past strenuous years grow hourly more snug and prosperous, entering no British fortress more formidable than a British Post Office or a British bank. Not an hour's imprisonment; not an hour on the run; not as much as a petty sessions summons came to interfere with the money making of Mr Duggan.'

The *Eagle* (11 February 1922) reported how James Duggan found himself spoken to 'with heat' by Tim Sheehy: 'How dare you try to monopolise Nationality? You never spoke on any platform of mine. Nobody could stand your ridiculous pretensions! You desire to wipe out the record of honest, unpretentious Irishmen!' The proposal was voted on and defeated.

There remained, however, the allegation that Jasper had likened the Irish tongue to 'Hottentot'. This was potentially very damaging, not because there was any great popular interest in speaking Irish – the language was rapidly dying out and was mostly not missed by ordinary people – but because Gaelic was a powerful symbol of the newly liberated Irish nation. An attack on Irish could too easily be understood, or represented, as an attack on the very soul of the native population. As soon as he learned of the charge (he had not been present at the council meeting), Jasper reached for his usual bag of tricks. In a letter to the press he opened by making fun of his accuser: 'If Mr Duggan wishes to beat his chest as an honest man – which I understand is a favourite pastime of his – he must surely have reasonably satisfied himself that the charge was true before levelling it at the head of an absent man.'

Jasper then proceeded to deny that he had ever, in the trial of Tadhg Barry, referred to Irish as a 'Hottentot language'. Such an accusation was 'a pure invention devoid of any foundation'. What was more, Jasper would prove that it was untrue: 'I will not merely expose the lie, I will proceed to unmask the liar.' To do this he offered to pay the Catholic Society of St Vincent de Paul, of which James Duggan was a member, £100 if 'the member referred to will satisfy any clergyman of his church, whom he may select throughout the diocese, that the charge he has brought against me is true.' However, Jasper perorated that, in the event of Mr Duggan not picking up the gauntlet, 'I demand a full and open public withdrawal and apology. Failing the acceptance of my offer, or the apology, I will brand Mr James Duggan as a reckless and cowardly slanderer and liar.'

It appears the offer was not accepted, but no apology was forthcoming, and so the matter rested, with Jasper the victor due to the no-show of his opponent. However, the fact was that Jasper delighted in making fun of the Irish language, a pastime that may well have originated in sibling provocations. Brother Willie had not only spoken Irish since the years he had lived on his grandfather's farm at Kilkeran, but loved to use it. Jasper no doubt found teasing Willie about his Irish a good way of annoying him. Later, Jasper discovered that one of the easiest means of pricking the pretensions of overly serious and narrow-minded Nationalists was to laugh at some of the more absurd acts of devotion to which worshippers of the language were prone. Although such sallies could be dangerous, as illustrated by James Duggan's attack, Jasper was aware that many Irish secretly agreed with him, though it was hardly politic or correct to say so.

As regards the charge that Jasper called Irish a 'Hottentot' language, I think it more than likely that he did so. However, he was on fairly safe ground in challenging James Duggan to prove the allegation. I searched through all the relevant numbers of the *Cork Examiner* and found no significant reference to the trial, let alone any verbatim reporting. The fact was that by this point in the Troubles (1921) newspaper reports and any other official accounts of Republican trials were almost always heavily censored. As Jasper well knew, it was extremely unlikely that anything other than hearsay reports of any contentious comment existed – at least in the public domain.

31

'From a few friends'

As soon as Jasper returned to Ireland in August 1922 he signalled publicly that he would be a loyal and active supporter of the Free State. With characteristic chutzpah, he stopped calling himself 'Crown Solicitor' and, on official documents and elswhere, took to referring to himself as 'State Solicitor'. Officially, he was still a Crown Solicitor, and State Solicitors, who would be the Free State replacements, had not yet been appointed. Furthermore, Jasper's chances of ever being appointed a State Solicitor were substantially less than zero. No matter. The point, which everyone grasped, was that he now saw himself, and wished to be seen, as acting in the interests, not of the vanquished British government, but of the new regime.

At last things began to go Jasper's way. In January 1923 he was honoured by a small gathering that presented him with a gold watch to mark the official ending of his time as Crown Solicitor. It was inscribed, 'Presented to J. T. Wolfe, Esq., C.S., from a few friends, 18.1.1923'. At the height of the Civil War, when travelling around West Cork was risky, these 'few friends' had taken the trouble to purchase, inscribe, meet together and present a valuable memento in honour of a man who had acted as prosecutor for the British adminstration.

Who were these 'few friends'? Since their demonstration of respect and affection for Jasper as Crown Solicitor would hardly have been popular amongst Republicans, their identity was always rather vague. Those present at the presentation could not have included any of the British forces with whom Jasper had worked closely during the Troubles. The military were long gone and the Royal Irish Constabulary had defiantly bowed out nine months previously, declaring 'an imperial force we were born, and an imperial force we wish to die'. Those who turned up must have been fellow lawyers of Jasper's and others who had been concerned in the administration of justice through the Troubles. Present no doubt were Eddie Swanton and Willie Wood, two of the very few Justices of the Peace who stuck to their posts, despite intimidation, until they were officially abolished, but most of those present would have been solicitors, barristers, clerks of the courts and possibly judges. The great majority of these men would have been Catholic, originally Home

Rulers, but all were now committed supporters of the Free State. Whatever their origins or beliefs, their allegiance to justice would have mattered to them at least as much as their patriotic loyalties.

Jasper wore the watch for the rest of his life. It meant much to him, because it was a symbol of the fact that his fellow professionals believed that, whatever the split loyalties, the fears and hatreds of the Troubles, he had sought to act in the interests, not of one side or another, but of justice.

All this had an immediate practical, and very welcome, implication. Those colleagues of Jasper's attending the presentation were not only honouring his past conduct as Crown Solicitor, but were in effect declaring that they remained ready to work alongside him in the future. As far as the lawyers of County Cork were concerned, Jasper would not be frozen out from either their camaraderie or their briefs.

Potential difficulties neverthess remained. It was, for instance, by no means certain that the Free State law courts, when they were established, would necessarily be ones in which Jasper would be able to prosper. When the Anglo-Irish Treaty was signed there were two competing legal systems in Ireland. One, the British, had been undermined by IRA hostilities to a point where it was in ruins, with only a few outposts still managing to function. It had no future. The other, the Republican, was flourishing at local level, but the higher courts barely existed.

The Free State government had to decide what to do about administration of the law, and fast. With the courts in disarray, doing nothing was not an option. The IRA, hard-line Republicans and many local people wanted to continue with the Dáil courts and build them up into a fully functioning system. However, the new Free State government was strongly opposed to this. There were difficulties to do with the embryonic and fragmentary nature of the Dáil legal system, particularly at its higher levels, but these were not critical. One major problem was to do with jurisprudence; the courts, despite appeals to Brehon law, lacked any sound, agreed, systematic body of law. Even more alarming was the influence exerted on the courts by the IRA. It was possible that the Dáil courts would become, not so much an independent judicial system as a wing of Republicanism. This, in turn, could sooner or later help to establish and underpin, not a democratic but a militaristic, even totalitarian, government. The stakes could hardly have been higher.

The Free State ministers moved urgently to set up a new legal system. The Dáil courts were abolished almost immediately and the British ones phased out more gradually. In their place came arrangements grounded in British jurisprudence, and in effect representing a modification of the British system for contemporary Irish circumstances. Locally, out went the Dáil parish courts and the British petty sessions and in their place came district courts, with a salaried Justice, sitting without juries. One step up, Dáil district courts and British quarter sessions were abolished and replaced by circuit courts of justice, with their own judges and juries, where were heard appeals from district courts, and all criminal cases except for murder, treason and piracy. Appeals to newly established high and supreme courts, in Dublin, could only be made by written transcript, an innovation which was to prove cumbersome and unreliable.[1]

The Republicans, and some locals, vehemently opposed these changes, but, as the Free State consolidated its power during and following the Civil War, there was little opponents could do to influence what was happening. Meanwhile, the legal profession was delighted. They had got all they could possibly have wanted, and even more. They would operate the new system as they had the old, so their status and independence were secure. Also, as important to them as anything else, the body of law and the forensic skills required to elucidate and apply it remained substantially intact. There is little a lawyer dreads more than being left without continuity and precedents, but now the Irish bench, bar and society of solicitors, together with all the attendant clerks and administrators, could adapt to a world which, while new, was yet familiar.

All this suited Jasper quite admirably. The conditions were now being put in place which gave him more than a fair chance of becoming as successful a solicitor in the Free State as he had been in Unionist Ireland. The introduction of the new arrangements, while quite complex, proceeded remarkably smoothly and swiftly. In March 1923, even before the last shots of the Civil War had been fired, the opening session of the new Free State district court was held in Skibbereen. Jasper, as the senior member of the legal profession present, stood to give an eloquent welcome to District Judge Crotty, the sole heir of all those departed Resident Magistrates, Justices of the Peace and, more recently, Republican parish court judges. And so it went on. A few months later, in Skibbereen and throughout West Cork, legal hearings were held to review decisions of the now illegal Dáil courts and to reject them or incorporate them into the already developing corpus of Free State judgements. Finally, on 17 May 1924, the last quarter session court was held in Skibbereen.

32

'VERY EXCITED AND BUSY AS USUAL'

Jasper now began to settle back into something like the life he had enjoyed before the Troubles. The Free State troops had moved out of Norton and Minnie was busy supervising repairs and renovations. The plan was for the family to be back in residence by Christmas. Meanwhile, the first Free State circuit court opened in Skibbereen during the third week of November 1924. It had to be held in the Town Hall, since the courthouse, damaged by the IRA during the Troubles, was still being repaired. Minnie, writing to Dorothy, who was beginning her last year at Oxford, reported that 'Sessions has started today in the Town Hall, and Daddy is very excited and busy as usual.'

Jasper had been working hard to keep those of his old clients who were still around, and to win new ones. On one front he had been very fortunate. The Free State government was well aware that many landless agricultural workers and 'unpurchased tenants' (tenants who had not yet bought their holdings) were extremely discontented. The land question was still capable of causing dangerous unrest, so, following the end of the Civil War, one of the first moves of the Dáil was to do something about this threat. In 1923 an act was passed setting up a new, strengthened Irish Land Commission. In the same year, another act gave the Commission powers to purchase compulsorily any tenanted or untenanted land that was needed for purposes of either 'facilitating resale of tenanted land' or of 'relieving congestion' (overcrowding).

The legal arrangements were complex, which could not have suited Jasper better. He was an acknowledged expert on land law and many of the landlords whose land was being compulsorily purchased, whether or not they still lived in Ireland, were Anglo-Irish Protestants, natural clients for Jasper. Moreover, numbers of tenants also signed up Jasper to act for them. As thirty years previously, if not in quite the same volume, estate work rolled into the offices of J. Travers Wolfe & Co.

Something like the old normality was also returning in another part of the legal woods. Many of West Cork's inhabitants resumed (or were once again being brought to court for) their habits of ebullient delinquency. In Skibbereen, the gardaí charged a member of the clan O'Driscoll with assaulting one of the Collins sept in the square. In Schull, some men were brought to court by the Skibbereen Fisheries Conservators for allegedly poaching salmon with a net. In Dunmanway, a cottager found to have a quantity of poitín in his possession was charged with a breach of the Illicit Distillation Act. A fisherman was accused of failing to hand over goods from a wreck to the authorities. A father summonsed two of his daughters and a son for assaulting him. Such cases, and many like them, provided plenty of work for Jasper.

Every now and then some dispute would attract particular attention. The *Southern Star* (11 April 1925) reported how a Rosscarbery publican, Denis Driscoll, was charged with a breach of the Licensing Act by serving liquor on a Sunday. Jasper appeared for the innkeeper, while a garda superintendent from Clonakilty conducted the prosecution. It transpired that, early on the evening of the Sunday in question, Denis Driscoll had met a couple of acquaintances, local farmers, on the pavement outside his pub. These two, he discovered, were organising a ploughing match the following Thursday and were wondering what to give the competitors to eat.

'There's a fine pig I'm keeping around the back. Why not give that to the fellas?'

'You'd not be giving it to us?'

'Sure, I'd sell it to you for next to nothing.'

The three went into the pub, and it was in what happened next that the court was particularly interested.

Mr Justice Crotty cross-examined the publican. 'How long were you on the premises?'

'A couple of minutes.'

'How many bottles of stout did you give them?'

'I gave them three bottles each.'

At this point the superintendent intervened, to make clear why such generous amounts of drink had been offered: 'That was before they saw the pig. It was enough to make them see two pigs.'

In answer to a question of the superintendent's, Denis Driscoll stated, 'It is usual to give drink in a purely business transaction.'

Mr Wolfe: 'You must soften your man first.'

The court then proceeded to the nub of the matter – the pig itself. The superintendent asked one of the farmers, 'Did you see the pig?'

'Yes, sir.'

'What kind was it?'

'A bit disabled. He had cramps.'

The defendant admitted, 'It is a pig I wouldn't send to a fair.'

Despite not having actually sold alcohol, the defendant was found guilty and fined ten shillings plus costs. The two farmers had to pay two shillings plus costs.

The *Southern Star* (3 May 1924) reported a rather more serious case, one that revealed why Jasper was once more becoming much sought after as an advocate, particularly for the defence. In this instance it seems likely that

Jasper's cleverness, together with his ability to play to the jury, enabled him to win a case which, if justice had been done, he should probably have lost. In May 1924, at the last Skibbereen quarter sessions before the introduction of the Free State circuit court, Jasper's successor as Crown Solicitor, the renamed State Solicitor, prosecuted a Jerh Daly for larceny. Jasper defended the accused. The case was heard by a jury. The State Solicitor and the Civic Guard must have thought a verdict of guilty was inevitable. They charged Jerh Daly with stealing £490 from the house of his brother, Cors. One day Cors went to a fair at Bantry and it was when he returned that he found the money gone, together with part of a letter referring to the money. Within the next few weeks it was proved that Jerh paid £240 into his account at Bantry Post Office and repaid a shop debt of £40. Six months later the Civic Guard raided the house of the accused and found in it the portion of the letter that had been taken from his brother's house.

Jasper opened the defence. He began by showing that the money paid by his client, Jerh Daly, into the post office and to repay a shop bill could well have had perfectly innocent origins. He then turned to the history of the Daly family. It turned out that the Dalys' mother had, a few years previously, been left about £600 by an American relative. This hard-up family were not used to dealing with such a large sum and they soon fell out. Apart from the two brothers, there was a sister. When old Mrs Daly died, she left all her inheritance to the two boys, and the sister promptly started a lawsuit to get her share of the money. Cors, in whose house his mother had died, took the money out of the bank, where it had been deposited in his and his brother's names, and hid it in his house. Jasper asked him if he had done this to make certain his sister could not get hold of the money. Cors admitted this was so: 'I took the money out because of the proceedings my sister had brought. My solicitor advised me to take the money out. My sister had no claim against it.'

Then the cash was stolen. Cors, like most others, pointed the finger at his brother Jerh. Jasper now set about discrediting Cors. In cross-examination, he uncovered the following facts. Cors had been an officer in the Irregulars during the Civil War. He reluctantly admitted, under threat of gaol by the judge, that he had arranged with two of his men to search Jerh's house. Which they did. When they failed to find anything, they returned to Cors (as he again only admitted under pressure from Jasper) for instructions. Following his orders, they returned that night and gave Jerh two days to produce the money. They threatened that they would hang him if he failed to deliver. Forty-eight hours later (as a nephew who was present testified), the men, together with Cors, duly returned with a rope. The money not being produced, they took Jerh outside. He returned, alive, but badly beaten – 'flogged', it was said in court. Jasper concluded by suggesting that the piece of a letter that the Civic Guards later found in Jerh's house had been planted there by Cors' men.

In his closing speech to the jury, Jasper, employing the well-tried tactic of attack as the best form of defence, went straight to the offensive:

There is no evidence to connect the defendant with the larceny of this money. This case has broken down. It will be a scandal if the accused is turned into a thief and loses the excellent character he has borne. The author of the whole thing is in the witness chair to turn his own brother into a thief, and himself into a pillar of the State. It is a disgrace to the cause of justice that Cors Daly and his two confederates have not been brought to justice. I confidently ask the jury to acquit the prisoner.

The judge, in his summing up, was sceptical of Jasper's case:

I have heard a good many defences, but I do not know that I have ever heard a defence such as that put forward by Mr Wolfe. He has accused the man who lost the money of stealing the money himself, and of planting the letter, apparently taken from his house, in his brother's house. It strikes me as an extraordinary defence.

His Honour may have had his doubts, but the jury did not, duly finding the accused innocent.

33

COUNSEL FOR THE IRA

Jasper at this point could quite easily have settled for running a modestly successful local practice, but that was not enough to satisfy him, even though he was now in his early fifties. He wanted J. Travers Wolfe to become once again a dominant player. To achieve this he needed, first and foremost, to get more briefs.

One potentially rewarding source of work lay in the wild country of West Cork, where life had not yet returned to normal. In these parts, law did not rule. As Rachel Wolfe wrote to her granddaughter Dorothy in Oxford: 'The only things that are out of the usual routine are the raids and robberies carried on by the brigands that are wandering in the surrounding hills.' These 'brigands' were men from the defeated Irregulars, who were facing every sort of trouble. Despite a powerful Republican campaign, no amnesty had yet been granted, nor would there be one until November 1924. This meant that any former 'Rebs' could face charges for their actions during the Civil War. Many of these one-time Volunteers had also spent months, sometimes years, living rough and on the run. Adapting to life now that there was peace, particularly in an impoverished land where unemployment was high, proved for many next to impossible. Since there was an abundance of arms and ammunition still available, it was almost inevitable that numbers of these trained fighters should turn to crime, or be plausibly suspected of so doing.

So Jasper decided that, if the opportunity presented itself, he would act as defence lawyer for the Irregulars. Neither constitutionally nor professionally would this cause him any difficulties. The Free State guaranteed an independent legal system and the prerogative of a fair trial to any citizen charged with wrongdoing. As for lawyers, they believed that all parties in a dispute had a right to be properly represented, and indeed had to be if justice was to be done.

Acting for Irregulars might have seemed an odd career move. After all, these were men who belonged to an organisation whose members Jasper had been prosecuting for several years and some of whom, in turn, had been attempting to get rid of him, by whatever means. However, in the new Ireland of the Free State, reaching out to help his former adversaries made a lot of sense to Jasper. For a start, he believed it was the right thing to do. He was committed, as were many others, to working for a land where old grievances and hatreds could, in a spirit of forgiveness, be laid to rest. It would be a powerful gesture of reconciliation if a former Crown Solicitor, prosecutor for the British government, were now ready to be a legal voice for desperate, defeated Republicans. In short, this was a chance for Jasper to identify himself once more, notwithstanding his loyalist past and sympathies, as a patriotic Irishman. There could also be considerable practical benefits from defending Republicans. It would bring in at least some more money, it could help to re-establish his reputation as an advocate for all-comers and it might even reopen the possibility of entry into political life.

Jasper believed in making things happen. Shortly after the end of the Civil War, in the summer of 1923, he put an advertisement in the local papers announcing that, since he was back in full-time private practice, he would be ready once again to act for anyone who required his services. The message, reading between the lines, was obvious. Within a few months the first friends and relations of imprisoned Irregulars had quietly sidled through the doors of J. Travers Wolfe & Co. Jasper, always at his best when acting for the defence, soon enjoyed great success. He rapidly became renowned for his ability to get Irregulars declared innocent of alleged wrongdoing or – where the evidence was incontrovertibly damning – at least getting them off with light sentences.

Some of those successfully saved by Jasper from long sentences, or worse, never forgot what he had done for them. Years later Jack Wolfe, nephew of Jasper and a son of Willie Wood, was studying medicine in Dublin. Jasper, who was frequently in Dublin at the time, would take Jack out for a meal at the start of term and, since he knew he was often short of money, slip him enough to cover his expenses for the next couple of months. Jack boxed for the college (a fact he kept secret from his mother, who feared that his good looks – inherited from his mother, but unusual for a Wolfe – might be spoiled) and amongst his friends was the college heavyweight. This fearsome fellow lived to fight, whether in or out of the ring. Before long he joined the army, where he allegedly started a brawl in the mess and several officers got injured. The heavyweight was charged with affray and threatened with dismissal from the armed forces. By chance the heavyweight's father had been a key figure in the Irregulars and, when charged with serious offences, had been defended in court by Jasper. When this former Republican learned that his son was friendly with a nephew of Jasper's he was delighted. 'Sure, that man saved my life!' So it was that Jasper was booked for the heavyweight's defence. He met up with him for a drink but, rather to the consternation of the accused man, did not so much as mention the case. At the trial Jasper put various officers in the witness box and got them to contradict each other so often that the accused was never even called to appear.[1]

One of Jasper's first cases defending an Irregular, a certain Denis Byrne, came before the newly established district court in Dunmanway and was heard within less than six months of the ending of the Civil War. Dealing with unauthorised possession of firearms, the case was reported in the *Southern Star* (15 December 1923) and was typical of many that were to follow. In early November a party of the National (Free State) Army had entered Calnan's public house, on the main Skibbereen to Cork road, at the foot of Rosscarbery hill. Those present (Denis Byrne, a friend and an elderly man) were ordered to raise their hands. Byrne did so, but not before throwing off his overcoat, in which was discovered a revolver. He was accused of illegal possession of firearms and held in custody by the army until December. Jasper cross-examined the soldiers who had made the arrest.

'Had the gun been fired recently?'

'No, it had not.'

'Was any ammunition found?'

'No, it was not.'

'What make is the gun?'

'It is German.'

Jasper then questioned the accused: 'You served in the British army, fighting against the Germans in France?'

'I did, sir.'

'And is that when you acquired this gun?'

'It was.'

'So you could say the gun was a sort of souvenir?'

'That's what it is, sure enough.'

Jasper went on to establish that the prisoner had been interned by the Free State for a year without charge, had been released after the Civil War was over and then held for five weeks after his arrest for possessing the revolver. Jasper then addressed the judge:

> This offence is purely technical. It would not be surprising if the prisoner feels he has already been treated rather harshly. At most the prisoner is guilty of an indiscretion. There are several released internees, like the accused, around Rosscarbery, and they have all been instructed by those to whom they look for guidance to live in peace and fellowship as good citizens, to use no firearms, and also to abandon the campaign of destruction and armed force. I trust – and I make such remarks to the Civic Guard as well as to other citizens – that such men on return to their homes and districts will be treated fairly. I ask that the accused be allowed out on his own bond, to return to his family and home, free from molestation.

Judgement was reserved for a month, but before that time was up the state had withdrawn its case and Byrne was set free.

A few months later Jasper defended two former IRA men in another case reported by the *Southern Star* (3 May 1924). This was heard at Skibbereen quarter sessions (not yet replaced by the Free State circuit courts). The charge, like many others at the time, dealt with an offence that had occurred before the signing of the Anglo-Irish Treaty. The facts were not seriously disputed. John Shanahan and Denis Hurley were accused of assault and theft. They had entered the farm of Samuel Levis, punched him, threatened him with a revolver, broken down the door of a room and removed a harness and cushions. They had then taken a horse, harnessed it to a trap (which was new) and driven off. The horse came back that evening, but the trap, harness and cushions never reappeared. Jasper quickly established that the whole area around Durrus, the site of the farm and a few miles south of Bantry, had been completely under the control of the Republican army. The accused were Volunteers and acting under orders. Jasper cross-examined Samuel Levis:

'Did you see the trap after?'

'I did, often.'

'And were the accused ever driving it?'

'No, sir.'

'But you claim they stole it?'

'I would not say they came to steal anything. I never said that. They commandeered my property.'

In his closing address to the jury Jasper was indignant.

'These men have never stolen anything. They had no thought of personal gain. They were soldiers acting under orders. What is more, after being detained for two weeks by the Free Staters, they came home and have lived a peaceable life.' Jasper now shifted into top gear. 'I have come to the conclusion that the dead past should be allowed to bury its dead. Only if that happens will we have peace in this country. There is no use creating a fresh blaze. It is a deplorable thing to bring a prosecution of this kind. But it would be far more deplorable if it results in a conviction. The government should stop prosecutions like this, and not be helping to promote internecine strife. The issue you, the jury, have to try is this. Can there be peace, which we are all anxiously looking forward to? If so, you should acquit the prisoner.'

The State Solicitor intervened to say they were all very sorry that Mr Wolfe was threatening war unless the jury found the prisoners innocent, causing some amusement in the court. The judge, as Jasper no doubt knew, was very much in sympathy with his argument, commenting: 'After the Republicans laid down their arms I am sorry the government did not pass a general amnesty. That might have been best.' His Honour was also much impressed by Jasper's conduct of the case, and in his comments incidentally revealed that Jasper was already well known for his successful defence of Republicans. 'We have before us,' he said, 'one of the cleverest prisoners' advocates in the whole of Ireland. The prisoners should be very grateful for the able way in which he has defended them.' However, despite all this, the law as it stood posed a difficulty. As His Honour reluctantly explained, it was so clear that not even the most brilliant lawyer could question its meaning. 'Whether these men acted under orders or not, they were out in arms against the government and had no right to take another's property.'

The jury, after half an hour, found the accused guilty but strongly recommended mercy, as they were now at peace with their neighbours. The Civil Guard superintendent, asked for his views, commented, 'Matters have been peacable in this locality lately.' The judge, in passing sentence, commented, 'It is rather hard that certain men should be prosecuted after the lapse of some time, and others be let go free.' In discharging the prisoners, on security of £10, he advised them to attend to their business. They now had a government of Irishmen making laws for Ireland. Men should not be killed because others disagreed with them. Whatever was done should be done constitutionally.

What really worried the authorities, and indeed the law-abiding citizenry of West Cork, were marauding bands of gunmen. These were threatening public confidence (which was little more than brittle anyway) in the ability of police and army to keep order. Jasper acted for the defence of one such gang that came from Drinagh and its surrounding hill country, a few miles inland between Skibbereen and Rosscarbery. From these badlands, they raided the not-so-badlands to their south. There were just three of them, all ex-Republican Volunteers, Dempsey, Donovan and their leader, Andrew McCarthy, a former captain of the Drinagh company in the IRA West Cork fourth battalion. From the end of the Civil War, in which they had fought as Irregulars, until their eventual capture by the Free State army near Drinagh in March 1924, this crew, armed with a single double-barrelled shotgun, rampaged across the central townlands of West Carbery.

The *Southern Star* (5 and 12 April and 5 July 1924) reported how Inspector Troy of the Civic Guard brought a whole battery of charges against the accused. A preliminary hearing was held in Rosscarbery district court. There was intense local interest in the case and the army were taking no chances. The accused, who had been imprisoned in Cork since their capture five weeks previously, were brought under armed escort in convoy from the city. Andrew McCarthy and the two others were handcuffed to each other and, when not in court, were kept locked up in the local barracks. They were brought to and from the courthouse by motor car. In the car with them were members of the Civic Guard, while armed soldiers travelled on the footboards. Soldiers, pistols at the ready, stood within the court building, at the entrance and all around it. Outside, large crowds watched the comings and goings, while inside the public squeezed into every possible space. To the relief of the authorities, there were no demonstrations of support for the prisoners.

Jasper's main tactic in dealing with the charges against his clients was to challenge the credibility of the army and gardaí. He went on the offensive as soon as the prisoners were delivered to court by strongly objecting to their being manacled.

'I fail to understand,' said Jasper, 'why the prisoners should be kept hand-cuffed while in court awaiting trial. There is no necessity for such a step, especially while there are bevies of armed military all over the place. During my experience as a prosecuting and defending solicitor for a period of over thirty years I never saw parties tried under such circumstances.'

The civic guard inspector reluctantly agreed to remove the handcuffs while the court was in session, but not before or after.

As it turned out, the spectators at Rosscarbery court were to be disappointed. Other cases were heard first, time ran out and the trial of Dempsey, Donovan and McCarthy was adjourned to the next district court at Skibbereen. On this occasion, the prosecution was undertaken, not by Inspector Troy, but by the State Solicitor.

Once the trial started, it was alleged that the three men had assaulted and robbed members of the Civic Guard. The prosecution stated that on the afternoon of 22 August 1923, McCarthy, Dempsey and Donovan had ambushed gardaí Healy and Smyth, who were on uniformed patrol a couple of miles north of Skibbereen. The gardaí, they told the court, first had their bikes removed and then were led into a field. Here their whistles and caps were taken and they were ordered to strip off their uniforms, which they refused to do. After all this, they were asked if they wished to be blindfolded, as they were going to be shot. They refused the offer and were then taken to a cowshed, where a fountain pen was taken from garda Healy, together with a watch and one shilling from garda Smyth. At ten o'clock that evening the gardaí were released, led back to the road and pointed in the direction of Skibbereen.

Jasper did not question the account of the events but concentrated on trying to prove that the gardaí had charged the wrong men. The accused had been formally identified by garda Healy, but that identification, Jasper argued, was a put-up job.

'Where,' asked Jasper in cross-examining Healy, 'did you first see the accused after allegedly being held up by them?'

'In an identity parade, with seven or eight other men, at the barrack yard in Rosscarbery.'

Jasper then got Healy to agree that he had seen the handcuffed men immediately before the parade in two cars being brought to the yard and that, besides the accused, those present in the identity parade were the two chauffeurs, whom he had just observed, together with two children and the district court clerk. Next, he moved on to the question of the names of the accused. Was it true that garda Healy had identified them by name at the parade? Yes, Healy was persuaded to agree, it was. So, how did Healy know how to fit names to faces? In a lengthy cross-examination it emerged that members of the public had given the Skibbereen gardaí, including Healy, the names and descriptions of those who took part in the ambush. Up to a dozen individuals had volunteered the information and this only ever varied in minor details.

'So,' asked Jasper, 'can you give any explanation why you did not mention, before the identity parade, that you knew the names and descriptions of the accused better than you knew your own prayers?' (Laughter.) 'I put it to you that you may be making a mistake regarding these three men.'

After these preliminary hearings, the case finally ended up in Dublin, at the Central Criminal Court. By that time, Jasper had succeeded in getting most of the charges dropped. What remained was an indictment against the three for holding up garda Healy with a gun on 22 August 1923 and stealing from him a bicycle and fountain pen. McCarthy and Donovan were found guilty, but Dempsey was declared innocent. So the final outcome was that one of the three was not convicted on any charges and the other two on only a couple of those they had originally faced. However, the authorities had managed to keep all three in custody for several months, with a custodial sentence for two to follow, so they probably were not too dissatisfied with the result.

34

THE COBH SHOOTING

In the spring of 1927 a general election was due and Jasper put himself forward as an Independent candidate for the West Cork constituency. In his campaign, Jasper was able to benefit from his standing as a friend of the Republicans. In particular, he made political capital out of a notorious incident that had taken place three years earlier. In order to understand what Jasper was up to, it is necessary to look at this happening, and its complex ramifications, in some detail.

At seven o'clock in the evening of Friday 21 March 1924 a British military launch, the *Cambridge*, was approaching the waterfront at Cobh. Various installations at this port town of Cork harbour, formerly known as Queenstown, had been retained as a United Kingdom naval base under the Anglo-Irish Treaty. The launch was coming from Spike Island, where major British facilities were sited, bringing mainly soldiers, some with wives and children, who were hoping for an evening's entertainment in the town. On board were upwards of fifty people, none of them armed.

Cobh is built on a steep ridge. Parked high up on one of its streets, overlooking the harbour, was a yellow Rolls Royce. This machine had once belonged to the former Lord Lieutenant of Ireland, Field Marshal Lord French. It had, however, in obscure circumstances, been permanently borrowed from him by the IRA and subsequently used in various operations, usually at night. 'The Moon Car', as it was popularly known, moved off when its occupants saw the launch leaving Spike Island and drew up on the broad parade which separated the fine, high buildings of Cobh from the waterfront. The jetty at which the British sailors were about to tie up was parallel to the waterfront and was reached from the parade by a short pier, perhaps about twenty yards long. This pier, guarded on either side by iron safety railings, reached out at right angles from the parade to the jetty. From where they waited in their Rolls, the four men inside had a clear view down the pier and onto the jetty.

As the party from the launch began to land, the windows on the side of the Rolls facing towards the sea were lowered and a Lewis machine gun was aimed from each. Several bursts of rapid fire followed. Passers-by on the promenade scattered. On the jetty the passengers, some of whom were still disembarking, 'fell', as one witness recalled, 'the same as corn before a scythe. It was a most appalling sight, the like of which I never hope to witness again.' Thirty soldiers were shot. Also hit were two local women, sisters, and a butcher's boy who had been delivering meat to the island. One soldier, eighteen-year-old private Aspinall of the Royal Army Medical Corps, died of his wounds. So, too, several months later, did the butcher's boy. The slaughter could have been much worse. Numbers of bullets hit the iron railings on the pier and ricocheted into nearby trees and buildings. On the jetty itself, a young woman, thought to be a nurse, rushed down from the parade and started to care for the injured. Pools of blood spread over the ground. After some minutes of chaos, the wounded, some moaning and screaming, were carried back into the launch, which returned to Spike Island.

Immediately after the gunfire, the Rolls Royce accelerated away westwards at a tremendous pace. At Rushbrook it slowed, while two more bursts of fire were aimed, harmlessly as it turned out, at a British destroyer moored midstream. The car, again driving ferociously fast, then made for Belvelly Bridge, the only exit to the mainland, Cobh being on an island.

What triggered this outrage? And who was responsible? A fortnight previously two senior army officers, General Tobin and Colonel Dalton, had presented a document to the government. They represented a powerful faction in the army known as the 'Old IRA'. Its members, while they had signed up for the Free State Army, remained loyal to the Republican ideals for which many of them had fought during the war of independence. The officers demanded a major reorganisation of the army and the creation of a Republic. Furthermore, they threatened the use of force if their ultimatum was not met. In support of Tobin and Dalton, approaching a hundred officers resigned or absconded, many taking with them Lewis guns, rifles, grenades and revolvers. The civil government, including the Minister of Defence, together with the army chief of staff and top generals, regarded these actions as mutinous. President Cosgrave described the action to the Dáil as 'a challenge which no government could ignore . . . The attempt . . . is a challenge to the democratic foundations of the state'.

The government handled the crisis with considerable, if devious, finesse. A week after the mutiny broke out, President Cosgrave announced in the Dáil that he would set up an army enquiry committee, thus going some way towards meeting the rebels' demands. In response, Tobin and Dalton, who had evaded initial orders for their arrest, rescinded their ultimatum. Nevertheless, on 18 March the army GHQ in Dublin learned that a meeting of leading mutinous officers was being held. There were rumours, and some evidence, that plans were being hatched to stage a coup, kidnap the cabinet and assassinate the leading government hawk, Kevin O'Higgins, Vice-President of the Executive Council and Minister for Home Affairs. The premises (a public house) were raided. The Parnell Street raid, as it became known, ended without a fight and, as the days passed, the threat of mutiny appeared to subside.

In Cork, however, the spirit of revolt was not reduced so easily. From the start the government and army high command had regarded it as the region most likely to ignite. Early on, General McMahon, the chief of staff, had been sent down there to quell any signs of disaffection. At the time of the Parnell Street raid, he was still in Cork city shifting particularly rebellious officers from their posts, listening to grievances and insisting that the army stay clear of politics. He was largely, though, as it turned out, probably not entirely successful in preventing the mutiny from sparking locally into an armed conflagration.

It was three days after the Parnell Street raid that the Cobh shooting took place. There are strong circumstantial reasons for believing it was related to the army mutiny. For a start, the reasons for carrying out the operation made little sense outside the context of the mutiny. The killing and wounding of British soldiers at Cobh had a good chance of inspiring diehard Nationalist patriotism. The daring attack, carried out in the spirit of heroic nationalism, looked as if it was intended to encourage a coup, by triggering, or at least facilitating, widespread unrest within and outside the army. The incident would also have harmed relations between the Irish and British governments, making it more difficult for the Free State to respond to any internal unrest.

The timing of the shooting was also highly suggestive. Not only, when the outrage occurred, was it by no means clear that the mutiny was dying down, but it seems likely that the original idea had been to mount the attack earlier. A week previously, the Rolls Royce had been seen in Cobh and telephone wires had been cut. Many believed that an attack only aborted because the car failed to reach the pier before the arrival of the government launch from Spike island.

Finally, there were more obvious signs that the attackers were in close touch with the mutineers. Just as the Rolls Royce scorched away from the scene of the massacre, one of the men leaned out of a window and shouted the name of the mutiny's leader, 'Up Tobin!' What is more, all four occupants of the automobile were wearing the uniforms of senior Free State Army officers. Since no thefts of uniforms had been reported, it is quite possible that there had been, not just collusion, but careful joint planning.

Who actually carried out the attack? Many inhabitants of Cobh, and a good number of others, seem to have known, but, at the time, nobody said anything. It was only a safe half-century after the events that a local IRA insider, Kieran McCarthy, published an account which left little to the imagination. According to this author, the attack was a freelance operation carried out by local Cobh Republicans in association with 'discontented elements within the Free State Army', but not sanctioned by the IRA leadership. In Cobh itself, the whole affair, McCarthy implies, may well have been masterminded by Seamus Fitzgerald, a long-time Volunteer activist and at the time chairman of the Cobh Urban District Council. Probably because he was so well known, he did not take part in the actual attack. Of the four who did, two were locals, one of whom immediately emigrated to the States. McCarthy has nothing to say about the other two.

Repercussions reverberated for weeks, months and years. The immediate reaction was one of widespread horror, and denunciation. The Lord Mayor of Cork, local councils, church dignitaries and senior political figures throughout Ireland joined in what one newspaper headlined as 'Universal Condemnation'. Even those who might have been, or indeed were, suspected of being responsible instantly expressed their abhorrence and denied having played any part in the outrage. General Tobin wrote to the Dublin papers disclaiming any complicity in what he described as 'a cowardly act'. The IRA chief of staff refuted any idea of involvement, as did Mary McSwiney and David Kent, leading Republican figures in Cork city and east Cork.

The Irish government might have been expected to move fast. And on the diplomatic front it did. Its leadership, only too aware that the Free State may have been weakened by the army mutiny, could not risk the further instability which would almost certainly result from any sort of a showdown with the United Kingdom. President Cosgrave immediately sent a telegram to Ramsay McDonald, the United Kingdom Prime Minister, apologising for the attack on British soldiers, expressing deepest sympathy and promising to bring the perpetrators of the outrage to justice. The British, for whom the Free State was the least bad Irish regime on offer, were not looking to make trouble. Apologies and in due course compensation were accepted. Little more was said.

Now the authorities had to track down the attackers. However, they and the Rolls Royce appeared to have vanished. Their escape was due to a great deal more than luck. Kieran McCarthy recorded Seamus Fitzgerald's account of what happened. Prior to the attack, three cars were stationed to the east of Cobh to cut off any attempt at pursuit by the National Army, which had troops stationed nearby. Also, two cars waiting at Belvelly Bridge covered their flight to the mainland and then escorted the Rolls Royce northwards. Since by now dusk was falling, the convoy got clean away. It travelled first to Fermoy and then west to Donoughmore, about fifteen miles northwest of Cork. Here, by night, the car was set alight and buried in a bog. Because of fears that the flames and lights had been seen, rumours were put about that the place was haunted. The remains of the vehicle were not discovered until over half a century later.

What about the actual occupants of the Rolls, and their accomplices in what was generally believed to be a wider conspiracy? The government gave every appearance of striving hard to apprehend them. The day after the outrage, a reward of £10,000 was offered for information leading to a conviction. The Civil Guard were also active, even hyperactive, and within a few days several arrests were made. However, all the suspects were almost instantly released. One man confessed to the crime, but he too was freed: 'a cock and bull story', commented the gardaí. Enquiries continued at full throttle but without result. Nearly eight weeks after the shooting the Ministry for Home Affairs issued a proclamation, repeating its offer of a £10,000 reward, together with various lesser rewards, and naming five suspects, all from Cork city or nearby.

Still no credible arrests were made. Some people began to suspect that the government did not really want to track down the conspirators. They may well have been right. In the wake of the army mutiny the Executive Council (the Cabinet) had followed a policy which, to any outsider, might have seemed to swing between folly and insanity. On the one hand the senior military leaders who had remained loyal to the state were required to surrender their posts; any who refused were sacked. On the other, known mutineers were quietly allowed to resign. No trials took place, no retribution was exacted.

There were, however, good reasons for these moves. The main concern of the government was to secure effective civilian control over the military. It believed that lax and autonomous leadership by the senior army commanders had greatly contributed towards provoking the mutiny. It also gambled that these loyal men (who included the adjutant-general, Gearóid O'Sullivan from Skibbereen) would, even if dismissed, create no difficulties for the government. As for the mutineers, the government hoped that, provided they were not turned into martyrs, they and their sympathisers would gradually drift away from conflict.

March was over; spring, then summer, arrived. Things seemed to be calming down. Neither the sacked loyalist generals, nor Tobin and his followers and the Old IRA, made any trouble. It began to look as if the Executive Council's counter-intuitive way of securing peace might work. But, there was one matter which continued to cause public anxiety, and criticism of the government. Why were there still no arrests, so loudly promised, of those men responsible for the Cobh shooting? After all, suspects had been named and many inhabitants of Cork thought they knew exactly where at least some of these men could be found.

Eventually, in late October, to defuse public criticism, the authorities alighted upon a bizarre solution. To a terrific fanfare of publicity, the police and military carried out a series of dawn raids in Dublin and seven local men were arrested. These included not one of those originally named in the government's May proclamation. When the accused were brought to the district court, armed soldiers surrounded the building and searched all male passers-by. When the proceedings began, all the defendants, when charged with planning and carrying out the attack, loudly proclaimed their innocence. 'I know nothing about it', said one, 'It is pure invention', stated another, 'False and ridiculous', commented a third . . . and so on. The seven were remanded for a week. On their return to court, another mighty security operation was mounted. The prosecution withdrew all charges, which provoked a lengthy outburst of cheering and applause. Outside the court, the freed men were surrounded by ecstatic supporters, press photographers and weeping women.

As 1925 approached, memories of the outrage slowly began to fade. The authorities, after their humiliation in Dublin, stopped even pretending to look for the guilty men. It seemed as if the Cobh shooting was being relegated as just another, if belated, incident in the Civil War.[1]

That is, until Jasper decided to stir things up.

35

INDEPENDENT CANDIDATE FOR THE DÁIL

In April 1927 Jasper received a letter from Captain William Redmond, son of the late Irish National Party leader, John Redmond. It invited him to stand as a candidate for the recently founded Irish National League (more commonly known as the National League) in the forthcoming general election. Although he was broadly in sympathy with the ideas of this new party, which were essentially old Home Rule policies modestly updated to engage with modern Irish realities, Jasper declined the offer. He probably judged that the new Redmondites had little chance of gaining many votes in West Cork.

Besides, a maverick like Jasper would have been far too much of a free spirit to fit happily into the regimentation of any political party.

However, as Redmond had guessed, Jasper was indeed interested in the idea of putting himself forward for election to the Dáil. His life was getting to be rather predictable, even boring, and he fancied the idea of some excitement. So he decided to stand as an Independent. This idea was rather less crazy than it seems. For a start, something like normal democratic political life was beginning to re-establish itself in the south of

Jasper Wolfe, 1927.

Ireland. This was largely thanks to the success of supporters of the Free State. In 1923, as the Civil War drew to a close, a new political party, Cumann na nGaedheal, had been founded. Its main aims were to support the Anglo-Irish Treaty of 1921 and to implement the constitution of the Irish Free State. Under the presidency of William Cosgrave, an effective and honourable, if uncharismatic, leader, Cumann na nGaedheal secured a parliamentary majority and governed effectively, albeit in an understandably cautious and conservative manner.

For Jasper and others like him, playing an active part in politics presented few difficulties in a country where the tone was being set by such as Cosgrave. Many of those active in Cumann na nGaedheal were pragmatic, middle-class, professional Catholics of the sort Jasper had always found easy to get on with. In matters of principle, above all in support for the Free State itself, he and they shared similar outlooks. As for disagreements over specific policies, while these would undoubtedly arise, it seemed unlikely that debating them would cause any serious problems.

So Jasper decided to try his luck. He did have some chance of being elected, even though, when the starting gun sounded, many would have considered him an outsider in the field of thirteen. However, if you were going to put money on this Protestant and former Crown Solicitor, what were the points in his favour? First, candidates like Jasper who represented minority interests were now given a fair chance by the voting system. The Free State, in an effort to ensure a hearing for all significant voices, had replaced the British first-past-the-post voting system with proportional representation.

Secondly, Jasper's general political outlook was shared by a substantial majority of the electorate. Like him, they supported the Free State and were inclined to endorse candidates who were committed to making the new constitution work. As for Republicanism, although West Cork had acquired the reputation of being an IRA hot spot, when it came to elections relatively few voters were prepared to back its candidates. From 1923, when Nelius Connolly came top of the poll as a Cumann na nGaedheal candidate and Free State supporter, to the 1933 election when Jasper stood down as a candidate, the Republican and Fianna Fáil first preference votes ranged between 20% and 30% of the total cast. So, neither Jasper nor any other candidates who supported the Free State were in danger of being swept away by a Republican landslide.

When it came to actual votes cast, Jasper could count on at least a modest constituency of his own. Most of those Protestants who remained in the constituency would be in his camp, and so, out of local loyalty, would many in Skibbereen, whatever their religion. And then, right across the constituency, there were the clients of J.Travers Wolfe & Co., many of whom felt some personal gratitude and obligation towards Jasper. Numbers of these, too, could be relied on to put their cross beside 'WOLFE'.

What about his programme? As is the prerogative of all Independent candidates, Jasper was able to cherry-pick those issues most likely to gain him votes. And some were ripe and ready to fall into his lap. While the West Cork electorate may have wanted to keep the present Cumann na nGaedheal goverment, it was fairly unenthusiastic about some of its policies. President Cosgrave and his party, who were focused on laying the foundations of a secure, financially viable, democratic state, were rather too high-minded to play mere party politics. And, in any case, they mainly represented the Catholic middle and professional classes and so were not particularly attuned to the needs and views of those many Irishmen rather closer to the earth.

In his published address to the electors Jasper expertly played on all the electorate's key anxieties. He opened up with references to unemployment and the unity of the nation, pledging to support any measures intended to get people back to work, and to 'labour in the hope . . . that the boundary between North and South, so hateful to patriotic Irishmen, may eventually disappear'.

There were three further issues, in particular, which he highlighted. First was old age pensions. In 1924 the government, in an effort to balance the books, had reduced the old age pension by a shilling to ten shillings and introduced strict means testing. The measure was very unpopular, not least within Cumann na nGaedheal itself. Jasper reached for the rhetoric: 'I consider the reduction . . . an indefensible outrage on a most deserving section of the community, and I shall do all in my power to restore such pension.'

Second was commercial fishing. While crucial to West Cork, it was not something the government power-brokers of middle Ireland greatly cared about and they had given the industry almost no financial support. Again Jasper orated: 'The wealth of the seas is at our doors . . . I shall not cease to advocate the fisherman's right to advances by the Government for necessary boats and equipment for his great and hazardous calling.'

Third, and perhaps closest to the hearts of both Jasper and his electorate, was the drink trade. Only months before the election, the government had passed an act intended to reduce the extraordinarily high number of public houses in the Free State and to recompense owners whose premises were closed by a tax on those that survived. This legislation provoked outraged hostility among publicans, brewers and drinkers – taken together, a significant percentage of the electorate – many of whom were Cumann na nGaedheal supporters.

Jasper was particularly well placed to exploit the controversy over licensed vintners. Quite apart from his personal partiality to liquor and pubs, one of his closest friends was, and had been for many years, a leading figure and publican in Skibbereen. John O'Shea, originally appointed town clerk twenty-five years earlier (thanks to Jasper) and still holding that position, knew all there was to know about the vintner's business. In late 1926, just as the government's plans to control the drink trade were being hatched, Jasper and John set off together on a continental tour. It was the only time the home-loving Jasper ever left the British Isles. The two visited Paris and Geneva. A photo survives of John, clad in dark suit and tie, on a steamboat on Lake Lucerne.

Advised by John, Jasper sounded the most solemn and uplifting of notes in his attacks on the 'Intoxicating Liquor Act': 'To legislation tending to lessen rights of property, recognised by law . . . I am opposed. The stability of the Free State . . . can be established only if people are assured of their right to possess and retain what they have lawfully inherited or purchased.' So there it was. Any attempt, or certainly this attempt, to reduce an Irishman's intake of alcohol was an attack at once on fundamental property rights and on the very foundations of the nation.

If Jasper succeeded in getting the votes of the elderly, the drinkers, the unemployed and the fishermen, he would assuredly be elected without difficulty. However, as the campaign opened the signs were that there was not much interest in his candidature. He decided to do something about that.

Just after Easter and more than six weeks before polling day, due on 9 June, Jasper addressed his opening meeting in Skibbereen. What he had to say was immediately picked up by the local press. The *Cork Examiner* (23 April 1927) headlined its report:

GRAVE CHARGES

WEST CORK CANDIDATE AND COVE SHOOTING

GOVERNMENT ACTION

Remarkable Statements by Mr Jasper Wolfe, Solr.

First and foremost, Jasper simply needed to get himself noticed, so he chose to talk about the Cobh shooting, which was bound to excite interest. In his opening remarks to the voters of Skibbereen he said, 'Everyone of you will remember that terrible incident when a number of British soldiers, after the Treaty, were fired at, killed and wounded in the town of Cove.' They did indeed. He also had to distinguish himself in the electorate's eyes from Cumann na nGaedheal, who, like himself, were advocates of the Free State. Accordingly, he attacked its handling of the Cobh shooting. It had, he said, issued a proclamation for the apprehension of several men but had totally failed to make any arrests, thus leaving damaging charges hanging over the heads of the accused. What is more, he alleged, the government had deliberately avoided making arrests. 'Search parties took uncommonly good care to pass by the gate which they knew, as all in this country knew, would lead to the culprits.' As for those named in the proclamation, he announced, in words which were shortly to get him into serious trouble: 'I saw two of them walking in the streets of Cork a few days previously, and they could have been picked up just as easily and innocently as myself.'

Jasper did not stop there. To distance himself from his past as Crown Solicitor and to build on his reputation as successful defence counsel for the

Irregulars, he needed to signal that he was sympathetic to Republicans, if not Republicanism. He had little hope of gaining many IRA votes, but he could well win over some of their less committed sympathisers. So he argued that Republicans had been falsely suspected by the government of responsibility for the shootings: 'Everyone knows that the Republican Party had as much to do with that [the shooting] as I, and yet all over Munster the camouflage was gone through of searching for notable Republicans.'

Jasper had had to perform some very clever legalistic juggling to keep his various points from slipping out of his hands. It was technically true that neither the Republican Party (Sinn Féin) nor the IRA had been responsible for the shooting. Amongst the prime movers had been the Old IRA, members of the National Free State Army. It may even have been that one or two of the men in the Rolls Royce had not formally been members of the IRA, but few doubted that at least some Republican sympathisers not in the National Army had been involved. To claim, as Jasper did, that the Republicans were whiter than white was pushing his luck.

Jasper implied that the government's failure to make arrests was wilful incompetence. In fact, like most other people, he had a pretty good idea that the real reason was the government's anxiety to avoid creating unnecessary confrontation with, and thereby possibly reviving, a Republican movement which, for the time being at least, was on the retreat. Jasper was taking an undoubted fact (the failure of the government to bring charges) and providing an explanation which had rather more to do with his own political needs than anything else.

Jasper had gambled that his speech would create a stir locally. He also guessed that most in West Cork, knowing full well the reality and the intricacies of the situation, would realise exactly what he was up to and would be entertained by his shameless nerve. In both calculations he was right. From the moment the press reports started appearing, his personality, and his campaign, began to move from the wings to centre stage in the West Cork election. So far, so good.

However, local politics were one thing, national politics quite another. Enter a most unusual figure on the Irish scene. Thomas Johnson was a working-class boy from Liverpool.[1] At the age of nineteen, he got a job as a fish merchant and started to spend half the year in Ireland, dividing his time between Kinsale in County Cork and Dunmore East in County Waterford. At the age of twenty-eight he moved to Belfast as a commercial traveller, where he became an active trade unionist. By the time of the Troubles he was sympathetic to Sinn Féin and in 1922 was elected to the Dáil as Labour candidate for County Dublin. After the 1923 election, as head of the Labour group of fourteen members, he became official leader of the opposition (elected Republicans, who were the largest opposition party, refused to take their seats, since to do so required taking an oath of allegiance to the British Crown, as agreed in the Anglo-Irish Treaty).

Thomas Johnson, TD. (Courtesy of the
National Library of Ireland).

It was Thomas Johnson who inaugurated a national fuss about Jasper's remarks in Skibbereen. He had been in touch with West Cork since his days in Kinsale and he was a close colleague of Timothy Murphy, a respected Labour TD for West Cork who had come second to Neilus Connolly in the 1923 general election. So it was that Johnson was informed about happenings in the southwest. Unfortunately he did not have a clue about what was really going on. A decent, principled man and a competent leader of the opposition, he took events at their face value. A literal-minded English-man, his feet planted in the ground of industrial life and breathing the air of socialist ideals, he had little under-standing of rural life and even less of the often devious games played by the inhabitants of West Cork in order to amuse and outwit one another. Like many an Englishman in Ireland, he was foolish enough to believe what he thought he had heard and seen.

What Thomas Johnson observed as he looked south in April 1927 was a small-town solicitor, a candidate for the honour of representing his people, withholding information about wanted men and vilifying the administration of Irish justice. Accordingly, he alerted the Minister for Justice, a post now held by Kevin O'Higgins. This powerful member of the Executive Council had connections in West Cork, mainly through his family. Furthermore, his brother, Dr T. F. O'Higgins, likewise an active politician, was a close friend of Jasper's. So, through his local contacts, the minister had a shrewd idea of what was going on. However, as events would soon show, unlike Thomas Johnson he did not regard what Jasper was doing as a threat to the state.

Nevertheless, O'Higgins was a member of the government and had received an official complaint, so he had to take some sort of an initiative. What he did was to send a senior police official to interview Jasper in Cork. Rumours abounded that Jasper was about to be arrested, and indeed Johnson had called for him to be thrown into gaol. In terms of his candidature, all this did Jasper no harm at all. While having spent time in prison was one of the surest ways of getting elected to the Dáil, being threatened with arrest was a good deal better than nothing. Jasper had little difficulty in dealing with the Assistant

Commissioner of the Garda Síochána, who arrived from Dublin in Cork on Wednesday 4 May to interview him. Exactly a week later, on 11 May, in response to a question by Thomas Johnson, Kevin O'Higgins made a detailed statement on what had occurred to the Dáil (which had not yet dissolved prior to the forthcoming election). His statement was subsequently given full coverage in the press (Dáil Debates, 11 May 1927; Southern Star, 14 May 1927).

In his encounter with the gardaí (the Chief Superintendent of Cork also being present), Jasper began by claiming that the press article which had caused all the excitement was unreliable: 'The report contained in the Cork Examiner was inaccurate, and probably deliberately so, inspired from political sources with a view to injuring me in my election campaign.' As for that part of the article which dealt with the search for those who carried out the Cobh shootings, he stated that, when he was reported as saying that he had seen two of those named as wanted in the government proclamation 'walking in the streets of Cork a few days previously', he meant a few days previous to the proclamation, not to his speech in Skibbereen. Consequently, there was no failure by him to carry out his civic duty by giving the authorities information likely to lead to the arrest of officially wanted wrongdoers.

Jasper also had to explain away his claim that search parties had taken 'uncommonly good care to pass by the gate which they knew, as all in this country knew, would lead to the culprits'. He admitted that he had implied that search parties had taken care to 'pass by the gate' but explained that 'I really wished to convey that the search parties would have been better employed searching houses, gates, etc. . . . rather than searching the mountainside for noted Republicans'.

Finally, the gardaí drew up a statement containing the main points made by Jasper. In the words of the Minister of Justice to the Dáil, 'Mr Wolfe admitted its accuracy, while refusing to sign it.' Kevin O'Higgins concluded by attempting to close the incident, saying, 'In view of Mr Wolfe's repudiation of the press reports, it is not proposed to take further action in the matter.' That, however, was not quite the last word on the affair in the Dáil. A few days later, none other than Neilus Connolly, not a frequent speaker in the Dáil, in a final intervention argued that there was evidence to show that the press reports repudiated by Jasper had indeed been correct. However, Kevin O'Higgins was having none of it. 'I have come to the conclusion', he announced, 'that for the moment Mr Wolfe's political ambitions are overriding considerations which the Deputy [i.e. Neilus] and I would agree ought to prevail even in the weeks preceding an election.' That was as close to the truth of the matter as anyone was likely to get and did finally put an end to government and national interest in the incident (Dáil Debates, 20 May 1927).

After Jasper's skirmishes with the authorities he became a bit of a star attraction, a fact which he did his best to capitalise on, holding one meeting after another throughout the constituency of West Cork. The first took place in Bantry a few days after his interview with the senior gardaí in Cork, but before Kevin O'Higgins' statement to the Dáil announcing that no further action would be taken. From the start of the Bantry meeting, it was obvious that Jasper's campaign was taking off. The hall, reported the *Southern Star* (14 May 1927):

> was filled to overflowing . . . the Independent candidate for West Cork was given a rousing reception, and the crowded meeting listened with close attention to his speech, which at every telling point was loudly applauded. All classes and creeds were represented, and as one surveyed the great audience there was no room left for doubt about the popularity of Mr Wolfe.

Jasper hammered away at his key chosen themes (old age pensions, the licensing laws, unemployment and the fishing industry), but majored on the Cobh shooting and his brush with the government: 'Some talk of arrest has been heard, but I have no use for humbug. It has not the slightest effect on me. I am too old a soldier to be in the least alarmed by such threats.' He then turned to the failure to arrest any of the men named in the government proclamation:

> In that proclamation those men were named as murderers. That stands today. And up to the present no steps have been taken to arrest them. I have said it before, and I will say it again. It is a shame to keep a charge hanging over the heads of innocent men for three years and three months, let them be Republicans or otherwise [shouts of 'hear! hear!']. In the past there have been various criticisms of me. I have been called a Republican. The only thing I say in reply is that anyone who said that a Republican had to get fair play was called a Republican.

Jasper's campaign was now rolling along at a fine pace. The triumph at Bantry was followed by visits in the west to Schull, Castletownbere, Berehaven, Allihies and Eyeries, and thence eastwards to Kinsale, Carrigaline and Crosshaven. 'At each venue', as the *Cork Examiner* reported (18 May 1927), 'there was a large gathering, and Mr Wolfe was extended cordial and encouraging welcomes. The proceedings throughout the tour were of a harmonious and enthusiastic character.'

Jasper pursued carefully targeted and sharp-edged tactics. With the government unpopular and Neilus Connolly, the previous TD, retiring, Jasper, as a Free State supporter and a former Home Ruler hoped to pick up good numbers of the first preference votes which in the last election (1923) had gone to Neilus. Consequently, he drove home his attacks on the government's most unpopular policies. He also made fun of their three candidates, one of whom was none other than his old stablemate Timothy Sheehy. He laughed at the way those standing for selection as Cumann na nGaedheal candidates had quarrelled among themselves: 'Those men who were chosen had not left the selection meeting before they started mud-slinging at one another.' (Laughter.) 'One of them said the other was a ruffian, another [not chosen] said that there were three candidates going forward out of four, and that during his whole life he never knew three greater tricksters going forward to an election.' (Cheers from the audience.)

Jasper, however, took great care not to upset supporters of candidates from the other main parties, for he hoped to win at least some of their alternative votes. He was particularly polite to the Labour Party. Unusually in a predominantly rural constituency, Labour had polled very well in the previous election and the signs were that it would do even better this time. This was partly down to the appeal of their candidate. Timothy Joseph Murphy, an O'Brienite in his youth, had, most exceptionally for a young man at the time, been more attracted to the universal doctrines of socialism than to the intense, but necessarily confined, appeal of nationalism. He picked up votes because he was personally popular (always important in West Cork), understood local issues and could speak for the poorer classes, many of whom, with their natural spokesmen, the Republicans, refusing to take their seats, felt they lacked representation. So Jasper politely commended Mr Murphy for voting against the reduction in the old age pension (against 'the cutting down of the old man's miserable mess of potage') and he congratulated him for his efforts to promote full employment. 'It is', said Jasper, 'the duty of the state to provide work for its able-bodied men who are willing to work. One might call that socialist doctrine. You may hear it from Mr Murphy's platform. I think you would hear the same from heaven.'

Since Jasper also hoped, under the Irish voting system of proportional representation, to pick up second, third or even fourth preference votes from Republicans, he was polite about them too. He dealt sympathetically with their refusal to take the oath of allegiance and to take their seats in the Dáil. 'I hold no brief for the Republican candidates, but I would like to say in their favour that they told the public what they intended to do if elected. They told the people they would not represent them in the Dáil unless a miracle happened. It is a great pity Mr de Valera and his representatives are not in the Dáil.' And, as Jasper pointed out, the West Cork Republican TD, Sean Buckley, by his very absence at least recorded an abstention when it came to government motions on such matters as reducing the old age pension.

Came polling day, and the results. It turned out that Jasper's analysis of the election and his tactics had been spot-on. Labour, with Timothy Joseph Murphy, came an easy first, both in the overall result and in first preferences. Cumann na nGaedheal slipped badly. Only one of its candidates, Timothy Sheehy, avoided the cut, coming in fourth on first preferences and third overall. The Republican Fianna Fáil, likewise with three candidates, only got one elected, with their top man, Thomas Mullins, coming fifth on first preferences but picking up enough further votes (very probably from Labour) to reach second overall. The only other significant grouping, the Farmers' Party, a pro-Treaty grouping representing the more prosperous agricultural interests, came in fourth overall.

That left Jasper. He came second on first preferences and must have taken, as he planned, a good number of the Cumann na nGaedheal votes cast for Neilus Connolly in the previous election. He did not, as he had foreseen, do as well on second and later preference votes but proved to have secured just enough to slip in as fifth of the thirteen candidates. He had thus succeeded in securing the last position which qualified for the honour of being a Teachta Dála (TD).

36

"Twas Jasper, and not Jinks, saved the Irish Nation'

Having achieved a toehold in the arena of national politics, Jasper exerted himself to convert it into a secure footing. Within days of the opening session of the new Dáil he was on his feet pursuing some of the issues on which he had fought his election campaign. He attacked the government for its parsimonious attitude to old age pensioners: 'Regulations are being carried out in a spirit of marked hostility towards the Old Age Pensioners. That is not the spirit that should prevail. On the contrary, the regulations ought to be carried out in a spirit of friendliness and kindness' (Dáil Debates, 5 July 1927).

Jasper was also highly critical of the government's record in dealing with the fishing industry. He charged the minister responsible with presiding over what he described as, 'in effect, the complete, tragic and dismal breakdown of a great Government department, vital to the interests of the people who live on the seaboard'. He was particularly critical of official reluctance, or simple inability, to deal with vessels from other countries which caught fish within the three-mile limit around the coast of Ireland.

> I represent a division which, taken from Crosshaven to Ardgroom is about 110 miles long. Along that sea-coast lies the greatest wealth of West Cork and Cork County, one of the finest seaboards you can find in Europe. That seaboard is being destroyed every day by foreign invaders . . . They come to our shores day after day and take away our fish . . . Fines amounting to thousands of pounds have been imposed . . . but the minister is unable to enforce them.

Then, there was the problem of foreign fishermen taking catches allegedly just outside the internationally agreed three-mile limit.

> We can control the foreign boats if a little common sense is used . . . We have a minister for foreign affairs, as I understand. Why not send him to France and Belgium with the object of seeking a reciprocal agreement, and

so keep their boats ten miles off our coast? If that were done it would bring
a new era for the fishing industry. (Dáil Debates, 7 July 1927)

These interventions by Jasper, and others like them, were part of the normal,
if vigorous, operations of parliamentary debate. There now, however, occurred
one of those cataclysmic episodes from which the Irish body politic had
suffered repeatedly for many, many years.

Kevin O'Higgins, who only recently had dealt with Jasper's attack on the
government for its handling of the Cobh shooting, was now, following the
election, confirmed as the most powerful figure on the Executive Council. He
was extremely able, ruthless and at the same time principled. He was the hard
man of the administration, and he used his authority at once to uphold the
democratic nature of the constitution and to bring Republicanism to heel. On
Sunday 10 July 1927 Kevin O'Higgins walked, alone and unarmed, from his
home near Dublin to attend mass. Three gunmen waiting in a parked car
opened fire. The first shots missed and the minister ran for cover. The assassins
pursued him, shot him down, fired repeated shots into his fallen body and then
drove off. They were never brought to justice.

The government reacted instantly, as it had to, with both its own existence
and that of the Free State all too evidently under threat. On the security front
it moved to forestall any attempted insurrection. Constitutionally, it demanded
that Republicans either behave democratically or get out of political life. Like
many others, Jasper found his career significantly affected by all this.

Jasper probably knew more of the workings of emergency laws than anyone
else in the Dáil. He had, throughout the Troubles, acted for the British
government at courts martial, special and other courts in cases brought under
the Criminal Law and Procedures Act (1887), under the Defence of the Realm
Act (1914) and under its successor, the Restoration of Order in Ireland Act
(1920). He had also appeared for the defence in Irish Free State courts under
successive Public Safety Acts. Consequently, when the government introduced
a new, extremely tough, Public Safety Bill, Jasper soon emerged as someone
with the experience to speak with authority on its provisions. He made major
contributions to the debate. In principle his view, as he told the Dáil and
subsequently his constituents, was that, 'while I did not agree with certain
sections of it, it was a bill which the government were entitled to introduce as
the custodians of public safety, and a measure which no man could reasonably
refuse them' (Dáil Debates, 16 August 1927). The bill proposed, amongst other
things, that the government could outlaw any association aiming to overthrow
the government by force, that the authorities could enter premises and search
for suspects virtually at will and that special courts (without juries) could
be set up with powers to execute anyone convicted of illegal possession of
firearms.

Jasper's main criticisms were aimed at the powers and nature of the
intended special courts. He referred to his wide experience in arguing that

'whenever courts were turned from ordinary courts martial into "special courts" they turned out to be a failure . . . It is suggested that this House should set up in its worst form these special courts, and that with the knowledge that they have proved a disastrous failure. I will be no party towards allowing my fellow-countrymen to be tried by a court absolutely unfit to try them' (Dáil Debates, 3 August 1927). In the event, a few changes were made to the bill but none of them significant. However, the criticisms of Jasper and others were not ignored for long. Many in the government and throughout the country were deeply uneasy about the attack on the liberty of the citizen which the legislation represented.

Immediately following the assassination of Kevin O'Higgins the security services took rapid action in an effort to extinguish any further, and possibly escalating, outbursts of violence. As part of a nationwide crackdown, on Monday 11 July, just twenty-four hours after the death of O'Higgins, armed forces in Cork city arrested the brothers James and Jeremiah Grey, two of those suspected of the Cobh shooting and named as wanted men in the government proclamation of May 1924. The speed and ease with which the Greys were picked up seemed to prove that the gardaí had indeed known all along exactly where they were to be found, just as Jasper had argued earlier in the year.

The brothers were formally charged with the wilful murder of Private Aspinall. Representing them in court was Jasper. He had been signed up by the IRA, which suggests that it accepted at least some responsibility for the men allegedly involved in the Cobh shooting. That it was Jasper to whom the Republicans turned for help confirmed the high regard they had for him and showed that, as far as they were concerned, bygones were bygones. And they stuck with him, even when it became clear that he supported, at least in principle, the new Public Safety Bill.

The Greys were taken to Cork gaol, where they remained for several weeks. On several occasions, under armed military escort, they were taken to court in Cobh. Every time the prosecution asked for, and was granted, further remand of the prisoners, Jasper protested. On the final occasion he became particularly eloquent.

I respectfully, but emphatically protest against the further torture of the two untried and innocent accused. The state prosecution has complained of the shortness of time they have had to investigate the case, but they have had three years and three months . . . The state says it has not been able to trace all the witnesses, but that it has been able to trace some. Why have they not produced them? For the sake of public safety, in which we are all interested, scandals like this should not be allowed to occur. We are living in what is supposed to be a civilised country, and the accused are entitled to be brought to trial at the earliest possible moment, or at least discharged, leaving it to the authorities to rearrest them at any moment they like.

Despite Jasper's pleas, the justice ordered yet a further remand. Jasper was not happy: 'Do I understand that on Thursday next the same performance will be gone through? Won't somebody put a term to this period of torture?' During his oration, Jasper had referred quite frequently and emphatically to the 'torture' of the prisoners. Eventually, as the *Southern Star* reported (6 August 1927), the prosecuting State Solicitor was provoked into responding: 'I do not think the word "torture" should be used. Many prisoners have been on remand and we know the treatment they receive. I think it is going too far to use the word "torture".'

Mr Wolfe: 'I have no complaint to make with regard to the prisoners' treatment in prison.'

Mr O'Connor (State Solicitor): 'Then there is no reason to use the word "torture".'

Mr Wolfe: 'When I use the word "torture" I am merely talking about the torture every man must be subjected to when his liberty has been taken from him. Cork gaol is a place where every courtesy is shown to untried prisoners.'

Mr O'Connor: 'If Mr Wolfe says much more about it we will all be anxious to go there' (laughter).

The court duly reconvened the next week, on Thursday 11 August. The State Solicitor announced that he still had been unable to trace his witnesses and so could offer no evidence. The judge finally ordered the accused to be discharged, but not before Jasper had had a final say. He demanded that the original proclamation – a 'libel', as he called it – naming the Greys and three others as wanted for the Cobh shooting be officially annulled.

> In common fairness and in common decency I think the libel should now be withdrawn, and it should be intimated to those lads that they are leaving this court, as they entered it, after thirty three days imprisonment, without witnesses against them – nay, rather with witnesses for them, to the knowledge of the state, who if they had produced them, would have entirely proved their innocence – that they were leaving court with every charge made against them entirely and freely withdrawn. They are in justice entitled to that. (*Cork Examiner*, 12 August 1927)

The State Solicitor prevaricated, but Jasper insisted: 'Will the proclamation be withdrawn?' However, Mr O'Connor had 'nothing to say to the proclamation', and there things finished. It was finally the end of the Cobh shooting affair. The Free State appeared to have suffered a defeat. It had, however, almost certainly succeeded in its main aims. It kept two men it considered to be very dangerous sidelined during the dangerous weeks following the assassination of Kevin O'Higgins. And it proved conclusively to the Cobh suspects that they were under close surveillance and could be picked up at any time.

While all this was going on in Cobh, at Leinster House – home of the Dáil – events were coming to the boil. Following the assassination of Kevin O'Higgins the government had taken steps to deal with the ambiguous political position of the Republicans. Since the founding of the Free State, Sinn Féin had participated in elections, but its elected members refused to take their seats in the Dáil. In general, they would not accept the legitimacy of the new constitution, but, in particular, they objected – and strongly – to the oath of allegiance to the British monarch which all members of the Dáil and Senate were required by law to take. As Ireland settled back into a more or less normal, democratic way of life, the Republicans became ever more distanced from political power. Their sense of frustrated impotence led to internal splits and in late 1925 the political and military wings of Republicanism parted company. The IRA, renouncing de Valera's leadership and opting to travel the road of violence, set up its own, autonomous Army Council. Six months later, Sinn Féin itself broke apart. De Valera proposed that, if the controversial oath of loyalty to the British Crown were scrapped, then Republicans could consider entering the Dáil. However, at an Ard Fheis (party convention) a narrow majority rejected its leader's suggested compromise. Within two months, de Valera set up a new political party, Fianna Fáil. This, in principle at least, was prepared to consider working within the existing constitution, provided – and it was a massive proviso – that the oath was scrapped. After a short struggle with Sinn Féin, de Valera succeeded in driving that band of diehards into the wilderness. In southern Ireland, Fianna Fáil now became the only credible party of Republicanism.

Fianna Fáil candidates had duly stood in the June 1927 election, but they had failed to secure a majority and so had little hope of securing the removal of the oath. Mainly for this reason, like Sinn Féin members before them, they did not take their seats in the Dáil. The existence, out in the country, of absentee Republican TDs had, from the start, weakened the Free State, as it was intended to do. Now, however, following the assassination of Kevin O'Higgins, it looked as if many Fianna Fáil supporters might be tempted into joining any further illegal and subversive action. Fears were provoked of a coup, even of a second civil war.

To put an end to this situation, President Cosgrave and the Executive Council introduced two bills. One proposed that every candidate for election to the Dáil should swear, if elected, to take the oath of allegiance. The second put forward various measures to make abolition of the oath more difficult. De Valera was cornered, and he knew it. He had rejected violence but had not yet fully accepted the existing constitution. He was in no position to go back, but could he go forward? Then, all of a sudden, with one bound, he was free. In a bravura display of the political conjuring skills for which he was widely famous and admired (or reviled, depending on one's allegiances) he led his followers into the Dáil, where he and they apparently took the oath. Only, de Valera had succeeded in persuading his adherents, who wanted to believe him anyway, that what seemed like the act of swearing fealty to the Crown was nothing more than an illusion: the words of the oath were covered, the bible was placed face down, and de Valera himself and the other Fianna Fáil deputies, as they wrote their names, all proclaimed that they were not signing any sort of declaration of allegiance to the British. Thereafter, Fianna Fáil became notorious as, in the words of one of its leaders, 'a slightly constitutional party'.

This parliamentary spectacular, with its drama of the oath-taking, had the whole country agog – and nervous. At this point, with the political climax approaching and with Jasper having appeared in Cobh court on behalf of the IRA, Dorothy reappeared on the scene. Since she had smuggled her father out of the country in the back of a car, she had graduated from Oxford and moved to London, where she was studying to be a barrister. Now she was back in Skibbereen for the summer vacation. Being fascinated by Irish politics and close to Jasper, she picked up various bits and pieces of inside information. As luck would have it, a diary survives which she kept during 1927. The first relevant entry in Dorothy's diary occurs on Monday 8 August. Watching events from Norton, she recorded that 'all much exercised by the decision of Fianna Fáil to enter the Dáil on Friday [12th]. It is still raining intermittently.'

With the swearing in completed and Fianna Fáil now able to put its full complement of TDs through the voting lobbies, it looked as if the Republicans might be able to gain enough support to outvote the government and so take its place. It did not have enough seats to achieve this on its own, but it was confident of forming an alliance with Labour. It was also optimistic of winning over to its side the Irish National League. Captain William Redmond, its leader, might have seemed a more natural partner for the government, but, his Home Rule background notwithstanding, he and his followers looked as if they might forget their principles and surrender to the temptation of power. Fianna Fáil moved in for the kill.

Thomas Johnson, as official leader of the opposition, proposed a motion of No Confidence. Originally it had been intended to do this on the Friday, immediately after the swearing in of Fianna Fáil members. However, it had been delayed for a few days. The weekend was spent by both opposition and government in desperate lobbying. It took Fianna Fáil some time to get the Irish National League on side. On the Monday Dorothy commented, 'The National League is still an unknown quantity, but no doubt Redmond's passion for a portfolio will make him support Johnson.' Within twenty-four hours she was proved right.

Meanwhile, the government, which was able to count on the Farmers' Party, was working on lining up the votes of the few Independents. However, they faced strong competition. Jasper found himself suddenly much in demand. Although known as a strong supporter of the Free State and thus, in this crisis, of the government, he was nevertheless approached by the opposition. On Monday 15 August Dorothy recorded, 'Johnson it seems has tried to bribe Dad with the Ministry of Justice, but unless unforeseen events occur he will vote with the government.'

Jasper had actually found himself in a potentially embarrassing position. After the Cobh shooting trial ended, he had other, unavoidable business in the south. On the Friday, Dorothy, who was now seeing her father daily, wrote, 'Fianna Fáil took their seats today, but the Vote of No Confidence is postponed until Tuesday. Just as well, because Dad has to go to Castletownbere today, and thought there might be adverse comment on his absence from Leinster House. But he can be there on Tuesday.'

As Jasper travelled back to Dublin on the Monday, it was generally felt that Fianna Fáil and its allies would just win the No Confidence vote. If it did, what would happen? One notion, probably the most hopeful, was that a coalition government would be formed, with Thomas Johnson as President, but with Fianna Fáil holding the key ministries and de Valera, with Fianna Fáil, calling the shots. But there was a quiverful of other, far more alarming possibilities. Republicans, for instance, feared that the ultra right, particularly in the senior army ranks, might itself try to seize power, in order to forestall Fianna Fáil participating in government.

As for Free State democrats and Cumann na nGaedheal, they, for their part, were also deeply anxious. They did not know whether de Valera intended to participate in constitutional government and, even if he did, whether he would be able to. His deputies were, for the most part, politically inexperienced. Many had made their names, not in council chambers, but in the conflicts of the Troubles and the Civil War. Still mostly in their twenties or thirties, these young guns had trigger-happy fingers which were still twitchy and heads which were still far from cool. Whether they would prove capable, or even desirous, of ruling constitutionally was open to question.

The greatest fear of those who supported the Free State was that a Fianna Fáil victory might signal an attempt at a hard-line Republican coup. They knew full well that the IRA, and those behind the assassination of Kevin O'Higgins, would be willing to try and take over the government by force. Furthermore, if militant Republicanism did succeed in seizing power, some form of dictatorship appeared to be a real possibility. As democrats looked towards Europe, they could see one country after another – Russia, Italy, Portugal – falling into the grip of despotic regimes. And who was to say that Ireland would not be next?

Unbeknown to him, Jasper was now about to play, for the second time in the year, a cameo role on the national scene; and this time he would be cast, not as a subverter of the Free State, but as a saviour. By the evening of Monday 15 August, the Cumann na nGaedheal whips had counted heads, done their sums and concluded that the government would indeed lose, but only by a single vote. At this bleak moment, the government had just one last hope. There was a solitary member of the Dáil who still appeared to be wavering. The fate of the government, and perhaps of the nation, depended on a certain Alderman Jinks. This deputy, representing Sligo, was one of eight members belonging to Captain Redmond's Irish National League. It seems he was having doubts. On the one hand, his party, on the orders of its leader, was to support Fianna Fáil in the No Confidence motion, but, on the other, his conscience told him that the only party in Irish politics which could claim direct descent from John Redmond's Home Rule National Party should not really be supporting Republicans. And he was not alone. One of his colleagues, prompted by similar anxieties, had actually declared he would vote for the government. It was not thought that Jinks would actually support the government, but, if he could be prevailed on to abstain, it seemed there was a fighting chance that the government might be saved.

So, the whips looked everywhere for Alderman Jinks. But, throughout Tuesday 16 August, with the vote approaching in the evening, the much sought-after deputy for Sligo proved elusive. Some reported sightings here, others there. In the next few days, rumours abounded of what had happened to Jinks. One claimed that sympathisers of the government had met Jinks on the Monday evening and had beered, dined, wined and spirited him so effectively that he was still legless by the crucial Tuesday evening. Another version had him suffering the same fate over Tuesday lunch. In some of these stories, Jasper featured. Over twenty years later, following an article in the *Cork Examiner* about the 1927 No Confidence vote, one reader who had been in Dublin at the time wrote in to give his view of what had taken place (6 March 1956). He claimed that it was Jasper who had been responsible for the disappearance of Jinks. According to him, when it came to the vote:

> All deputies were in their place except two – Deputy Jinks of Sligo and Deputy Jasper Wolfe of West Cork. Anxious enquiries failed to reveal to either side where these deputies could be. The only news of them was that they had been seen that morning in a Dublin hotel. Just at the last moment Deputy Wolfe arrived to cast his vote for the government, but Deputy Jinks was absent from the division.

One theory, however, nows seems to have become established as the favourite. According to this, R. M. Smyllie, editor of the *Irish Times*, and Major Bryan Cooper, an Independent deputy from Sligo, got hold of Jinks and managed to push, or pour, him onto the train home before the vote.[1]

All these speculations contained some truth. None, however, were fully aware of the role played by Jasper. When, two days after the vote, on the Thursday, Jasper returned to Norton, he was, said Dorothy, 'pleased with himself'. He, told the family of what had actually happened and of how he had become involved in the drama. Dorothy recorded that:

> Dad . . . provided us with the true story of the redoubtable Jinks. It seems that the intention of Jinks not to vote with de Valera etc. was well known to the government lobby, but when the speaker was about to call Johnson to wind up it was perceived with panic that Jinks was still in the House. The government whip rushed to the smoking room where Dad was and implored him to come in and speak. Dad manfully rose to the occasion and delivered

an unprepared and highly provocative speech (I think too provocative) during which Jinks unobtrusively vanished.

This account tallies with the official record. The Report of Dáil Debates shows that Thomas Johnson opened the No Confidence motion at 3 p.m. on Tuesday 16 August, proposing that 'The Executive Council has ceased to retain the support of the majority of Dáil Éireann.' At about 6.30 Jasper rose to his feet. He spoke for at least half an hour and made the longest contribution to the debate. Apart from rehearsing, at some length, the line he had taken on the Public Safety Act (which followed the assassination of Kevin O'Higgins) and the Electoral Abuses Bill (which led Fianna Fáil to taking the oath and entering the Dáil), he fired off a terrific attack on his old enemy, Thomas Johnson, the proposer of the motion.

Thomas Johnson was the only figure in the whole of Jasper's public life, not forgetting those who had planned to execute him, towards whom he revealed real animosity. He was not ready to forgive the Labour leader for trying to get him into trouble over the Cobh shooting. Furthermore, Jasper, a liberal son of rural Ireland, simply had no use for and less understanding of Johnson, an Englishman, a socialist and a man from an industrial background. He pelted Johnson from every possible angle. He complained, for instance, that, while the leader of the opposition had been quite prepared over the Cobh shooting affair to demand in the Dáil that Jasper be imprisoned without trial or hearing, he had nevertheless only a few months later opposed the Public Safety Act on the grounds that it interfered with the liberty of the citizen. But Jasper's main complaint was that the nationalist-minded Republican Party was being hypocritical and cynically opportunistic in supporting an Englishman as leader of a potential coalition government. It was, Jasper pointed out, a main principle of Fianna Fáil that there should be 'government of Ireland by the Irish . . . and what,' enquired Jasper rhetorically, 'have we today? . . . We have a motion which must have the support of the 43 members of the Fianna Fáil party, and (if it is successful) we are going to have the Dáil ruled over by an Englishman. I am off that job. I will have nothing to say to it.' Jasper's words, as no doubt he had intended, stirred an outraged reaction. Fianna Fáil and Labour deputies jumped to their feet. The debate lasted another good hour. By then, Deputy Jinks had vanished.

The result was a tie. The speaker, as convention demanded, cast his vote against the motion. The government was saved. That evening in Norton, Dorothy, like almost everyone else, was expecting Fianna Fáil to triumph. Learning the news almost instantaneously, probably by radio, possibly by phone, she was amazed and delighted, writing, 'An astonishing thing has happened. The government has won – by the Speaker's (sorry! Ceann Comhairle's) casting vote.'

In the aftermath, everyone gorged on theories as to how the government had managed to save itself. On the Wednesday Dorothy wrote, 'All Ireland is ringing with the name of John Jinks.' Why had the alderman not turned up for the historic vote? Dorothy wrote:

> Some say he was kidnapped, spirited away, but this rumour would appear to be merely a newspaper stunt. Jinks left the Dáil, simply walked unobserved out of it before the division on the No Confidence motion was taken. It is certainly 'ighly 'umorous – except for his party and the other coalitionists.

However, there were some, particularly in West Cork, who knew exactly what had happened. They were in no doubt that it was Jasper who had saved the day. As a Republican opponent of Jasper's was to acknowledge, generously and publicly, ''Twas Jasper, and not Jinks, saved the Irish Nation'.

37

'Possibly the most "independent" member of Dáil Éireann'

What did the electorate think of the crisis in the Dáil? The answer was not long in coming. In two Dublin by-elections held less than ten days after the No Confidence motion, Cumann na nGaedheal thumped all other parties. With virtual deadlock in the Dáil, President Cosgrave saw his chance and declared a general election. So it was back to the ballot for Jasper. In his previous campaign, in the spring, he had suffered from a problem common to Independent candidates in all times and places – inadequate organisation. Cumann na nGaedheal could boast paid organisers (albeit of questionable efficiency) and Fianna Fáil had an excellent grassroots set-up inherited from years of Republican activism, but Jasper had little more than his solicitor's office.

It was now that Dorothy, who was still on vacation, signed up as, in effect, her father's campaign manager. She filled this post not only for the 1927 election but for the remaining elections which Jasper was to contest. In some ways, this was surprising. She certainly did not share his political outlook, having little sympathy for any Irish nationalist aspirations, however mild. She was a natural Unionist. From her Oxford days she had been an active member of the Conservative and Unionist party. Jasper, an inveterate Liberal, in British terms, had consoled himself by writing to her that 'you will probably change your politics later, as did Gladstone and many other great men, so you will be following in illustrious footsteps'. However, by the time of the British general election of 1929 she was a fully fledged and valued Tory worker, being allocated by an appreciative Conservative Central Office to a particularly difficult constituency.

However, in West Cork Dorothy's deep affection for her father and sensitivity to the pulse of Irish politics made her an invaluable recruit for the maverick Jasper. Dorothy rapidly installed herself in the offices of J. Travers Wolfe & Co., where she set up her control centre. Here she took command of operations, but not without some initial difficulty: 'I anticipate unpleasantness with my second in command, Mr M. McCarthy.' Three days later she was writing with grim satisfaction: 'A day of violent activity in the Committee Rooms. I exercised great firmness, and they are resigned to the inevitable.' Thenceforth it was the frantic routines common to all elections: 'Addressed a couple of hundred envelopes . . . we are getting rid of great batches of the stuff . . . very busy dictating letters and appointing personation agents . . . It has been discovered that Paddy can forge Dad's signature *à merveille*, which is most useful.'

Canvassing, for most candidates, relied heavily on family support. For Jasper, it was vital, and Wolfes and Vickeries came out in force: 'Uncle Dobby [Robert Vickery, Minnie's brother] took Mum, Travers and me on a canvassing expedition round by Caheragh and Clohane [former IRA strongholds]. It was very successful.' But the most effective of Jasper's champions was his older brother. Willie, still a town councillor, remained a well-liked and much respected local figure. Long experience had taught him the most effective method of winning votes, even if it hardly came cheap. His daughter Mary, aged ten at the time, recalled her father's electioneering tactics well. Early in the evening, accompanied by Mary, a bright and lively girl, he would visit a pub. On leaving, with drink taken and rounds stood, he would call out, 'Now, you'll be voting for my brother alright.' Came the reply, 'We're all for Jasper here, right enough.' And so it went on, from one public house to another, night after night. Luckily the campaign only lasted a couple of weeks.

Jasper was doing what he did best – holding meetings. At Skibbereen the occasion was a great success. 'Meeting at the Town Hall to-night', reported Dorothy. 'Dad's speech was very good, and the Hall was crammed.' Jasper continued with his tour, speaking across the constituency, always to large and enthusiastic audiences. He could, and did, emphasise his contributions in Dáil debates to all the local interests he had promised to promote in the last election, in particular raising old age pensions and supporting the fishing industry. But the Independent candidate for West Cork majored on his role in standing up for law, order and justice. He reminded audiences of how he represented those accused by the government in the Cobh shooting affair, he justified his decision to support the government's Public Safety Bill following the assassination of Kevin O'Higgins, and, above all, he played up his part in saving the government in the No Confidence vote. 'I voted', he told voters in his election manifesto, 'for Order as against Chaos, for Peace as against War, and I am convinced that in doing so I rightly interpreted the wishes of my constituents'.

Nor was Jasper reluctant to play up his own part in the dramatic events of the No Confidence debate. In this endeavour he received a great boost from one of his opponents. It was Thomas Mullins, the leading Fianna Fáil candidate, in a campaign speech at Bantry who had said ''Twas Jasper, and not Jinks, saved the Irish Nation'. Jasper pounced on the quote, flourishing it, to much laughter and applause, at every one of his meetings. To appear before the electorate as a saviour of the nation, and to have been called such by an opponent, can have done him no harm at all.

Although clearly the campaign had been a success, the general belief was that, while Jasper would hold on to his seat, he would do well to improve on his fifth place of the last poll. At the start of the election, with two Cumann na nGaedheal candidates, two Fianna Fáil, one Labour and one Farmers' Party, Dorothy was worried. She feared that Jasper's support for Cumann na nGaedheal in the No Confidence motion would have cost him support: 'his voting with the government means 1000 Republican votes lost'. She assumed that Jasper and the second Cumann na nGaedheal man would be battling it out for the fifth place. In the event, come election day, Jasper routed all-comers, coming top of the poll on the first count. Even after other preference votes had been counted he managed to hold on to second place, being beaten only by the main Fianna Fáil candidate, the helpful Thomas Mullins. (Overall, not including Jasper, each party won one seat each.)

But how to explain Jasper's success? Anyone would have been considered insane if they had predicted, back in the days when Jasper Wolfe was Crown Solicitor and being hunted by the IRA, that he would within five years succeed Michael Collins as the most popular politician in West Cork. Jasper must have garnered most of the available Protestant votes, he must also have won huge backing in Skibbereen as a favourite local son, and perhaps more votes arrived as a tribute to his sheer entertainment value, but, apart from his willingness to fight for his constituents, it may have been admiration for his nerve and courage that counted most. Then again, he probably seemed to many to be the best available spokesman for what, irrespective of their political allegiance, they desired most: a forgiving, fair-minded, quick-witted and mostly peace-loving land.

At Norton, Jasper, Dorothy and the rest of the family, as the election results came in, were almost as delighted with the national as with the local vote. The unprincipled Captain Redmond and his Irish National League had lost almost all their seats, being reduced from eight to two, the uncompromising Republican Sinn Féin were wiped off the board completely and the Labour Party was down from 22 to 13. When Dorothy heard that their leader was amongst those defeated, she was absolutely ecstatic: 'Johnson has lost his seat! Wild Rejoicings!!' (Johnson managed to return to the Dáil before long, standing for Cork city. Jasper every now and then remembered to give him a gentle tease, referring to him, for instance, as 'the Cork member for Liverpool – sorry, the Liverpool member for Cork'.)

As for the major players, Fianna Fáil had done quite well but only emerged as the second largest party. It seemed that the electorate, not fully satisfied with the party's reliability, was putting it on probation. As for Cumann na nGaedheal, it had secured a majority of ten over de Valera's members. The outcome of all this was that Cosgrave was able, despite a few early anxieties, to form a stable administration in partnership with his long-standing and natural ally, the Farmers' Party. As for the Free State, it soon became clear that it had taken a firm step towards a viable, two-party system of government, and one in which all citizens were represented. The big question, however, was this: would Fianna Fáil bed down contentedly into a constitutional way of life, or would it find the constraints and obligations of this cohabitation insupportable?

The new Dáil opened in mid-October. Dorothy was still at home, benefiting from the long summer vacation enjoyed by students for the bar. As a reward for her hard work in the election she accompanied her father to Dublin. The trip was not without incident. She gave a full account of events in her diary.

Monday 10th. Dublin. Travelled hither, in great luxury, with Dad. Explored the city with him, as far as we could, by moonlight.

Tuesday 11th. First visited Mrs O'Reilly [the one-time Miss Browne, Jasper's apprentice who had been with him when he evaded an IRA ambush at Caheragh; now married to a successful Dublin solicitor and a firm family friend]. Then spent some time at the Courts which now live at the Castle, the Four Courts being still not ready.

Proceeded to Leinster House. The visitors were admitted by a winding staircase of stone. We waited in a weary queue for the door to be opened. When the appointed time came the attendant could not unlock it. Commotion, naturally, but nothing to the commotion when, the first gate having eventually yielded to the hundredth key, and the queue having mounted the stairs, the second door would not move. Wit, annoyance, a little locksmith with spectacles, crashes, expostulation from the sixth Dáil assembled within, at last entrance at 3.10 – 40 minutes after we should have got in. There was longer opposition than we expected to Cosgrave's nomination for the Presidency of the Executive Council – a Fianna Fáil member, Seán T. O'Kelly, opened with a spiteful and very poor speech – followed by O'Connell, the new Labour leader, fluent and authoritative, but unsound. Heffernan, Farmers' Party, dreadful. Redmond, quite efficient and mercifully short. Blyth [from the North, Cumann na nGaedheal minister and vice-president of the Executive Council] has a bad style, but made a good point. Seán Lemass, Fianna Fáil, a good speaker. The division was Tá (!) 76 – Níl 70. Uncomfortably and ominously close. Cosgrave spoke shortly. There was some small interruption in the gallery from a good lady who was noisily impolite to the government and speaker. Maud Gonne MacBride, in Celtic draperies of black was also there.

For many Irish, the next few years were a time of continuing anxiety. In both town and countryside there was real economic hardship, exacerbated by the worldwide depression. Once again, there were families throughout the land who were ill-fed, were poorly clothed and who feared starvation.

Nor had the threat of Republican violence blown away. The IRA, now entirely unhinged from political control, carried on sporadic campaigns of intimidation, shooting and bombing. As for de Valera, he continued to play his cards so close to his chest they might as well have been behind his shirt. During his speeches to the Dáil, he at one moment could appear, if ambiguously, to support the legitimacy of the government ('If there is no authority in this House to rule, there is no authority in any part of the country to rule') but, another time, equally ambiguously, he could seem to be the old, recalcitrant Republican ('I stood by the flag of the Republic, and I will do it again'). In reality, everyone knew that the vision of an Irish republic had not evaporated. It seemed all too possible that a final crisis, possibly military, perhaps political, had not been defused but merely postponed.

Despite all this, life for Jasper was definitely improving. He had no more financial worries, since his practice was as prosperous as it had ever been. Throughout West Cork he was a well-established public figure, while in Skibbereen itself he was now the leading citizen, and as such involved with numerous public and other organisations. One of these, the Skibbereen Lodge of Freemasons, of which he was an active member and had been Master in 1908 and again in 1924, he certainly found both congenial and useful. However, most of the posts in his portfolio were not only undemanding but shared one common factor: his minimal personal aptitude for any of the activities concerned. Thus, though showing little private interest in religion, he was circuit accountant and legal adviser to the Methodists, and, while never having played sport if he could avoid it, he was president of the Skibbereen Hockey and Rugby Clubs and on the committee of the Skibbereen and West Carbery golf club. Most incongruously of all, although he had seldom muddied his boots on a farm, he was a member of the Skibbereen Carbery Agricultural Show Society.

Finally, he became involved with the *Eagle*, for which he was also minimally qualified, being neither any sort of businessman nor putting pen to paper if he could possibly avoid it. However, unlike his other local public positions, this one involved a serious commitment. The *Eagle* had ceased publication on 8 July 1922, when the Irregulars invaded Skibbereen. In 1926 Jasper bought the company, whose assets now mainly consisted of premises and machinery, reorganised it as The Eagle (1926) Ltd. and became managing editor. By 1928 the paper had spasmodically resumed publication. However, it did not prove a success and in January 1929 Jasper (apparently being the sole shareholder) amicably agreed the sale of the *Eagle* to the *Southern Star*. Since he was partly paid in shares, he became a shareholder in what henceforth was to be known as 'The Southern Star incorporating the Skibbereen Eagle'.

All this, though, was little more than background colour to Jasper's life. His main interest lay in Dublin, and here he – and indeed various of his fellow politicians – was beginning to have a good time. For a start, the job of a TD was not, in this sixth Dáil, particularly demanding. The government could rely on a majority, as Fianna Fáil showed little sign of wishing to create another confrontation and no major emergencies arose. So relatively calm was the atmosphere that the Dáil only met infrequently. In 1930 it sat for a total of only fifty-nine days.

Reading through the official reports of Dáil debates one is struck by the freewheeling, informal style in which business was conducted. I was reminded not so much of a House of Commons as of an extended, highly argumentative and combative family gathering. Here, almost everyone knew almost everyone else, if only slightly. What was more, not only did many present have an encyclopaedic knowledge of the past deeds, and misdeeds, of other members, but they did not hesitate to refer to them in the various clashes which erupted every now and then. That some sort of peace, nevertheless, prevailed for most of the time owed much to the remarkable open-mindedness and tolerance of the Ceann Comhairle (or Speaker). Like all good referees, he was mainly interested in letting the game flow and was reluctant to make a fuss about minor misdemeanours. In the end, though, the Dáil worked, and often worked quite well, because many members actually enjoyed each other's company. When all was said and done, and a lot was said and done, these deputies, whatever their beliefs, were beginning to feel at home in the Irish political family.

Perhaps more at ease than anyone was Jasper. This was something the political journalists quickly noticed and enjoyed commenting on. Jasper was at home in the smoking room, in the lobby and in Dublin's main hotel, the Gresham, where he usually stayed. He was, noted one Dublin paper, 'genial, kindly, and almost embarrassingly hospitable'. There are memories of him always surrounded by friends, drinking, smoking, talking, arguing – scenes of endless conviviality.

Jasper knew a great many of the Dáil's members (properly called deputies) from his earlier life. There was, for instance, Gearóid O'Sullivan from Skibbereen, former adjutant-general of the IRA and the Free State National Army, the man who had raised the tricolour over the GPO during the 1916 Easter Rising and was now TD for Dublin County. (O'Sullivan was also a fluent Irish speaker, and Jasper used to consult him if ever he needed help with Gaelic.) Also from Skibbereen was another figure even better known to Jasper. Timothy Sheehy, former Town Council stalwart and now a deeply and vocally loyal member of Cumann na nGaedheal, had secured the fifth and last seat for West Cork in the September 1927 election, thus succeeding to Jasper's place. He had not taken kindly to this lowly position and hinted that his opponents had 'voted early and often'. However, this veteran, on reaching Leinster House, discovered to his delight that he was 'father of the Dáil', an eminence which he greatly enjoyed. A piece in the *Sunday Independent* called 'Political Sketches' described how, when de Valera attempted to introduce a bill restricting the age of deputies to 70 because beyond that age men were liable to 'lose grip', Timothy Sheehy was outraged. 'What', he demanded of the now leader of the opposition, 'has the Deputy to say to men over 75?' The great Republican leader, ever the political realist, swiftly backed down.

Many of those Jasper knew he had first encountered as Crown Solicitor, when dealing with them for alleged law-breaking. Nobody, however, seemed in any way fazed by this. As for Jasper himself, if his loyalist past was referred to he was more than happy to respond. Thus, in dealing with one Fianna Fáil interruption, he responded by saying: 'I prosecuted my fellow countrymen on both sides of the House, and I am bound to say I prosecuted more members on the government benches than on the other side. The other side were far more agile. They escaped prosecution' (Dáil Debates, 20 March 1928). As the *Irish Statesman* (3 November 1928) noted, 'he has more than once informed the House that he has prosecuted members of both front benches, and instead of hanging his head chuckles contentedly over the experience. It is quite impossible to be angry with Mr Wolfe.'

Jasper's former opponents were often ready to make friends in part simply because they warmed to him, but they also accepted his often reiterated claim that he 'played the game'. By this he meant that he never broke the rules of British justice. However, he also meant, and was understood to mean, that he was simultaneously playing a very different game, one conducted by Irish rules. Here, any subterfuge, trickery and quiet deviousness was justified if it helped life to go on as normally as possible and managed to save Republicans and their families from those such as the Black and Tans who were not playing by any recognisable code. Morally, Jasper had always observed the golden rule 'Do unto others as you would have them do unto you'. It was because all those veterans of the recent conflicts who now sat in the Dáil recognised this to be so that they were happy to fraternise with the Independent deputy from West Cork.

It was in the debating chamber that Jasper became a star attraction. To observers of the House he seemed to feature as a cross between an elder statesman and a mischievous uncle. His age (approaching sixty) and his experience certainly qualified him as a potential Grand Old Man. However, his speed of wit and pin-pricking accuracy in dispute inspired at once affection and admiration. Many journalistic pen portraits survive of his appearance and style. According to the *Irish Statesman* (3 November 1928), 'When you look at the Independent benches, you find Mr Wolfe's seat occupied by a ruddy, jovial, good-humoured person . . . a precise, square shouldered figure in decorous black'.

But it was Jasper's way of debating which really caught the imagination. Various political writers had a word or two to say about Jasper.

There is only one deputy who is master of the art of saying cutting things about opponents without exciting the suspicion of the chair. He is Mr Jasper Wolfe. Mr Wolfe can insinuate delightfully vitriolic things about people who incur his displeasure. And when they stand up to remonstrate nobody is more pained and surprised that the honoured and honourable deputy should take the references to be to himself than Mr Jasper Wolfe.

Mr Wolfe has a witty and whimsical style of speech which tickles the ear of the House . . . It is reminiscent of that type of forensic address which used to make our country courthouses places in which one could spend an enjoyable afternoon . . . Mr Wolfe can drive his point home by raillery and banter more effectively than many of his colleagues by ponderous phrase. But he is at his best when dealing with the personal aspect of things. (*Sunday Independent*, September 1928)

Jasper's performances could arouse rather differing reactions amongst the legislators of Leinster House. For a government that was looking to build secure majorities on particular motions, he could be a headache. As one paper put it, 'Possibly the most "independent" member of Dáil Éireann, he was regarded – unless the Treaty or some other major issue was at stake – by party whips as being entirely hopeless.' However, for those other than ministers and his immediate opponents, Jasper, as reporters regularly observed, was generally, although perhaps not exclusively, looked on as high-class entertainment: 'His oratory has a flavour very much to the liking of the Dáil, and empty benches fill rapidly when . . . he takes the floor . . . he does know how to tickle the Irish sense of humour' and 'Mr Wolfe draws the absent ones from the smokeroom and the lobby.'

Jasper's popularity may well have achieved more than just providing light relief and scoring some ephemeral points. Amongst his most appreciative listeners were many of the new Republican recruits: 'Nowhere,' reported the *Irish Statesman*, 'are smiles of anticipation more radiant than among the younger bloods of Fianna Fáil, who know exactly what is in store for them at his hands.' These men who had recently fought for their country's freedom, as they sat and laughed were probably also learning, if unconsciously, that, with irreconcilable principles more or less dealt with, it was possible to use the light word rather than the lethal bullet to advance one's cause. Jasper was one of those influences helping to acclimatise 'the younger bloods' to the ways of peace.

To the government whips Jasper may have seemed maddeningly unpredictable, while to the back bench ranks he was a great entertainer. In fact, his frequent and sometimes substantial speeches were pretty faithful to his own 'one man, one party' line and reflected the longstanding and consistent preoccupations of his public life. Equally, his wit and the tricks of his rhetorical trade were deployed not just to amuse or to irritate or to score clever points, but to enhance his arguments.

Few deputies can have been in doubt for long about Jasper's agenda. In the first place, like all conscientious elected representatives, he had an active concern for the interests of his constituents, and not least for the many who were deprived or impoverished. During a debate on a Dentists' Bill he said, 'My wish and intention will be to safeguard . . . not merely the interests of the medical profession, but of the poor' (Dáil Debates, 19 October 1927). In a discussion of the Education Estimates, he called for the wider introduction of school buses: 'I know of no more distressing sight than that of little children travelling on foot two or three miles to school on a wet morning. They face the day's work damp and shivering, and they are unable to learn' (Dáil Debates, 21 May 1930). More generally, he was vocal in support of government relief schemes to provide work, such as road building, in impoverished areas.

Then there were the interests of those trying to make a fair living in West Cork. Butchers, for instance, were worried that their livelihoods might be threatened by an Agricultural Produce (Fresh Meats) Bill. 'The traders', announced Jasper, 'thoroughly approve of the principle of the bill, but in detail they do not approve it. As it would have the effect of driving them out of business one can hardly expect them to approve of it' (Dáil Debates, 23 October 1929).

Still on the topic of food, there was the question of fisheries, always a great concern to Jasper. He attacked the government over a Sea Fisheries Bill, which neglected the interests of fishermen while concentrating on the sale of catches. 'This bill deals with the selling, not catching of fish. The minister would have been well advised to have commenced at the other end and said, "First catch your fish, and then sell it".' Nor was he happy about the vending proposals, which, he alleged, favoured retailers over wholesalers: 'A great many of us who live in the country get our supplies . . . from a wholesale fish buyer. I would much rather buy fish through one of the wholesale men in Bantry, Skibbereen, Clonakilty, or elsewhere along the sea coast than through any fish merchant in the city of Cork' (Dáil Debates, 3 December 1930).

Jasper likewise supported local builders and fuel merchants threatened by a Mines and Minerals Bill: 'It would be a very serious matter if to-morrow the country were to awake to the fact that the Dáil had passed a bill which would prevent the further cutting of turf, and the taking of sand and gravel' (Dáil Debates, 21 October 1931).

A worrying issue arose for poor agricultural areas when a bill was proposed making it an offence for anyone other than a qualified vet to deal with sick animals. Jasper protested strongly: 'There are remote parts of the country which could not possibly support a properly qualified veterinary surgeon . . . but there are people who are well versed in veterinary science, and who of necessity have received fees . . . By this bill that type of man is to be sent to the workhouse' (Dáil Debates, 19 February 1930).

Nationally, Jasper, as ever, worked to maintain the tricky balance between maintaining law and order and defending the liberty of the citizen. He soon found himself crossing swords with various of the younger Fianna Fáil deputies, who tended to be more concerned with personal freedom than public safety. One young man destined eventually to sit in the Dáil for over forty years emerged as a particular opponent of Jasper's. Martin Corry, a deputy for East Cork and a member since 1924 of Cork County Council (though also until rather more recently a very active member of the IRA), had sufficiently distinguished himself in the War of Independence and the Civil War as to warrant imprisonment, first by the British in Cork, Belfast and Wormwood Scrubs, and later by the Free State in Newbridge detention camp. When Martin Corry talked of security, he spoke with the authority of detailed experience – at least from one perspective.

To begin with, things went fairly smoothly. One of the first acts of the government after the September 1927 election was to introduce a bill repealing the stringent Public Safety Act passed after Kevin O'Higgins' assassination. This Jasper supported, along with Fianna Fáil and almost all other deputies. However, as disturbances and IRA-inspired law-breaking increased, the government took a tougher stand and there were complaints in the Dáil about the poor treatment IRA prisoners were receiving in Free State prisons. Martin Corry compared the new regime (which he had experienced) with the good times he had enjoyed when imprisoned by the British. Evidently, it was more important to him to shame the Free State than to denigrate the British. Or perhaps he was just telling it like it was.

> Speaking from my prison experience of a short time ago, I do not think the treatment which prisoners are receiving at present, as regards food, is as good as the treatment given to political prisoners or prisoners under sentence in, say, the years 1918 or 1919. I remember the happy time when we used to be presented every morning with a chop. (Dáil Debates, 16 November 1928)

Later in the same debate, he applauded the way Republicans treated their prisoners, remarking, 'I wish deputy Jasper Wolfe would tell a little of his experiences when in our hands'. Unhappily, the Ceann Comhairle ruled such a reminiscence out of order, so Jasper merely commented, 'A characteristic of my prison experiences was that I never grumbled'. He went on to recall that a large number of Republican prisoners, on a recent occasion, 'publicly thanked the prison authorities, through their advocates, of whom I was one, for the treatment they received in gaol'. When a Fianna Fáil deputy complained that prisons were overstaffed, Jasper intervened with a proposal: 'Would the minister be prepared to meet the deputy's concern by raising the number of prisoners?' To which the deputy retorted, 'And by putting Deputy Wolfe in'.

The alleged intimidation of juries was another matter for debate. In 1929 the government passed an act, which Jasper strongly supported, to provide for the protection of juries. Two years later, when a bill to close one or two loopholes was introduced, it – and indeed the whole notion of jury protection – was vehemently opposed by Fianna Fáil (as it had been with the previous act). Jasper not only supported the new bill but praised the effects of the earlier legislation. He described the situation as it had existed before the war, when juries had not been entitled to any protection. The result was that the accused were nearly always found innocent. 'When I left the bar in 1916', said Jasper, 'I was able to say that over a period of sixteen years in my area there had been no conviction against any professionally defended criminal . . . Friends of the dock, like myself, look back with great affection to the old days . . . I agree that there are more convictions now than there were in the good old days. That is bad for the felons. But I do not know of any case in which a person got an unfair trial since the present government came into existence' (Dáil Debates, 11 June 1931).

Through such debates, Jasper and Martin Corry sparred away in what became virtually an end-of-the-pier show. One journalist commented, 'even Mr Corry, that impenitent irreconcilable, who serves so often as a whetstone for Mr Wolfe's wit, would miss the Mutt and Jeff interludes that never fail to tickle the Dáil'. One clash came when the need for local authority officials to take the oath of allegiance was being debated. Martin Corry spoke at length of individuals in his constituency (whom he failed to name) who had, he alleged, 'lost their positions and their daily bread because of their refusal to subscribe to the declaration'. He demanded an enquiry. As the debate continued, Jasper joined in. He was attacked by Martin Corry for receiving a pension as an ex-Crown Solicitor. Jasper responded by wondering how many TDs present were sons of parents who had taken the oath, were receiving pensions and whose sound financial situation had helped their sons' careers. He went on to muse about a Cork family, not named, who had always defended the law, one of whom had been a highly respected head constable in the RIC. Such a man had taken the oath and now enjoyed, like himself, a pension. Would the minister, asked Jasper, enquire not only into the circumstances of families allegedly suffering from failure to take the oath, but also of those who had benefited from taking it? At this point, Martin Corry stood up. His father, as everyone well knew, had been a chief constable in the RIC.

'Deputy Wolfe has made an allusion here. I take it to my parent?' said Corry.

'Why Deputy Corry should take it to himself I do not know', replied the redoubtable Wolfe (Dáil Debates, 15 February 1928).

In this exchange, as in several others, Martin Corry suffered at the hands of the more experienced debater, but he was not always the one on the receiving end. When, for instance, Jasper was questioning whether the IRA was prepared to accept any responsibility for the various outrages committed in 1921 at the height of the Troubles, Martin Corry interjected that they certainly accepted one responsibility: 'The responsibility of letting Deputy Wolfe go – a very serious responsibility' (Dáil Debates, 20 March 1928).

Jasper balanced his support (admittedly qualified) for the government on major issues such as public safety and the preservation of the Free State with guerrilla campaigns against the conduct of the tax authorities and imposition of the Irish language. On tax, Jasper took the line, guaranteed to be popular with voters, that the revenue inspectors were too harsh. In debating a finance bill he told the minister: 'Over the last twelve to thirteen months I have known two prominent West Cork men, whom I have followed to their last resting place. They were there, according to medical opinion, as the result of unfounded and unjust tax assessments made upon them.' The rest of his lengthy contribution made a great impression: 'I desire', said one deputy, 'to congratulate Deputy Wolfe on his powerful and eloquent speech. The voters who sent him to the Dáil know their business' (Dáil Debates, 3 July 1929).

Two years later, the Minister for Finance was still smarting. This time Jasper began by attacking the attempted introduction of retrospective legislation aiming to tighten up revenue collection: 'I put it to the minister that he is creating a precedent which is not merely against the constitution, but is also against the best interests of the state.' He followed this up with another onslaught on what he now called 'the blackmailing methods' of income tax inspectors. The minister commented: 'This year Deputy Wolfe recorded no fatalities as a result of the burden of income tax' (Dáil Debates, 25 June 1931). A few months later, provoked yet again by Jasper, the minister responded irritably: 'The deputy speaks strongly because he wages relentless war against the department' (Dáil Debates, 5 November 1931).

Over the years one of Jasper's favourite ways of amusing himself, and sometimes others, had been by taking pot shots at what he saw as over-zealous efforts by officials to promote the Irish language. Now, in the Dáil, he was offered many opportunities to indulge in this pastime. When a bill was put forward to provide subsidised housing in Gaeltacht areas, Jasper enquired why various West Cork districts – Schull, Skibbereen, Bantry, Casteltown, Dunmanway and Clonakilty, all with serious housing problems – were omitted? The minister, said Jasper, alleged that it was because, from the census, it appeared they were not Irish speaking. He went on to say:

> But if it were known when they were taking the census that the speaking of Irish had anything to do with the provision of houses, I would guarantee that every man-jack of them would speak Irish, and I would say they speak Irish there as well as they speak it anywhere else. I would not say they speak it as well as the people of Cape Clear, which to anybody who wishes to study Irish is the one bright spot. (Dáil Debates, 27 November 1929)

Jasper's main gripe was attempts to make the passing of exams in Irish compulsory for entry into various professions, not least the law. The proposer of a Legal Practitioners (Qualifications) Bill had said, after much questioning about his reasons for requiring a qualification in speaking Irish, 'The reason is this: I want to get rid of the difficulty of persons who cannot instruct solicitors in English. In Cork, there are 39,271 persons speaking Irish.' Jasper was scornful.

> In forty years, on only two occasions have I met people who could not converse with me freely in English. Both of these persons have long since gone to their immortal reward. If there is a suggestion that there are 39,271

persons in the County of Cork who are unable to speak English, I never heard a more almighty lie. (Dáil Debates, 24 October 1928).

The Irish language was supported, as an article of faith, by Free Staters and Republicans alike. It was one of the few things on which they still agreed. To these men and women, it expressed the spirit of the nation. For anyone to attack Gaelic would have seemed close to treachery. Accordingly, Jasper was pretty much on his own in questioning some of the wilder plans to invigorate what was, to all appearances, a native tongue dangerously close to uttering its final words.

Some deputies took the obvious course, when responding to Jasper, of accusing him of being no true Irishman. Jasper did not trouble to expend much effort on trying to disprove such charges. Rather, he suggested that many of those who waved the banner of the Irish nation were themselves far from pure-blooded Gaels. Here he was on firm ground. After all, the leader of the Republicans in the Dáil was half Spanish and numerous other members, belonging as they did to a gregarious race, had generous infusions of non-Celtic blood.

So, when a Deputy Flinn was foolish enough to charge that all those in favour of making the qualification in Irish mandatory for legal practitioners were pro-Irish and anyone against it anti-Irish, Jasper galloped into the assault.

I am Irish both in Dublin and in Cork, and I object to Deputy Flinn suggesting to me that I am anti-Irish. Deputy Flinn came here as an Englishman. He was not above appealing to the British Government as an Englishman, and of relying on his services to the British Government in 1918. Later on the deputy took an oath of fealty to his King and his country. I have no doubt he took it, not as an empty formula, but as meaning what it does . . . Those who vote against this bill have more Irish blood beneath the nail of a small toe than Deputy Flinn has in his whole composition. (Dáil Debates, 8 March 1929)

There were, however, Nationalist deputies who found it hard to repress the politically incorrect feeling that maybe, just occasionally, Jasper might have a point. Nor could they resist being entertained by his way of mocking opponents. One journalist reported (*Irish Statesman*, 3 November 1928) that he had been in the Dáil when the proposal to 'Gaelicise the legal profession provided Mr Wolfe with an opportunity of making one of his favourite horses cut a whole series of new capers . . . I saw stern, unbending Gaels who were hard put to it to wear an air of becoming gravity as he sprayed with irony the Gaeltacht, which is to them what Mecca is to devout Muslims'.

As an Independent, Jasper had little opportunity to make – as opposed to criticise or influence – policy. One chance, however, did appear and he took it. Legal matters were generally seen as non-political, and Jasper was amongst the leading lawyers in the Dáil. While the system of justice set up by the Free

State was, mostly, working remarkably well, there were a few procedures and rules which clearly needed reform. Jasper's main criticism concerned the way appeals from local circuit courts were handled. Under the British system, high court judges had travelled on circuit to deal with appeals, whereas now, if aggrieved parties wished to challenge a verdict, they had to go to Dublin to have their cases heard. This often resulted in increased expense for litigants, delays and at times miscarriages of justice, since testimony was mainly reviewed on the basis of evidence provided by stenographers' records of the original hearings. Jasper wished to have the old system of high court judges travelling on circuit to be restored. He proposed that a joint committee of the Dáil and Senate report on amendments to the 1924 Courts of Justice Act. During the debates which accompanied this motion, Jasper learned what it was like to be pot-shot at rather than be a pot-shooter. After a particularly lengthy speech going into various technical legal details, Jasper was challenged on one of his points, to which he replied, 'I did not say that. I am sure the Deputy was unable to follow what I said.' Upon which another another deputy commented, 'Nobody could' (Dáil Debates, 4 July 1929).

Obscurities notwithstanding, the Minister for Justice duly established the proposed arrangements and Jasper was appointed a leading member of the committee. Its report, including a recommendation to restore the high court circuits, was accepted and legislation was promised. Bit by bit, and in due course, this pledge was kept, although it was another ten years before the high court circuits were actually restored, by which time de Valera and Fianna Fáil had been in power for some time. The legislation initiated by Jasper could be seen as a contribution, in its modest way, to a new-found continuity, even occasional bi-partisanship, in Irish politics.

Every now and then Jasper let fly on topics which he felt called for rigorous comment. On a piece of failed land legislation he commented, 'It was a bill that was conceived in ignorance, born in dishonesty, and died at the hands of the Minister for Agriculture of exposure' (Dáil Debates, 4 July 1929). On another occasion he enquired, 'Are we to take it that it is the settled policy of the government to defy the Supreme Court in cases in which they are parties?' (Dáil Debates, 14 March 1929).

In his various outings in the Dáil debating chamber, Jasper remained remarkably sure-footed. In part, at least, this was because he seldom, if ever, lost contact with his bedrock principles. He knew where he stood and he made sure that his fellow deputies knew too. First, he believed that religious tolerance was a cardinal virtue. He also believed, as he always had done, that this was widely practised in the public life of southern Ireland. So, for instance, in a debate intended to prevent possible corruption and bigotry in local authorities, he intervened. (He diplomatically never referred to Irish religious life, for he was as aware as anyone that both the Church of Ireland in its heyday, and now the Catholic Church, were very ready to be ruthless in imposing their own orthodoxies.) In his speech Jasper said:

I was a member of various public bodies for over thirty years. When I ceased to be a member of them I ceased to be a member of them because I became an official of at least ten different public bodies. And I assert that there could be no greater tribute to the toleration and freedom from bigotry that exists in this state than that I should have been appointed by these boards as their solicitor. (Dáil Debates, 8 June 1928)

This intervention earned Jasper praise in the *Catholic Times* (15 June 1928). Under the heading, 'A Southern Tribute', his 'tribute to the absence of bigotry amongst Irish Catholics' was quoted at length.

Another guiding principle for Jasper was his commitment, as an Irishman, to a free Ireland. He was not a Nationalist as Republicans understood it, but he had always stood for Home Rule, albeit within the community of nations allied within the British Empire – or Commonwealth, as it was becoming known. As usual, he was not reluctant to inform the Dáil of his beliefs, particularly once Fianna Fáil eventually succeeded in forming a government. In an early debate following de Valera becoming president of the Executive Council, Jasper underlined the fact that he was no Unionist but a stalwart, unwavering veteran of Nationalism. 'I have', he said, 'never altered my beliefs. They are the same now as when I was twenty years of age' (Dáil Debates, 29 April 1932).

38

'I REMAIN, AS FROM THE BEGINNING, A SUPPORTER OF THE IRISH TREATY'

Jasper Wolfe, 1932.

The sixth Dáil eventually approached the end of its life and an election was duly called, to take place on 16 February 1932. The Wolfe election machine, by now well travelled and just about roadworthy, chugged into action. Dorothy, recently qualified as a barrister but evidently not overworked, arrived from London to take up her post as the Wolfe election organiser. Willie Wood and his daughter took to the public house circuit. Other members of the family went their canvassing way.

Jasper's message to the electorate lacked some of the variety of his previous appeals. There were few critical local issues. The major question facing the electorate, in West Cork as in the rest of Ireland, was whether it wanted to hold on to the safe, if somewhat governessy, hand of Cumann na nGaedheal or if it wanted to risk voting for

Fianna Fáil, as yet untested in government and with Republican aspirations. Jasper was in absolutely no doubt where he stood. In his Address to the Electors he warned of the fearful cataclysms that would erupt if the people deserted Cosgrave and his followers:

I remain, as from the beginning, a supporter of the Irish Treaty. That international compact is not only the corner-stone of the Free State, but the guarantee of every liberty we possess. Destroy it and no longer will our Irish Parliament function . . . Nothing but ghastly confusion and irreparable injury to the economic and social structure of our country could result from any violation of the Treaty, and therefore I shall do all in my power to preserve it from overthrow.

Armed with this message, Jasper took to the now familiar routine of meetings across West Cork. He was often driven to the various venues by Dorothy, who also, on occasion, gave supporting speeches. In the traditional opening gathering in Skibbereen Town Hall, Miss Dorothy Wolfe, BL, proposed the vote of thanks to the chairman. A short while later, after a meeting in Bantry, she was thought sufficiently prominent by at least one member of the audience to receive the following letter:

Dear Miss Wolfe,
    Please allow the liberty I take in writing you.
    At the impulse of the moment I cannot help doing so. I happened to be among the audience tonight in the courthouse, and I congratulate you sincerely on the fluent and lady-like manner in which you addressed your crowd. If without any inconvenience to yourself, you could see your way to recommend a boy of mine, who have already sent in his application for a post at the coming election I would be very grateful. I don't want to trouble Mr Wolfe as I can understand what a strain he has on just now.
    Thanking you in anticipation,
I remain,
Yours sincerely,
Mrs Costigan

The audiences at Jasper's meetings also seem to have been mostly supportive, nor do any of these events seem to have suffered from the sometimes rather hostile attentions that some members of the IRA paid, in a number of other constituencies, to opponents of Fianna Fáil. February in West Cork, when the campaign took place, may have discouraged any outrageously flamboyant misdemeanours.

    Came the election. Nationally, Fianna Fáil overtook Cumann na nGaedheal to become the largest party. However, it failed to secure an overall majority and could only form a government in coalition with Labour. It had

DAIL ELECTION, 16th FEBRUARY, 1932.

Your Vote and influence are respectfully requested in favour of the

INDEPENDENT CANDIDATE, J. TRAVERS WOLFE.

Your Number on Register is shewn on Envelope

Your place for Voting is **Town Hall, Bandon.**

☞ *Vote for the last name appearing on the Ballot Paper, as follows—*

1	**WOLFE**
	(JASPER TRAVERS WOLFE),
	Norton, Skibbereen, Co. Cork, Solicitor.

Printed and Published for the Candidate, J. Travers Wolfe, by the "Southern Star," Ltd., Skibbereen.

79 TDs on its side of the chamber, compared with 74 for Cumann na nGaedheal and its allies – hardly a landslide.

In West Cork the electorate, true to its tradition of independent thinking, swung against the national trend. Fianna Fáil candidates filled three of the last four places and secured only one seat, the fifth. Last of all was a vet, Eugene McCarthy, who in a few years time was to reappear in Jasper's life. (Fianna Fáil was probably damaged by a quarrel with its previous TD, Thomas Mullins, who had temporarily become an 'Independent Republican' and did not seek re-election.) Also a loser was Timothy Sheehy, who, failing to get re-elected, finally disappeared from the political scene.

Of the more successful candidates, Jasper slipped to second on first preferences and third in the final count, ceding his place at head of the poll to the Labour candidate T. J. Murphy. Cumann na nGaedheal, as in the previous election of September 1927, secured one seat but succeeded in moving up from fifth to second place in the final count. On first preferences, candidates supporting the Free State secured a fairly narrow majority over those in favour of Republicanism.

Jasper, and many others, had prophesied apocalypse if Fianna Fáil won sufficient seats to form a government. This day had now arrived. As Jasper looked out of his train window on his way to the opening of the new Dáil, it was not difficult to imagine the horsemen of Disease and Famine again threatening the land. In fact, as it turned out, it would be several decades before they were finally driven away. However, of that even more familar pair, Conflict and Death, there were few signs.

There were, nevertheless, reasons for fear. Domestically, both the main parties still included extremists. Internationally, authoritarian regimes were taking power in one country after another. Indeed, as Fianna Fáil formed its first government in Ireland, in Germany the National Socialists, following a similarly modest election success, were preparing to use their new authority to found a one-party state. In the 1930s, the wind was blowing against democracy. Why should Ireland be sheltered?

Deputies entering the new Dáil were extremely apprehensive. As when Fianna Fáil took the oath of allegiance in the summer of 1927, each main party feared that the other side might stage a putsch. Many members were armed, or 'carrying'. De Valera looked particularly anxious. It was later rumoured that he was worried mainly because his son, not known for his markmanship, was among those who had been handed a revolver. However, it turned out that everyone was on their best party behaviour. All the rules were observed. It soon became apparent that southern Ireland, at yet another turning point in its modern history, was now, far more decisively than anyone had foreseen, about to follow the road to peace. This was partly because de Valera and Cosgrave had managed to edge their ultras away from the control room of politics. Much as the wild men might want to seize power illegally, they lacked the necessary clout. Nor was the government about to fall apart through inexperience. The Fianna Fáil deputies (who in 1927, to quote the words of a later leader of Fianna Fáil, Seán Lemass, were 'a pretty raw lot') had learned, at the hands of Jasper and others, some of the ways of parliamentary democracy. Like many revolutionaries before them, they had come to see that membership of the legislators' club offered a preferable way of life to being chased from hedgerow to hedgerow, and quite possibly ending up shot or in gaol.

That Fianna Fáil proved capable of governing, remained true to democracy and established a remarkably robust and long-lasting regime was ultimately due to the genius of its political programme. This resonated with historic, romantic Republicanism and was rooted in the original name, the rallying cry and motto of political Republicanism, 'Sinn Féin' – 'Ourselves' or 'Ourselves Alone'. (Unfortunately de Valera and his followers could not actually use this term, since it had been left with the diehards when Fianna Fáil and Sinn Féin split.) The new government proposed populist policies of economic protectionism and political separation from Great Britain and the Commonwealth. Just as in the previous century there had been across the Irish Channel a Little England party, so now, in what was no longer John Bull's Other Island, an Irish political movement – Fianna Fáil – had in effect become a Little Ireland party.

The main opposition in the Dáil proved ineffective in its attacks on the government. Cumann na nGaedheal, having built the foundations of a democratic state and honourably handed over power following electoral defeat, was bereft of ideas and terminally exhausted. It was now that Jasper, unwearied by years of office and fired up with indignation, emerged as one of the more effective voices amongst the government's critics. In Cork at least he was considered to be 'The Man' in the Dáil. With an edge of anger that was unusual for him, indeed uncharacteristic, Jasper went into the attack – gloves off. His main targets were the government's two keynote policies.

During the election, Fianna Fáil had proposed the suspension of various payments being made to the British government that had been formally agreed a decade earlier by the Irish and British governments. The most significant of these were the annuities, or mortgage repayments, on lands purchased by tenant farmers from their original owners, and paid for with money lent by the British government. This policy, which the new ministers immediately set about implementing, delivered, from their point of view, a highly desirable double whammy. It was popular with farmers, who were led by many members of Sinn Féin to believe that their payments would cease altogether (in fact they did not, although they were reduced), and it was popular with strong Republicans, who believed that the British had taken the land by conquest and so it was never the landlords' to sell in the first place. In any case, the sight of the Irish government repudiating a dependent financial relationship with the imperial power gave them great satisfaction.

Jasper viewed the situation differently. He charged that, in suspending the payment of annuities, the government was 'breaking its bond with the government of another country'. This he saw as not only perfidious and illegal but also foolish, for, as he pointed out, the British would retaliate with economic sanctions so as to ensure that they got their money anyway – as indeed they did. The result, combined with various other protectionist measures, was to push up prices. By November 1932, the economic effects of government policies were already becoming evident, and Jasper was not slow to comment. 'What', he demanded, 'is the position our people have been brought to in the last eight months? I will not talk of poverty. We have had to face poverty before. But today it is not poverty they are faced with. They are today faced with absolute destitution' (Dáil Debates, 16 November 1932).

The other major policy of the government's that Jasper laid into (Dáil Debates, 29 April 1932) was the removal of the oath of allegiance. Here he was in less sombre mood, not least because it had long been clear that, if any Republican party ever got into power, removing the oath would top their list of must dos. In his major speech on the subject Jasper, in the words of an *Irish Press* reporter, 'presented the House with a Cork accent, Cork forcefulness, and that sardonic Cork humour which is famous'. Jasper attacked the bill from every possible angle, and not least because 'we are condemned, as a result of this debate, to be held up by England as the country of the violated treaty'. Not content with this sally, he then proceeded to attack the president himself for hypocrisy. Back in 1922, when the Dáil was debating the Treaty with the United Kingdom to set up the Irish Free State, de Valera had produced his own alternative version, famously known as 'Document No. 2'. However, there had been earlier drafts of this that had been widely leaked. These included a wording of the oath that did not feature in the final version, but which evidently de Valera, at that point, had been prepared to accept. Jasper had got hold of a copy of this wording of the oath, which in any case was hardly a secret (the *Irish Press* journalist covering the 1932 debate for removal of the oath commented that 'Mr de Valera is said to have dictated it to the plenipotentiaries'). He reached the climax of his speech thus: 'The President is prepared to swear this: "I, Eamon De Valera, do hereby swear faithful allegiance to the constitution of Ireland and to the principle of association of Ireland with the British Commonwealth of Nations and recognise His Britannic Majesty as head of the Associated States".' At this, de Valera rose to speak.

> The President: 'Where did the Deputy get that?'
>
> Mr Wolfe: 'Does the President suggest that I am not quoting Document No. 2 correctly?'
>
> The President: 'Where did the Deputy get it?'
>
> Mr Wolfe: 'I am taking it from Document No. 2.'
>
> The President: 'It was not in Document No. 2.'
>
> Mr Wolfe: 'Old Document No. 2. The President has so far forgotten Document No. 2 that he does not recognise the oath.'
>
> The President: 'The Deputy has no idea what he is talking about.'
>
> Mr Hogan: 'Does the President not recognise it?'
>
> The President: ' I do. I have heard it many times from the other side.'
>
> Mr FitzGerald: 'And dictated it.'
>
> Mr Wolfe: 'We have got the President's admission that this is a document he recognises . . . Does he now propose to adhere to his former declaration that he was willing to sign and subscribe to Document No. 2?'
>
> The President: 'It would require more time than we have at our disposal to discuss that matter.'

With that, the debate moved on. Both wily gentlemen, de Valera and Jasper, could feel they had preserved their honour. Jasper was not proved wrong, while Dev did not admit to being wrong. The bill to remove the oath was eventually passed in May 1933. As for Jasper and de Valera, they developed a continuing mutual, if wary, respect. When the president secured the passage of a new constitution in 1937, one which only just fell short of declaring a Republic, he presented Jasper with a signed copy. While this was, no doubt, a gesture of courtesy to an old opponent, it was quite possibly also an act of typical de Valera slyness, subtly reminding Jasper who was eventually coming out on the winning side. In the end it was the Republicans, not the Home Rulers, who were looking like the victors in the long, long battle for the nationalist soul of Ireland.

Many years later de Valera had not forgotten Jasper. In 1965, long after Jasper had died, his nephew, Brian Wood Wolfe, Willie Wood Wolfe's first child, who had become one of Britain's leading aeronautical engineers, received an honorary doctorate of science from the National University of Ireland. Conferring the degree in Dublin as chancellor of the university was de Valera. After the ceremony, de Valera and Brian Wolfe had a chat.

'Wolfe?' said de Valera. 'You wouldn't be related to Jasper Wolfe?'

'He was my uncle.'

'Well now, that man gave me an awful lot of trouble.'[1]

PART FIVE

'SOMEWHAT OF AN INSTITUTION IN COUNTY CORK' 1933–1941

39

'UPSETTING ALL SORTS OF APPLE-CARTS'

When Jasper returned to Skibbereen for the Christmas of 1932, he could well have been distracted from his political troubles by all that was going on at Norton. For the last time, as it turned out, all his children were home for Christmas. Dorothy and Ray were in particularly good form, both engaged and both planning to be married within six months. Each, despite all that was going on over the holiday, wrote almost daily and at length to their beloveds, the one in West Wales, the other in London. Since their letters survive, we have a detailed picture of the goings-on over the next few weeks.

People came and went endlessly. There were, Ray wrote, 'hordes of chattering female relations'; men in dark suits, frequently emitting aromas of whiskey, came to discuss serious matters with Jasper; and other lesser clients and constituents of Jasper's arrived bearing gifts, part gratitude, part down payment for future favours. Amongst these offerings was livestock. Ray wrote, 'We've had at least half a dozen turkeys given us – we've eaten two, sent several away, and there are still two prancing about in the yard. The unfortunate part about it is that mother can't remember who they all came from and she's afraid of thanking the wrong people.'

But Jasper remained depressed. The New Year message that he traditionally addressed to the electorate of West Cork was not one of good cheer. He said:

> I would dearly like to write in an optimistic spirit, full of hope for the future, but to do so under present circumstances would be nothing short of rank hypocrisy. Our country is darkened by an overhanging cloud of political insanity which has brought it to the brink of financial ruin, and has already lost us and will lose for a generation yet to come markets gained by thrift and industry of many generations.

On Monday 2 January de Valera announced a general election. With his assault on the oath and his suspension of payment to the British government of the annuities, he had retained, and perhaps even strengthened, his party's hold on its core constituency of Republicans and small farmers. Furthermore, he had governed democratically for nearly a year, so those voters who had feared that Fianna Fáil would set up an authoritarian Republican regime were reassured.

On the other hand, the government's opponents were in disarray. Not only had Cosgrave proved to be an anaemic opposition leader, but his party was fragmenting. An 'Army Comrades Association' was set up, effectively to defend the achievements of the Free State. Within a few months this was to morph into the 'Blueshirts', a militaristic set-up inspired by the British fascist Black Shirts of Oswald Mosley. A new, or newish, party also put in what was to be a brief appearance. The National Farmers' and Ratepayers' League (or National Centre Party) was essentially a broader-based version of the old Farmers' Party (in West Cork the same candidate stood for the Farmers' Party in 1932 and the Centre Party in 1933). Its main aim was to defend the interests of the professional and rural middle classes. While its policies differed little from those of Cumann na nGaedheal, it sought, in effect, to be a vigorous up-dated Home Rule party (one of its leaders was the charismatic young James Dillon, son of the last leader of the old Irish Parliamentary Party).

Polling was to take place in just over three weeks time. In West Cork, as elsewhere, Fianna Fáil's opponents were caught unprepared. Not for the first time, de Valera had succeeded in wrong-footing his adversaries. As Ray put it, 'the election is upsetting all sorts of apple-carts'.

From the start, the Wolfe electoral caravan had a bumpy ride. Dorothy and Ray did their best. Ray, who was not a political creature, nevertheless saw it as 'her solemn duty to stay at home to address envelopes and things for Dad'. A rather more demanding task also fell to her. Since Jasper did not drive, he had to be chauffeured everywhere. It was all hands to the wheel, not least Ray's. However, she had problems. The first, all too often, was actually getting the car started. The Wolfes now owned a splendid beige Armstrong Siddeley saloon, successor to the Maxwell that was taken by the Irregulars in 1922. Unfortunately, particularly in wet or cold weather, it could be very reluctant to start. Ray wrote: 'Re car. I am developing an extra specially colossal muscle in my right shoulder. The battery is on strike, and I spent half my day turning the old handle round.' When the vehicle was in its worst mood, only Cadogan could be sure of getting it moving. One evening, Cadogan failed to show up. 'I was left paddling about the yard in the rain, trying to start the brute. I couldn't even get her over once. So I tried the old game of draining the water out and filling her up with hot, a proceeding which takes time and is very splashy. In the meantime the maid had a happy thought of a man who was near, and what with the hot water and all we started it between us.'

Ray also worried about the driving conditions. For a start, there were the wandering animals, not least cattle: 'We met several and crawled most carefully past them while they weren't looking. Dorothy remarked that I was positively Hindu in my respect for cows.' Then there was the condition of the roads themselves, almost invariaby 'slippery and partly frozen'. Nor was that all: 'I've got to take the car out to a meeting on Thursday along a road which I'm told

is covered with sharp stones. No doubt I'll puncture all the tyres at once.'
Longer expeditions were a particular challenge:

> On Friday we start at the crack of dawn for Castletown – Berehaven, the
> uttermost outpost of Dad's colossal constituency, miles and miles away
> (about 80, I think), along the world's worst, steepest, and narrowest coast
> roads, which lie among superb scenery, which I've never seen. It's always
> been raining, or I've been driving or both . . . Think of me sitting in the car,
> in the cold, in the dark, by the roadside, while Dad chases votes and fills
> up all the country people with whiskey and stuff, and then they promise
> they'll vote for him, and when the election comes they go and vote for the
> Farmers' Union man or some other boob. Who would be a politician, or
> worse still a politician's female relative?

Dorothy made her now familiar contributions. Apart from organising things,
she, like Ray, did her fair share of driving, which brought her frustrations too:
'I had a long hunt in Bandon for petrol, the Cork garage having nothing but
commercial.' On another occasion she was late picking up Jasper: 'I found him
standing on the steps with a watch, in his usual fever of apprehension.' Most
of her time and effort, however, were devoted to meetings. She had now
graduated to having a speaking circuit of her own.

> I spoke in Ballydehob, Dunbeacon, Durrus, and Caheragh [a notoriously
> Sinn Féin village], and everywhere there was enthusiasm and eagerness to
> be told the facts . . . It was an immense satisfaction to me to reply to cries
> of 'Up de Valera' at the beginning of one of my speeches and gradually to
> hear them lessen and cease. Oddly enough my worst effort was made to the
> Durrus audience who interrupted only to cry, 'Up Wolfe', and who
> obviously would have stood for hours in the grey and driving mist to listen
> to what I had to say.

In the first days of the campaign Jasper went, as usual, to meetings across the
constituency, but his attention was really concentrated on Nomination Day,
Wednesday 11 January 1933. In many constituencies, including West Cork, it
was not yet at all clear who would stand for which parties. In particular, with
the political battle getting ever hotter, there seemed to be less and less room
for Independents. Furthermore, quality candidates were in demand.
Accordingly, it seemed likely that pro-Free State parties, in particular Cumann
na nGaedheal and the new Centre Party, might try to sign Jasper up (several
previously Independent deputies had already joined the Centre Party), or,
failing that, squeeze him out. If he could not be recruited and so bring his votes
with him, it were better he were removed from the scene, leaving his mainly
Free State support up for grabs.

The first few days of the campaign duly brought developments. Jasper
received a tentative approach from Cumann na nGaedheal, which led to brief

but inconclusive negotiations. Towards the end of the week he heard from the Centre Party. 'Extraordinary new development', reported Dorothy. 'Dad has just come in. When he went to the office this morning he was handed a letter which had arrived *two days ago* inviting him to stand for the Farmers (i.e. Centre Party) – their convention to-morrow.' But Jasper was not showing his usual enthusiasm for the political game. 'Dad', wrote Dorothy, 'is really rather bored and cross with the whole thing'. He did not respond to the Centre Party: 'Dad doesn't appear to have much real regret about the lost opportunity. And if he had really wanted to stand for them he could have communicated with them tonight.' Jasper was beginning to show signs of being ready to give up the fight. He told Dorothy that, if a certain Robert Kelly of Bantry was a candidate for Cumann na nGaedheal, 'I won't stand at all'.

Through the week there had been ripples suggesting local Cumann na nGaedheal scheming. On Sunday word surfaced of what had been going on. 'Political events', wrote Dorothy, 'have taken a completely new turn today. It is now strongly rumoured that J. M. Burke is likely to be adopted as a C. na G. candidate.' This was none other than Jasper's old schoolfellow, Jim Burke. He could call on impressive support. He edited the *Southern Star*, was, as Dorothy put it, 'highly esteemed by the Catholic Church' and, as she also stated, unusually delicately for her, he was 'very widely connected in the local district'. The fact was, the Burke family, in true West Cork style, was a power in the land. It escaped nobody's attention that, if Jim Burke were to become a TD, his family would become even more influential. Jasper instantly decided that, if the rumour proved true, he would not stand. On simple electoral arithmetic alone, Dorothy agreed with him. He would, she believed, inevitably lose 'hundreds of Skib. votes, which are a solid and necessary nucleus of his poll'. Later, she had second thoughts, but in fact she was as much in the dark as everyone else about the likely outcome.

Jim Burke.

Jasper took the whole situation very calmly. He spent the Sunday afternoon, as Dorothy wrote, 'reading an Edgar Wallace, having completed his weekly puzzle (hidden girls' names!) in the paper'. Dorothy herself was a good deal less philosophical. She suspected dirty tricks: 'there must be a movement behind it all – I don't know whence – to get Dad out. It is sickening.' A few days later she had decided who to blame: 'there has apparently been some very dirty work on the part of the Burkes'.

From Monday until nominations in Cork on Wednesday, nobody was quite sure what was going to happen. Jasper consulted with his supporters and others. There was general agreement that, if he stood against Jim Burke, Fianna Fáil would probably benefit and that was a risk Jasper was not prepared to take. Although posters were already up, he cancelled a big meeting that was to be held on the Monday evening at Skibbereen Town Hall.

Jim Burke, who had played little or no part in the move to get him nominated, was in London. All his life he had been involved in local politics, and as a younger man he had stood as a Nationalist Party candidate for the House of Commons. He unquestionably still aspired to higher things than the Skibbereen District Council or the Cork County Council. However, he was only just recovering from a very serious illness. As soon as his candidacy was spoken of, people started saying he would never survive the demands of being a TD. And they were proved right. He must have been torn every which way: ambition, family loyalty and duty to his party, against self-preservation. By Monday, Jasper heard a rumour that Jim Burke had sent a telegram turning down the chance of nomination.

If Jim Burke was not going to stand, then Jasper would. On the Wednesday morning, driven by Dorothy, he travelled to the Cork courthouse, where he waited, £100 in hand as deposit for the nomination. Entries had to be in by one o'clock. By 11.45 there was no sign of the Burkes. Dorothy, jotting a letter in pencil, was in quite a state. As well as suffering from the political tension, she had had an accident on the way from Skibbereen: 'My faith in magpies is stronger than ever. After seeing one this morning I ran over a small dog and I don't think it will recover.' Just after writing this, she added, 'Jim and Dr Burke [brothers] have just passed in . . . Later. 2 men in great excitement just passed me and said, "Jasper is not nominated". I suppose it's true.'

Jasper's withdrawal was, as Dorothy described it, 'a first class political sensation', engendering headlines in papers, etc. The man himself, his daughter noted with some surprise, was 'quite cheerful about it'. In reply to all the speculation about his failure to stand, Jasper explained his position in an interview with the press:

He stated that owing to troubles which had arisen in his division it was conveyed to him that his candidature might lead to strife between supporters of the Treaty. On that possibility he had reluctantly come to the conclusion to retire'. (*Cork Examiner*, 14 January 1933)

As in the previous election, West Cork went against the national tide. In the Free State overall, de Valera, able to count on the support of Labour, secured a comfortable majority. In West Cork, however, while the Fianna Fáil candidates just held on to their one seat, their candidates had a reduced share of the poll and occupied the last four places. By contrast, Jim Burke emerged a convincing winner on both first and final counts. Cumann na nGaedheal also, for the first time since 1923, won two seats and greatly increased their share of the votes cast. What was more, the Centre Party candidate came a convincing second, so the Treatyite forces had much to be pleased about. It looked as if all the scheming, and possible skulduggery, had paid off.

As for Jasper, he retired with honour, his departure much regretted by many constituents. While there were good political reasons for him to leave the field, it may also be that he was one of those rare politicians who could recognise when his time was up. A new Republican era was coming in Irish politics, and Jasper would not have been as easy in that world as he had been in the Free State. He also probably did not miss having to deal with the two thousand letters from constituents, some requiring considerable work that, as he told one meeting, he had to deal with every year. In any case, he was now over sixty and at last, after nearly twenty years of public life, perhaps ready for a little less excitement.

40

WEDDING ROWS

Jasper could now hope, quite reasonably, to enjoy a congenial and more or less untroubled way of life. Skibbereen itself was settling back into familiar traditional routines. Indeed, if some emigrant relation of Jasper had turned up having been completely out of touch for twenty years, (say a lumberjack in the forests of western Canada), he would, on the surface, have found that remarkably little had changed.

In County Cork generally, he would, it is true, immediately have noticed that a generous measure of Home Rule had evidently been achieved. The postage stamps were now marked 'Eire' and no longer showed the king's head. The postboxes were green. He would also soon have learned that not only did southern Ireland have its own assembly, but that only a vestigial relationship remained with the Crown of the United Kingdom. Likewise, he would have discovered that Northern Ireland had been partitioned from the new Free State – and that would hardly have come as a surprise, given the the militant Ulster loyalism with which he would have been familiar before his departure.

In Skibbereen itself, the returning native would have seen hardly any signs of the traumas that the town had endured during his absence. Little revealed that the inhabitants, for nearly a decade, had suffered, in rapid succession, a European war, a war of national liberation and a civil war. Up and down the town he would have seen faces and shop-fronts familiar to him. As for his relatives, they were nearly all carrying on much as before. Robert Vickery, Wolfe Bros., Wood Wolfe, the Wolfes at the Corner House, the Wolfes at Ilen House and Grove House and J. Travers Wolfe all were still busy trading, socialising and worshipping. The only sign of any real violence was the ruin of the Catholic McCarthy residence at Glencurragh. The public life of the town, too, was much as might have been expected. The men who had been prominent in 1913 were even more prominent now. Willie Wood Wolfe remained a leading member of the Urban District Council, Jim Burke was editor of the *Southern Star* (now incorporating the *Eagle*), as well as a deputy of the Dáil. And Jasper Wolfe, still the leading solicitor in town, had just ceased to be a TD, as had Timothy Sheehy.

So Jasper began to settle down once more in his familiar surroundings. He worked hard at his practice, which had suffered rather while he was busy in

Dublin. At Norton, occasional late evening card parties, which he had started some years previously, now became regular occasions. Friends such as Eddie Swanton would arrive at the front, while Willie Wood, to avoid Minnie, would slide in at the back. From his room off the hallway, Jasper had a bell fitted into the floor, so that he only had to put his foot down for refreshments to arrive from the kitchen. Nor was there any shortage of whiskey or cigarettes. The deal in the Travers Wolfe marriage was that Minnie looked after domestic affairs, devoting her formidable energies to managing the children and the large household. As for Jasper, he dealt with public life, bringing in the money, securing status and reputation. This arrangement suited both very well.

Unfortunately, from time to time the public intruded on the domestic, and vice versa. Up to the present, Minnie had been the main sufferer from the unruliness of events. During the Troubles, the outside world had not only disrupted, but had for several years literally invaded and displaced her household. Now, for the first time, Jasper too was to find the marital division of labour failing to hold firm. Family matters threatened to trespass seriously on his time and thoughts. He was to cope rather less well than Minnie had with the demands of shared responsibilities.

Just as Jasper was hoping for some peace, the marriage plans of his daughters began to loom threateningly. Dorothy fancied a wedding at Easter, Ray wanted hers just three months later in July. The preparations inevitably provoked turmoil. And, in due course, Travers too succeeded in raising the temperature.

Dorothy had become engaged to Lynn Ungoed-Thomas, who in almost every way was, from both Jasper's and Minnie's point of view, ideal. A good-looking, Oxford-educated Welshman, son of a radical Baptist minister and beginning to make his way as a barrister in London, he ticked all the right boxes. On a visit to London, he had been vetted by Jasper, who approved: 'I liked that boy.' And when he came to Skibbereen, although he did not, as Ray suggested, ingratiate himself with Minnie by picking gooseberries, he soon charmed her. 'Mother', reported Dorothy, 'likes your looks and is glad you talk a lot having suffered recently from some strong and silent Saxons'.

Despite Lynn's high approval rating, the proposed marriage caused some difficulties. Minnie and Dorothy had never got on well and they found much to quarrel over when it came to wedding plans. Dorothy to Lynn:

> Another wedding argument, but not so bad because Ray was there to referee. I also find that the last scene has had a rather alarming hardening effect on me. I think the fundamental cause is a streak of cruelty in Mother's nature which one can see sometimes in her dealings with Murty [Irish terrier] to whom she is devoted.

Minnie's mood was not improved by often being in pain, something that Dorothy did realise and for which, in her more generous moments, she was prepared to make a few allowances: 'The poor dear has frightful sciatica and naturally feels rather unamiable.'

Jasper, too, had worries. While Minnie and Dorothy might quarrel over the details, they were as one in desiring a big, big wedding. And a big wedding there would certainly have to be. Jasper himself was a leading citizen, while Dorothy also, thanks to her electoral activities, had become quite well known. All this was going to cost a lot, and Jasper, after his years supporting himself as an Independent TD, was temporarily low on funds. Then there was the question of wedding gifts. The custom was for both friends and acquaintances of the bride's parents to give presents. Not only were these put on display in the bridal home, but lists of who had given what were published in the local press. In return for gifts given, professional and business contacts were liable to expect favours. A rather nervous Jasper could see himself becoming indebted in a number of ways.

Easter, and the day of wedding number one, approached. People came and went, including some who meant a great deal to Dorothy, the bride-to-be – such as Jasper's great friend, Father McCarthy, who had recently moved as parish priest to Aughadown. Dorothy had a great respect for Father McCarthy and he, in turn, had a soft spot for her. Dorothy wrote how:

> Father McCarthy turned up for tea, so the day ended well. I am commanded by him to buy myself a wedding present and send the bill to him, but if it's less than £5 he will not pay it! We have arranged that you are to come with me to see him on Easter Monday. That man is wasted as a country priest. Or indeed any priest.

Also putting in an appearance was Frank O'Meara, now an officer in the British army, with whom Dorothy had been in love ten years ago. That affair had, however, been ended. Frank was a strong Catholic and neither he nor Dorothy had been prepared to compromise over religion. A few months earlier, and with some trepidation, Dorothy had told Frank of her engagement. He took the news with equanimity:

> He was slightly amused, and amazed at my certainty. He hoped that I should still be 'allowed' (!) to go out with him on his next leave in London . . . I have offered to find him a wife, but it isn't easy as the sort of girl who could stand the army is the sort of girl he could not stand. He told me that he has made a list of the six qualities he demands in his wife and locked it up in his attaché case for reference and support in case he feels in danger of losing his head! He wouldn't tell me what the qualities were – though I think he might have been persuaded if Ray and Mother had not come marching in at the wrong moment.

As things turned out, everything worked out well for Frank. He met his perfect match when posted to India, a young Catholic lady of good family who had come out from England on what were known among the young officers as 'fishing trips'. They married, had children and lived happily ever after, even though Frank was captured and imprisoned by the Japanese during the Second World War. Frank and Dorothy remained close friends all their lives, while Lynn even became a godfather to one of Frank's children (how the Catholic Church agreed to this I do not know – Lynn was not merely a lapsed Nonconformist, but an agnostic).

In due course, Lynn, together with various young Welshmen and lawyers, arrived for the wedding, one in an open touring car. They were all put up in a local hotel at Jasper's expense. A cousin of Lynn's who was to be bridesmaid stayed at Norton. On the eve of the wedding, she had a bad night's sleep because her room was over Jasper's study and he was celebrating, or consoling himself, with an all-night card and drink party, which got rowdier as the hours passed.

The nuptials were celebrated in satisfactory style. A Methodist eminence, once a minister on the Skibbereen circuit, was imported from Belfast to perform the ceremony ('Sheer swank', commented Ray). The service, held at midday, was only slightly hindered by a pig market which was being held simultaneously behind the church. It was, nevertheless, unfortunate that the ceremony was performed to the intermittent sound of distant grunts. Thirty-eight guests sat down to lunch at Norton.

After the bride and groom had departed, a party of seventeen, bridesmaids and friends of Lynn and Dorothy, went off to a celebratory dinner in a hotel at Glengarriff (paid for by Jasper). They remained in Ireland for the next couple of days, sight-seeing, swimming and generally living it up. The high point, literally, of their stay was an outing to Castlefreke. Jasper still held on to his portion of this past investment (eventually purchased from him by the Land Commission in 1940), which consisted now of little more than the buildings, including the castle itself. This, although gradually decaying, Jasper occasionally used for entertaining guests. When Dorothy and Lynn's friends came visiting, they picnicked there and explored. A photograph still exists of them on the ramparts.

Minnie only just survived in one piece. 'This affair', commented Ray, 'has nearly laid out mother completely, even though we had extra domestic help'. As for Jasper, he took himself off for a few days' rest in Dublin. Here he could count his losses and regale himself in the company of old friends. One brief press report mentions him being surrounded by welcoming deputies on a visit to the Dáil.

It was not long before things began to hot up once more at Norton. After a respite of a few weeks, Ray returned to begin planning her wedding. Her arrival was inauspicious. Minnie was not in good humour. Ray reported the event to her betrothed, Paul Walton:

I arrived home amidst a torrent of rain and abuse. The abuse came from mother. Apparently Jerry went off to his dinner without getting the pony ready. Result, she was late for the train. She drove up in a fearful rage, and polished off Jerry in a few well chosen words. I stood by, knowing my hat was doomed. Having finished with Jerry she turned to me, and sure enough started on the hat. Having told me how dreadful it was, she first of all ordered me to take it off, then she said I wasn't to wear it any more in Skibbereen – she wasn't going to have me looking odd – then she seized the side that is up and tried to tug it down. Finally, she implored me to turn it back to front!

The set-to over the hat was merely a preliminary skirmish. Full-scale battle was called over Ray's fiancé. Whereas Lynn had been approved of, Paul most certainly was not. His family were artisans and small traders from the East End of London. Minnie found him absolutely unacceptable, almost entirely because of his class (after a year or two, he, like Lynn, succeeded in charming his mother-in-law). Jasper, likewise, was unhappy about the proposed bridegroom, though for a different reason. Paul had left school with few, if any, qualifications. However, like Lynn, he was ambitious, clever and very presentable. Having started his career as a salesman, he was currently working in London's West End. Having just moved from Harrod's to John Lewis, he was beginning a rapid ascent from shop floor to ever greater responsibilities. Despite all this, from the perspective of Norton, Paul looked a poor prospect. Jasper even had suspicions that he was marrying Ray for her money.

Jasper now found himself caught up in domestic warfare. Ever since his boyhood in Snugville, his strategy for dealing with family turmoil had been to keep his head down and, if possible, do a bit of peace-keeping. While he thrived in the formal combat of courtroom and debating chamber, he hated any raw personal confrontation. Now he could not avoid it. Things were getting impossibly fraught and Minnie worked on Jasper to fire some of her bullets. The prospect of further wedding expenses and obligations, and of Paul as impecunious son-in-law, made him uncharacteristically prepared to take up arms. Now hopelessly cornered, Jasper got quite truculent. In Ray's words, he became 'particularly pig-headed'. He had a series of difficult confrontations with his daughter (the two did not get on well anyway – Dorothy, not Ray, was Daddy's girl). At various points Jasper even suggested that the wedding, if it did take place, could not be held at Norton. His actual words, as Ray reported to Paul, were: 'Well, you can marry who you like, but there aren't going to be any more weddings in this house. Get married in Cork, Dublin, or London if you like, but not here.' When pressed, he explained his reasons. These were, wrote Ray, '(a) Mother keeps him awake at night, and (b) Dorothy had about £300 worth of presents, and he's afraid the same would happen to me.'

Ray fought on. Eventually, she won grudging assent to the marriage being held at Norton. However, now a new terrain of worry opened up, which was related only marginally, if at all, to the wedding. Nevertheless, it effectively succeeded in raising the level of anxiety yet another few notches. Travers, of whom Ray was very fond, had reached his early twenties. While he had never done well at school, it was now becoming clear that he was close to being, in the language of the time, 'simple'. He was good-natured, loyal, tolerant and popular, but he could not cope with anything more demanding than the ordinary routines of daily life. Looking after money, earning a decent wage, were beyond him.

Travers was a huge disappointment to his parents. Neither of them knew how to cope. To them, Travers just seemed feckless and wilfully difficult. They could not make allowances (they had no idea of what they should be allowing for). As the only son, he had been expected to inherit the legal practice and further enhance the good name of the family. Instead, he was employed as an office boy in his father's firm. On a recent visit, Ray had tried to do what she could for Travers. He wanted a billiard table, a decent wireless and to be allowed to invite his friends home. Ray pleaded his cause with her parents, but to no avail: 'If I open my mouth to make any sort of suggestion about him I am literally shouted down by mother, and Dad just doesn't listen. I'm sure something could be done with Travers if he was given half a chance.'

Despite his parents' objections, Travers spent more and more time in the town, especially at weekends and in the evenings. Some of his pursuits could not be faulted. He was a keen helper in the scouts and he became secretary of the Hockey Club. But there were rumours that he was drinking – although he assured Ray he had given up. Even worse, he was reported to be enjoying the company of 'girls who have a very bad reputation'. Minnie, Dorothy and Ray would stay up at night awaiting the belated return of the wanderer, moaning to each other that he would bring ruin and disgrace on the family! Of course, what they really feared was that, like his uncle Willie before him, Travers would fall for or be entrapped by some wondrous black-haired Catholic beauty.

As the wedding tensions heightened, Travers began to find it all too much and, shortly before Dorothy's wedding, he simply disappeared. 'That ass Travers', reported Ray, 'went out yesterday at lunch time, and has not appeared since. Jerry was sent round town to look for him'. Nothing. 'He may', hoped Ray, 'have gone to see a friend who is camping on an island near Baltimore, and got stuck in the fog, which was pretty heavy yesterday at sea.' Some hours later, news arrived that Travers was indeed on the island. 'He is', commented Ray, 'due for an almighty rowing when he does come back. And I'm afraid he deserves it too.'

But worse was to come. Just two weeks before Ray's wedding, a really serious crisis erupted. 'Trouble', wrote Ray to Paul, 'has arrived in this family in large, illuminated letters. Travers has excelled himself.' Rumours had reached Jasper that Travers owed money. Minnie was sent on the trail. She in turn despatched her brother Robert (Uncle Dobbie, owner of the Vickery family hardware business in town) to investigate. He found that, besides owing around £15 to various people, Travers had run up a £100 debt as secretary of the Hockey Club. 'No member', said Ray, 'has the slightest intention of paying their share.

It is hard to blame them, as things were done on a considerably more lavish scale than was necessary.' Jasper, when he heard of all this, 'saw red'. He threatened Travers, not for the first time, with a one-way ticket to Canada. More immediately, he told Minnie that he intended to fire Travers from the office for dishonesty, but she and Ray, reinforced by Eddie Swanton and after much haranguing, got him to admit that he was being 'a trifle severe'. The debts were settled, but Ray was feeling very despondent about Travers. 'The problem is what to do with him, where to send him. He's breaking Dad's heart, and he's killing mother.'

At least the wedding show was now on the road. However, there was little sign of peace arriving. Hardly even a brief armistice was declared over the bridegroom himself. Paul had come to Skibbereen shortly before the wedding. When Dorothy arrived a day or so later, she instantly settled in as a participant observer. Supercilious but sharp-eyed, she commented, 'Mother and Paul had a significant little brush this afternoon . . . the truth about the parental attitude to Paul is that they are explaining away what is uncongenial about him by calling it 'English'. Dorothy herself was just as militant as her parents. 'God, I hate Paul – and so does Murty [the dog]. Absolutely refused to play at rings with him.'

It was not only Paul himself, but his family and friends who attracted disapproval. Paul's sister, Nellie, who was to be a bridesmaid, was the target of occasional sharp-shooting. Here, however, Dorothy at least was prepared to be tolerant, if condescending. 'Nellie', she judged, 'has been much maligned and is genuinely likeable'. Another possible victim was the best man. Ray herself could see all too clearly that he was vulnerable. 'For heaven's sake', she instructed Paul, 'inspect Douglas' proposed wardrobe. We will never hear the last of it if he appears looking like an 1880 cyclist! The chin and side-whiskers will be quite enough sensation by themselves.' When Douglas arrived, he duly caused a stir. However, Dorothy was ready to make allowances. He was, she considered, 'Good-hearted', despite being 'a terrific looking object with a tendency to side-whiskers, a green shirt, and checks'. Jasper was less forgiving. He considered Douglas incompetent in his duties.

But the bloodiest clashes were to take place over Paul's mother. Minnie would not invite her. 'I regret to say', reported Ray, 'that Mother has absolutely refused to have your mother here'. Mr Walton had retreated at the first whiff of gunpowder, never to be mentioned again, but his wife was much doughtier. She had every intention of seeing her beloved only son married.

Centrefield, trying to broker peace, was a desperate Ray. There was no hope whatsoever of making the teak-tough Minnie relent, so Ray had to persuade Paul that his mother should withdraw. Mrs Walton was rumoured to be a woman with health problems (although she was to live on for years). Minnie, as Ray wrote to Paul, seized on this. 'She said it would be absolute madness for your mother, who is far from strong, to attempt to do the double journey with only two days in between, for the sake of a half-hour ceremony.' Ray then developed the theme. 'It is really not fair to give us the worry of wondering when and where she will choose to collapse. I have already had two sleepless nights thinking of it, and several days' acute depression.' Mrs Walton still did not back down, so Ray wrote again, with dark warnings of the perils of travel between England and Ireland: 'I hope very much your mother will not come. The danger with sea-sickness of course is internal haemorrhage, and as she has a weak sort of inside to start with it might be fatal. It is no use bringing her short sea, either, as I know from bitter experience that one can be far sicker on that route, even for three and a half hours. I sicked up some blood myself last time I came that way.'

Still Mrs Walton was not deterred. So Ray attacked on another front. Now, she claimed, she had serious concerns over Minnie:

> I am getting really anxious about mother, and I am expecting her to crack up at any moment. She is insisting on doing far too much of course, and at midnight last night she was staggering round complaining of a violent head-ache and looking awful . . . This morning she picked up all the threads on the floor of my sewing room . . . I always know that when she starts doing really crazy things that she is liable to go smash at any moment . . . I'm afraid it will be a bad smash too . . . I am quite ridiculously disturbed at the idea of your mother coming over. She'll get ill for certain, and Mother will promptly do the same. And then we will have no honeymoon and probably no wedding either, as I shall have to stay and nurse the pair of them.

At last, Mrs Walton conceded defeat. However, just as the way ahead seemed clear, there appeared one final obstacle. Ray discovered that the day of wedding was also the day of 'a big cattle fair'. She supposed, correctly as it turned out, that 'there will be cows and drunken farmers all over the place' and added crossly, 'that would happen. Dorothy had a pig fair for her wedding which was not so bad.'

A cattle fair, as everyone at Norton well knew, was far too animated an occasion to be contained by the fair ground. The proceedings invariably cascaded out onto the road opposite the Methodist church. Minnie, however, finally operating at full throttle, took action to avoid calamity. With Jasper (still disaffected) and Ray (famously unpunctual) aboard, she drove her trap through the crowds to the church. Jasper was decanted into the forecourt, while she and Ray, still seated in the trap, surveyed the scene and awaited the arrival of the groom and best man. Each getting angrier and more anxious respectively, the two waited, and waited, and waited. No sign of Paul and Douglas. Eventually just above the tumble of bulls, cows, carts and country folk could be seen swaying uncertainly towards the church two top hats.

From then on, at last, everything proceeded more or less smoothly. Back at Norton, before the wedding feast, everyone took their positions for photographs. As well as bridesmaids, ministers and so forth, there were crowds of Wolfes and Vickeries. Several of these would not normally have featured, but they took the place of absent Walton family and friends. The result is that a fairly complete pictorial record survives of the various relatives of Jasper and Minnie who at that time still lived in Skibbereen. And quite numerous they are too, despite the dramas of the previous years, that God-fearing, decent-living, tenacious, quarrelsome, Methodist crew.

After the guests, bride and groom had finally left, Dorothy retreated to the back quarters of the house, where a good time was still being had. As she wrote to Lynn:

> There was great gaiety in the kitchen. Jerry was discovered parading in Travers' top hat and white gloves, and Mike Brien (an odd-job man) fell asleep in the stable singing 'The Rose of Tralee' and has only just – 11p.m. – been dragged to his feet by Cadogan and induced to leave the premises. I was talking to Ellie and Birdie [housekeeper and maid] for about one and a half hours to-night describing to their rapt ears all the details of our ménage. Ellie said she thought Miss Ray was lonely leaving home. I wonder.

As Jasper had feared, the presents did indeed pile up. For the first time, Dorothy, who throughout had assumed that she was on the inside track in the marriage stakes, was somewhat disgruntled. 'There are', she reported to Lynn, 'a lot of presents, and nice ones, in spite of all, including many things we didn't have at all, and no silver photo frames'.

41

GAELIC TRIBESMAN

Once Jasper had decided not to stand again for the Dáil, politics became for him a sideshow. However, on occasion it could be quite a dramatic sideshow. Thus, six months after Ray's wedding, on the afternoon of Sunday 28 January 1934, the Blueshirts, the fascist-inspired movement that had already been in serious trouble with the government, planned a massive rally in Skibbereen. But not everyone wanted it to take place. Early in the morning, three armed men drove up in a commandeered car and tried to set light to the wooden platform from which various speakers, including Gearóid O'Sullivan, were to address the crowd. Shots and fighting erupted, arrests were made. Despite the brouhaha, it turned out that little damage had been done and the day was able to go ahead as planned. Speeches were preceded by a 'monster' parade of, according to a 'prudent' estimate, over 2,000 Blueshirts, together with 1,000 ladies, or 'Blue Blouses' as they were derisively nicknamed by the *Southern Star*.[1]

The town remained in a state of high excitement for the next day or so. The following night, at 12.30, flames were seen coming from a shop (Collins') on Main Street. Minnie wrote to Dorothy describing the drama.

The fire spread to the Arcade (Eddie Swanton's shop), and he had a narrow escape, evidently the roof over his bedroom was burning and the room full of smoke when they got him out. All the goods had to be taken out. The whole place is saturated with water and a lot of stuff destroyed. The heat was so terrible it broke Uncle Dobbie's window opposite; he and the two girls [his daughters; he was a widower] were up all night, they were so much afraid of the fire spreading. Eddie had been up here till 11.30 with Wood Wolfe, Dr Scully and Jasper [playing cards, no doubt]. We are all sorry for poor Mrs Collins and the girls. The little black pom they were so fond of was burned. Mary Kate Carey brought a bottle of holy water and sprinkled it in front, but I'm afraid it didn't do much good. And of course a lot of looking was going on.

Charlie McCarthy's on the Bridge and the Cellar were open, so the helpers were able to get plenty of drink. (I suppose Eddie will have to pay for this.) Then they started fighting up-stairs in the Arcade drawing room, Blue-shirts, Fianna Fáil, and the gardaí all drunk. The noise was awful. Uncle Dobbie succeeded in bringing two of the worst down and putting them out in the street. Bertie Whitley [neighbouring chemist] was taken for a Blue-shirt and got a blow on the nose from a garda, and fell into Mrs Swanton's pram! She, by the way, is in Manchester for a holiday and will be sorry to have missed it all.

De Valera may have been implicated with gunmen earlier in his career, but once in power as a democratically elected leader he soon made it clear that he would stand for no nonsense from militants, under whatever banners they marched. It was not long before he dealt with the Blueshirts. Just a month after the Skibbereen affair, the Dáil passed a Uniforms Act, which effectively banned them.

A further source of trouble, as potentially disruptive as ever, was the IRA, which continued a campaign of random violence until, on 26 March 1936, it shot dead a retired British navy admiral. Boyle Somerville belonged to a handful of intermarried Anglo-Irish families who had lived in Castletownshend (on the coast a few miles from Skibbereen) since the seventeenth century. Now they represented one of the few surviving enclaves of the old ascendancy. They were well thought of locally. Jasper was in touch with Boyle's sister, the writer Edith Somerville, who occasionally presented him with signed copies of her books and corresponded with him (for instance, writing to congratulate him when Dorothy qualified as a barrister). Minnie came across a sister of Boyle Somerville's, Lady Coghill, when the two met, not always amicably, as judges at local horticultural shows.

Boyle Somerville was killed for signing references for local boys who wanted (at a time of widespread unemployment) to join the British army. He answered a ring at his door and was shot dead in his porch. Beside the body was left a piece of cardboard with the message, 'This British agent has sent 52 boys to the British Army in the last few months. He will send no more.' National outrage followed. Within three months de Valera introduced, and the Dáil passed, a Special Powers Act, making the IRA illegal.

As Jasper was soon to discover, although the IRA had legally been put down, in real life it remained quite capable of biting, or at least snarling. In 1940, having secured a conviction for debt that displeased some local activists, Jasper received a threatening letter. It read:

The gunmen are not yet subdued, and the Republic is still going strong. You must send £20 without delay anonymously and keep a silent tongue in your head. Fail to do as requested and meet the same fate as Somerville.
    Signed,
Irish Republican Brotherhood

Jasper did not comply, but instead read the letter out in court, as reported by the *Southern Star* (1 June 1940). When asked by the judge, 'Were you in any way intimidated?' he replied, 'Not in the least. If you had been three times sentenced to death you would not mind a letter of that kind'.

Jasper had not been alone in finding the 1933 election a turning point. As de Valera, now securely in power, pacified the country and observed the constitution, his popularity and that of his party steadily grew, which presented his political opponents with a problem. In response, the pro-Free State parties, and most prominently Cumann na nGaedheal, communed together and, within a year of their defeat by Fianna Fáil, combined to form a new party. Fine Gael, or 'Gaelic Tribesmen', stood for a united Ireland within the Commonwealth.

Jasper, with little regret, soon surrendered his Independent status and joined Fine Gael, thereby, in a sense, becoming a member of the Tribe of Gaels, or a Gaelic Tribesman. When, within just over three years of his election, Jim Burke, not unexpectedly, died, Jasper was considered a likely successor. 'The only name so far mentioned', reported the *Sunday Independent*, 'is that of Mr Jasper Wolfe, who was a useful and popular member of the Dáil for some years . . . If he were to go forward his candidature would be both forcible and popular, since he is somewhat of an institution in Co. Cork.'

Jasper, however, was not interested. But he did enjoy playing the elder statesman. In 1939 he was one of the Cork delegates to a national Fine Gael Ard Fheis, which required a welcome trip to Dublin. Even ten years later, in 1949, he was receiving a personal letter of thanks from an old friend, now the president of Fine Gael, Richard Mulcahy, for his help in a recent by-election. Political life in southern Ireland, after centuries of turmoil, was finally settling down. It was a sign of this new age that someone like Jasper had found a place in the constitutional establishment.

42

'AN EXCELLENT MEMBER OF THE PROFESSION'

In December, just before the general election of January 1933, Jasper was elected vice-president of the Incorporated Law Society of Ireland, the solicitors' governing body. Amongst many others, members of County Cork courts paid him tribute:

> We have always been very proud of our own 'Jasper' for there is no-one like him . . . No better person could be found to fill the position to which he has been elected . . . he has gained further lustre in the profession in which he has become famous . . . he has always been an excellent member of the profession. (*Southern Star*, 17 December 1932)

Some years later, in 1941, Jasper gained a yet higher distinction, being elected president of the Law Society. Once again, congratulations poured in. Local lawyers were particularly pleased, because Jasper was the first Corkman, and only the second solicitor from Munster, to hold this post. It was generally felt that until then a mafia of Dublin men had more or less kept the position to themselves. Now, as one colleague put it, he had 'brought back to his native county the blue riband of his profession' (*Cork Examiner*, 8 January 1941).

For Jasper, who was once more enjoying normal legal practice, amongst the highlights of the legal year were the visits to Skibbereen of the circuit courts. Even while Jasper had been a TD he and Minnie had entertained the retinue of lawyers and officials who accompanied the court, but this hospitality now flourished as never before. Seán Ó Faoláin, in his *Irish Journey*, described what happened:

> Barristers who have been on that old Munster Circuit have told me repeatedly that in Jasper Wolfe's house (and the phrase was constant), they were always 'made feel at home'. [With] the court sitting for a week, every day, there would be a buffet table and a warm welcome for every barrister and official.

Nor was hospitality restricted to midday. In the evenings, after a hard day's arguing, many on the circuit enjoyed a drink. Jasper always arranged that a private room was available for them in his favourite pub; this had once been run by the late John O'Shea, Jasper's great friend, but now his widow, known to all as 'Mam Shea', was in command.

Since many in the legal fraternity liked to drink not only hard, but late, Jasper also arranged with Mam Shea that alcohol would be available after hours. Normally, the gardaí, who were well aware of what was going on, acted as if they could see no evil and hear no evil. Unfortunately, in one particular court case Jasper gave the local superintendent a very hard time. This officer decided on revenge and organised a raid on the illegal drinking den. However, not wishing to be implicated, he arranged for colleagues from a nearby town to do the deed. Unwarned and unsuspecting, the merry lawyers were arrested without difficulty. Willie Wood Wolfe, who was also in the pub, as a sort of friend of the legal family, hid behind some curtains, but in vain. He too was apprehended.

The next day, the miscreants were brought before the court – their court – and charged. Jasper, who had not been at the scene of the crime, acted for the defendants. He was more than up to the job. He requested that the case be heard in Gaelic. From his time in the Dáil dealing with legislation on the administration of justice, he knew that the judge would have no option but to agree. Hardly anybody involved spoke Irish. Jasper insisted that the defence have its own interpreter, so the prosecution had to have theirs. The judge, naturally, could not use either the defence or the prosecution interpreter, for fear of being accused of bias, one way or the other, so he too had to have his own interpreter. The session was suspended while competent, independent Irish speakers acceptable to all parties were sought and found. This took a long time.

Eventually, proceedings began. The case, however, went very slowly indeed. The judge opened the case, speaking in English. His words then had to be translated by his interpreter into Irish. Since this was the official version, and was understood by few, it had to be rendered back into English, even though everyone had heard, and understood, what the judge had originally said. After a few days of this sort of thing, no end was in sight and the execution of justice throughout West Cork was stalling badly. The judge decided he had no option but to dismiss the case. And that was the end of the affair.[1]

Jasper made a couple of new appointments to Wolfe & Co. With no son or other relative to inherit the business, he needed to secure his firm's future, so he appointed a senior partner. Ronnie Boland was a member of one of the most talented and distinguished families to emerge in the Free State. He was also a highly competent lawyer and a well-liked man. Only Dorothy seems to have disapproved. To the end of her life, she always referred to him coldly as 'Boland'. She did not mind him personally, but she disapproved of his religion. He was a Catholic. For Jasper, this was one of his attractions. With a Catholic as heir apparent, J. Travers Wolfe & Co. gave the clearest possible signal that it was at ease in the new Ireland. As the years passed, Ronnie Boland took on, tactfully and effectively, an ever greater role in the day-to-day running of the practice.

Jasper, who throughout his professional life had from time to time indulged in some sharp, behind-the-scenes tactics to win cases, now realised that he was getting rather too old, and too distinguished, to carry on in this fashion. So he found himself a fixer. Alfie Regan fitted the bill perfectly. He rapidly became absolutely indispensable.

Some of the cases that appeared in local courts differed little from many which had featured in the years before the First World War. Animals on the highway continued to cause trouble. At Bantry district court Jasper appeared for the driver of a car who was being prosecuted by a local farmer: 'I observed,' said the farmer, 'a car coming, and it drove through my cows. Two were hurt so bad they had to be destroyed.' The driver, when cross-examined by Jasper, had a rather different view of events:

> I observed a lot of cattle on the road, and sounded the horn several times. I pulled the car up about 50 feet in front of the cattle. I could not see anyone in charge. As the cattle spread out across the road I tried to pass through. But one animal bounced out in front of the car, and then sat down on her hind legs. I could not say if she was hurt. I did not examine the cow. I know nothing about cattle. At the time of the incident I was travelling at about five miles an hour. I stopped for about three minutes and looked around. I did not see anyone, so I proceeded on my way. (*Southern Star*, 7 December 1935)

The accused was found not guilty of careless driving, but guilty of failing to stop.

Boundaries were another perennial cause of quarrels. Jasper defended one client who claimed that a neighbour was ignoring a boundary and trespassing on his land. However, on a preliminary visit to the disputed site no boundary could be seen. The day before the case was due to be heard, Jasper had a word with Alfie Regan. 'Tonight, you go and see if you can find that boundary. Just walk up and down, looking for it, where it might be.' The next day, the judge and all involved went to seek out the alleged boundary. And there it was. A neat, narrow, well-trodden track. Jasper won his case.

On another occasion, in the far west, a woman from Castletownbere claimed damages for personal injury. She alleged that, while lifting boxes in the grocer's shop where she worked, she had permanently strained, indeed crippled, her right arm. The arm, she claimed, was now useless. She could no longer even lift it. Jasper, acting for the grocer, cross-examined the plaintiff.

'So, you have lost the use of your arm?'

'I have.'

'Why, that's a terrible thing. Could you tell the court how you suffer?' The woman complied, at length. 'Well,' said Jasper, still all sympathy, 'and that's altogether true?'

'It is right enough, your honour, it is.' The woman had tears in her eyes.

'And,' enquired Jasper, 'you would swear to the court that every word is true?'

'I would, I would.'

'Are you prepared by Almighty God, on this Bible, to swear that all you have said is true?'

'It's true altogether!' cried the woman.

'Raise your right arm and swear . . .' Before her lawyer could intervene, the woman raised high her crippled right arm.

Paternity cases were much more frequent than in the past and of great local interest. Jasper appeared in several. In one, a girl claimed maintenance from a man who, she alleged, was the father of her child. The man denied responsibility and the evidence was inconclusive. The defendant was so outrageously ugly that the jury was clearly reluctant to believe that anyone would find him acceptable as a suitor. Jasper, acting for the girl's father, who, as was usual in such matters, had brought the case, asked for the baby to be produced as evidence. It was claimed at the time that this was legally unprecedented. Nevertheless, the infant was produced. It was so ineffably ugly that all doubts over paternity vanished.[2]

It was, bizarrely, on account of a paternity case that Jasper, for the only time in his life, suffered serious physical injury from assault by a Republican. The episode began, in November 1938, with a touch of farce. Cornelius Collins of Smorane accused a local vet of having seduced his daughter Kathleen and of being the father of her recently born child. The defendant, Eugene McCarthy, was an active Republican and had stood at least once for election to the Dáil as a Fianna Fáil candidate – coming bottom of the poll. When Kathleen appeared in court, Jasper was horrified to discover that, far from looking like a wronged woman, the girl was smiling, brilliantly lipsticked, attractively dressed and altogether turned out as if for a night on the town. Jasper managed to get the case adjourned and had a word with Alfie Regan.

The next day, a very different Kathleen showed up. Pale-faced, tear-stained, drably clad, she was the very picture of a betrayed and heartbroken lover. She and Eugene, under cross-examination by Jasper, differed sharply on her courting habits.

'No sir, I never kept company with other men,' said Kathleen.

'I did not seduce her. It was common property around the town that she had gone with other men. At the time, I did think of marrying her, but I would marry no girl under 25,' said Eugene.

The judge was clearly very taken with Kathleen. 'I have,' said he, 'rarely seen a more intelligent and fearless witness than Miss Collins. There is nothing brazen about her. She strikes me as being clean and upstanding.'

The *Southern Star* described how the jury (it was a Skibbereen circuit court) agreed with the judge and found the defendant guilty. Eugene McCarthy was ordered to pay, by instalments, damages to the plaintiff. He, however, appealed, but when the case was heard at the criminal circuit court in Cork the appeal was dismissed. McCarthy was extremely angry. A short time after, seeing Jasper about to enter the Cork garda barracks, he said: 'I see, Wolfe, you are seeking protection, because you will want it. I'll be throwing you in the river!' A little later, noticing McCarthy apparently lying in wait for him, Jasper had to hide in a nearby house until the coast was clear.

By the next summer McCarthy, thanks to his conviction, had lost his veterinary post with Cork County Council and was falling behind with his payments. When an officer of the court served him with an order to pay up, the vet shouted: 'Take that away, and tell Jasper to — ! Jasperene the — ; I will pull the guts out of him!'

In November, McCarthy was summonsed to appear at the Skibbereen district court for non-payment. There resulted a scene which the *Southern Star*, perhaps with some exaggeration, described as 'unique in Irish court history'. During the morning Jasper brought his case against McCarthy and the judge found against the defendant and ordered that he be imprisoned for a month. For some reason, McCarthy was not immediately detained – and he was in a foul mood. Late in the afternoon, when he calculated the court would have finished, he set out from the Shamrock hotel, where he boarded in Townshend Street, towards North Street. Like everyone else, the vet knew that Jasper, after a day in court, liked to have a drink before going back to the office for an hour or two. So McCarthy called in at Mam Shea's.

'Is Wolfe here?' asked McCarthy of the assistant, Madge Hegerty. When she said that she had not seen him, he swore 'I will get him!'

At this moment Jasper, having left the court, was on his way to the pub. He was just outside the Pro-Cathedral when he encountered the vet . McCarthy stood in front of him and blocked his way.

'You,' shouted McCarthy to Jasper, 'You said I am the father of the Smorane —.'

'Let me pass,' said Jasper.

'I will not, so.' The *Southern Star*, described how, according to Jasper, McCarthy then pulled him to the side of the pavement and, abusing him loudly, punched him hard in the face. He was, as Jasper said later when giving evidence, 'a very powerful man'. Jasper fell into the road, which at that point was nearly two feet below the footpath.

McCarthy subsequently gave a different story. He alleged that Jasper started it all by striking him 'a nice little blow in the solar plexus'. This Jasper denied ('I swear on my oath I didn't touch you'). At this moment a garda, who, 'by the mercy of Providence', as someone later said, was cycling by, intervened. He found Jasper bleeding freely from mouth and nose, with blood all over his collar and jacket. Asked what had happened, Jasper replied, 'That blackguard McCarthy struck me.'

The garda now tried to arrest the vet, but this was no easy task. McCarthy was swearing volubly at Jasper, using, as the garda later put it, 'very vile language'. 'You North of Ireland bastard!' he shouted, and so forth. He was also doing his utmost to have another bash at Jasper. However, with the garda intervening, Jasper was fairly safe. McCarthy, for all his shouting and struggling, only succeeded, as the garda reported, in 'touching Mr Wolfe's hand'.

While the garda battled to get the vet under control, he shouted at Jasper to go back to the courthouse, which, dazed and holding a handkerchief to his face, he did. Three gardaí on duty in the courthouse, alerted by the noise of the unholy fracas, came out on to the steps to see what was happening. The first thing they observed was the gore-stained Jasper approaching. Beyond him, they perceived one of their colleagues engaging in hand-to-hand combat and they rushed to the scene.

A few minutes later, Ronnie Boland emerged with Jasper onto the courthouse steps. He was starting to help him home when the gardaí arrived with McCarthy. By now various onlookers had assembled.

Cadogan.

Also watching was Cadogan. He, like everyone else, was in a state of high excitement and had found a gardening task conveniently close to the low wall that separated Norton from North Street and the adjacent courthouse. When McCarthy, with his escort, passed Jasper, the vet's fury surged to yet greater heights.

'I will get you again! I will give you the same again!' roared McCarthy to Jasper.

This proved too much for Cadogan. Appalled by Jasper's condition and burning for revenge, he leaped over the wall, crashed the gardaí aside and dealt McCarthy a fearful blow between the eyes. McCarthy, like a goaded bull, retaliated by lashing out in every direction. The gardaí hauled him into the courthouse building, but, proving impossible to subdue, he had to be taken out almost immediately. He was dragged bellowing to the barracks.

All this gave rise to a flurry of further cases. The following week, at a special court held in Skibbereen, McCarthy was refused bail and returned for trial at a higher court. The vet's case was heard in January 1941 at the criminal court, on circuit in Cork from the high court in Dublin. It cannot have helped Eugene McCarthy's cause at all that the election of Jasper as president of the

Irish Law Society was announced shortly before the circuit court proceedings began. These were initiated, with much pomp, in a ceremonial opening, when His Lordship, Judge J. K. O'Connor, was accompanied by the Lord Mayor of Cork, in tails and chain of office, and received by a guard of honour. The judge was joined on the bench by the lord mayor. Much of the introductory business which followed concerned Jasper. One after another, first the judge, then the lord mayor, followed by representatives of various branches of the legal profession, all proffered, some at considerable length and in florid style, their congratulations to Jasper on his recent elevation to head of his profession. Jasper then replied, wittily but, like numbers of his colleagues, not briefly. (It was also mentioned, and forgotten by nobody, that this high court was only on circuit thanks to none other than Jasper and the legislation he had been responsible for getting introduced in his time as TD.)

When the case against McCarthy came up a few days later, the unfortunate man found himself charged, in effect, with assaulting a local hero, indeed in the eyes of many, at least in Cork, a national treasure. Jasper, as the barrister prosecuting for the state put it, was a solicitor 'whose name was a household word in many counties, and not only Cork'. That was a bad enough start for the vet. He then made matters worse for himself by deciding to dismiss his solicitor and act in his own defence. He won few sympathisers. He was deemed guilty by the jury and received no mercy from the judge. Said Justice J. O'Connor:

> This was a cowardly assault – a lion of a man against a frail man twenty or thirty years his senior. If a solicitor is to be intimidated in doing fearlessly what is his duty towards his client, then all law and order in the country will be at an end. During the whole course of the trial I have waited for an expression of regret from the accused, but it has not been forthcoming.

McCarthy was sentenced to nine months' imprisonment with hard labour and bound to keep the peace for a subsequent year or face three months further in gaol.

The final case arising from the McCarthy affair concerned Cadogan. The gardaí were not inclined to overlook his over-enthusiastic behaviour in attacking the vet and he was summonsed for assault. Ronnie Boland, appearing for Cadogan, pleaded that the accused only struck the vet in defence of his master, an action which, said Jasper's partner, was recognised and allowed by the law. However, the prosecution, and not least the garda superintendent, were having none of it. What really upset the superintendent was that McCarthy had been in the custody of no fewer than four gardaí at the time and Cadogan had brushed the lot aside in order to get at his quarry. The judge found Cadogan guilty, but commented: 'I accept that the circumstances surrounding the incident caused great provocation, and I consider that in mitigation of the offence.' Cadogan was bound over to keep the peace for a year in his own surety of £5.[3]

Unfortunately that did not end Cadogan's troubles. Eugene McCarthy had supporters in the town. If they had attacked Jasper, it would have caused them more grief than they wanted, so they targeted Cadogan. Minnie, writing to Dorothy, told her of one particular drama that had occurred.

Cadogan had another encounter the other night with an IRA man, and friend of McCarthy's. He was coming back from the office on Friday evening before Christmas. A man, Croston, asked him into a public house for a drink. Another man came in collecting for some races and immediately attacked Cadogan.

'Let me out, for God's sake, I'm bound to the pace!' said Cadogan.

'To hell with the pace!' said Croston, and hit him.

I said to Cadogan, 'Did you do anything?'

'I made bruss of him. Shure he had to go to the doctor. His teeth and nose were flying —. I'm not the man I was.'

I said, 'Perhaps that's just as well.' I had to laugh, as May Levis says.

As for Eugene McCarthy himself, in the aftermath of all his troubles he seems in due course to have returned to life as normal. The Thoms 1947 *Directory for Ireland* lists 'McCarthy, Eugene, MRCVS' as one of two veterinary surgeons practising in Skibbereen.

43

'FORWARD WITH CONFIDENCE TO A GOLDEN TIME'

Dorothy used to say that Jasper was never quite the same after his encounter with Eugene McCarthy. From photographs, however, it can be seen that he was already ageing before the assault. As he reached his seventies, he began to suffer from deafness and in old age, in common with many others in his family, his memory began to go. But, like his brothers and sisters who survived early childhood, he reached eighty without too much difficulty and, while inevitably slowing down, was always the same old Jasper.

When Jasper and Minnie married, the year after Queen Victoria's Diamond Jubilee and at the height of Empire, he must have wished for a successful professional career, a happy family life and a respected place in public life. All this he achieved. He had built an extensive and prosperous practice; under British rule he had been appointed to the prestigious post of Crown Solicitor; and at the end of his career he headed his profession as president of the Law Society.

He could also feel proud of his family. He and Minnie had built an enduring and stable marriage. Their only son had been a disappointment, but their daughters were thriving. As the years passed, grandchildren arrived. Dorothy became Lady Ungoed-Thomas when Lynn, elected a Labour MP, became a law officer in the post-war Attlee government. Ray's husband became a leading businessman and was awarded an OBE for services to commerce. In 1948 Dorothy and Ray and their families celebrated Jasper and Minnie's golden wedding anniversary in Skibbereen.

And then, there had been his public life. Apart from holding, at one time or another, almost every available office, honorary or elected, in Skibbereen, Jasper had also represented his constituency of West Cork in the Dáil – as Jasper saw it, the national Home Rule legislative body for which he had always hoped, and worked.

Altogether, as His Lordship Judge J. K. Connor put it when publicly congratulating Jasper on being elected president of the Law Society, he had now reached a position where he could 'look back with satisfaction, and

Jasper Wolfe, president of the Irish Law Society (photo inscribed to his grandson Jasper on his birthday, 1 May 1942).

forward with confidence to a golden time'.

Thus described, Jasper's life story reads like a classic and familiar tale of ambitious, hard-working, talented, local middle-class boy makes good. If one did not know the background, it would be easy to assume that the times through which Jasper had lived were more or less settled and contented. What is extraordinary is that his conventional success was achieved, not in a time of relative peace, but through the mayhem of extended revolution and civil war. During those years, as an Anglo-Irish Protestant, a 'milk-and-water Home Ruler' and a prosecutor for the Crown, Jasper was a prominent and active official of a British government against which Republicans were waging a war of independence. At worst, Jasper was hated, and hunted, as a symbol of colonial authority.

The ending could never have been happy had it not been for Jasper's particular character and skills – but that alone was not enough. Jasper was blessed with friends who were loyal and opponents who, while they never forgot, were, with rare exceptions, ready to forgive. No wonder Seán Ó Faoláin wrote that:

> Wolfe and men like him *are* modern Ireland . . . It is [his] humanity, born of natural warmth of heart and long mingling with the simple folk of the country that, together with his immense talents, has made Jasper Wolfe an epitome of the natural unity of Irish life; to be remembered and quoted by everybody who knows West Cork.

There remained Jasper's lifelong political ambition for the country he loved. From boyhood he had worked for a Home Rule Ireland within the British Commonwealth. However, in old age, on the anniversary of the Easter Rising, he saw an Irish Republic, partitioned from the North, finally declared. This caused him some regret, but little more. The Irish and the British still carried on much as before, criss-crossing the Irish channel for work, holidays and family occasions alike. Southern Ireland itself, at long last, was a land at peace.

A democracy. A country where the law was respected and, by and large, observed. As for the North, Jasper had never felt any sympathy for those of his fellow Protestants who whipped up bigotry and spat venom at Catholicism. If north and south could not unite in amity, then better wait for history to sort things out.

Above all, though, as Ireland and Great Britain changed over his lifetime, so, gradually, had Jasper. Now that each country had its own flag, he found it ever more difficult to salute both. While he was hugely irritated by many of the policies pursued by de Valera, he understood perfectly well what they were about. When it came to the Second World War and the Fianna Fáil declaration of neutrality, he realised, as well as anyone, that there really was no other way forward. If the country was not to collapse back into civil strife, with the IRA utterly opposed to fighting alongside the British, then Ireland had to stay on the sidelines. As for the English, Jasper found them simply exasperating. Few of them had any real understanding of Ireland. They just did not get it. As Jasper, in words reported by Dorothy, said to some fellow politicians just before he resigned as a TD, 'Of course, the English don't understand, do they?' But Jasper did. He loved Ireland. He loved its ways. Along with the country, he had become, not Anglo-Irish, but wholly Irish.

In the end, however, it was an Englishman, or at least someone with an English father – his mother being American – who probably best expressed Jasper's feelings. When the Republic was declared Winston Churchill said in the House of Commons:

> Because of its long, terrible and tragic history, Ireland seems to me to have always had an entirely different position from other parts of the world – I mustn't say the British Empire! I have watched with contentment and pleasure the orderly Christian society, with a grace and culture of its own, and a flash of sport thrown in, which this quarter of a century has seen built up in Southern Ireland, in spite of many gloomy predictions.

EPILOGUE

AUGHADOWN
1944–1952

44

TRAVERS

Travers (on left).

For most of the war I lived in Wales, together with my mother, brother and sister. However, in 1944 we moved to London, where we all rejoined my father, who was working in the War Office. The dangers, and excitement, were not quite over yet though, as became clear when a flying bomb scored a direct hit on a nearby synagogue.

The smogs of London did not agree with me. I spent a good deal of time in bed, not seriously ill but wheezing quietly. A frequent visitor was my Uncle Travers. He and I would play draughts. He was easy going and benign. After a year or two, he ceased coming. My mother said he was not well. She visited him in hospital for months and looked more and more worried. Eventually, she told us our uncle was dying. He was suffering from cancer.

Many years later I learned that my Aunt Ray had been so upset by the frosty relations between Travers and his parents that, towards the end of the war, she had arranged for him to live in England and managed to get him a job as a storeman at John Lewis, where my

Uncle Paul was already quite senior. Whether this was a good idea, I rather doubt. Travers may have been unhappy at Norton, but he thrived in Skibbereen, where he was greatly liked.

The catalyst for the move may have been a serious car crash near Bandon. Travers, who had become Jasper's chauffeur and been given a car of his own, was driving his parents when he collided with a lorry carrying horses. All three were taken to hospital. Travers had never been the most reliable of drivers – he once managed to run into the Skibbereen to Schull light train where it ran along the road. However, Jasper and Minnie now became reluctant to be driven by Travers, which put an end to one of the few jobs he was able to manage. He could quite easily have been found somewhere to live independently in the town, perhaps with a housekeeper to look after him, but Jasper and Minnie, while they could deal with fatal and near fatal disease, death threats, deaths and all manner of crises, whether personal, social or political, could not handle a son who deviated slightly from the normal. In this, they were typical of their times. The life and death of Travers was, if in a minor key, a tragedy. And, in some respects at least, an avoidable one.

My mother travelled with Travers' coffin by rail and boat to Cork, and from there by hearse to Skibbereen. Local obituaries sounded a note of genuine grief, unusual in such public notices. Mr Wolfe was, wrote the *Southern Star* (June 1946):

> One of the most popular young men in the town. In every aspect of life he was big-hearted, unprejudiced and sociable. He was certainly a friend whose loyalty never wavered, while his unpretentious good nature was something that made his friends equally loyal to him.

When Travers' hearse began the slow drive from Norton through Skibbereen to the Wolfe family burial vault at Aughadown, it was met by a huge 'concourse of people'. The coffin was taken from the vehicle and shouldered through the streets: 'As the funeral passed through the town business houses were closed and shuttered, and blinds drawn in the windows of private houses.' After the crowds of mourners on foot came inummerable cars and traps. Elderly people in Skibbereen still remember the cortège as one of the greatest, and most moving, in their lifetime.

45

'Oh, Jasper'

A few years later, in 1952, at the start of the summer holidays, Grandpa fell seriously ill. My mother and I travelled over to Norton. I was fifteen years old. I slept in a room just across the landing from my grandparents' room. A nurse was also living in the house. She was reassuring, comfortable, warm, and clearly very competent.

Grandpa just seemed to be quietly retreating from life. I was allowed to look in on him occasionally. He certainly looked ill, his bones showing under his skin, his features reddened. I was rather awed, but not frightened.

Having spent a previous summer holiday on my own in Skibbereen, I was able to make outings by myself. I cycled to Glandore and went sailing with my mother's cousin, Jack Wolfe, Uncle Jackson's son. I did not know that he spent most of his time in Baltimore boating with my Catholic cousins, about whose existence I had not the slightest idea. I missed out on some very good times.

In Norton, for a day or two it appeared to my mother and various others that Grandpa might be rallying. Dorothy wrote to my father, 'He lies quite quietly for most of the time, very occasionally rousing and talking a little, even cracking a joke, and usually recognising us all. He reads the newspaper, or seems to.' As ever, there were visitors. My mother mentioned one in particular: 'Father McCarthy, looking wonderful, called yesterday. He and J. fell for each other at once.' In fact, although I remember visiting Father McCarthy, which must have been the following year, I don't recall this first encounter.

At the end of August, just before I had to go back to school, Grandpa died. The coffin was brought downstairs and placed in the library, where it stayed until the day of the funeral. Then the family assembled around the coffin, waiting for it to be put into the hearse. Grandma came in at the last moment and stooped over the coffin, laying her cheek on its surface. 'Oh, Jasper,' she said.

As previously, for Travers, the cortège moved slowly down North Street and through the centre of Skibbereen. Past, on one side, the courthouse and on the other the school that Jasper had attended. Past the Pro-Cathedral and its presbytery, where Father McCarthy had lived during the Troubles. Past Jasper's first office and opposite it the house in which he and Minnie had started their life as a married couple. Past Mam Shea's. Through Main Street to Bridge Street. Past the Wolfe family shop on the Bridge, where Jasper had been born. Past the Methodist church. Past the building that once housed the grain mill of William Wolfe of Ilen House. Finally, in cars and traps, the cortège travelled to the family vault at Aughadown, for Jasper Wolfe to join his parents, his brothers and sisters who died as young children, and Travers.

Funeral of Jasper Wolfe, 30 August 1952, passing through the Square, Skibbereen. Front row (l–r): Paul and Ray Walton, Dorothy, Jasper and Sir Lynn Ungoed-Thomas. Second row includes Jack Wolfe, Robert Vickery and Willie Wood Wolfe.

GLOSSARY

CONFLICTS AND ARMED FORCES

Anglo–Irish War and War of Independence

The 'Anglo-Irish War' is the phrase now most commonly used to describe the hostilities which lasted from 21 January 1919, when nine Volunteers killed two members of the Royal Irish Constabulary in Tipperary, until the truce of 11 July 1921. The term 'War of Independence' is now less commonly employed. Both these phrases have difficulties. The word 'war' in particular is problematic. On the Irish side, the IRA fought a campaign of guerrilla tactics, subversion and threat, which were hardly 'warfare' in the sense recognised at the time. As for the British authorities (not specifically 'Anglo'), they saw themselves not at war but as dealing with an explosive security situation. Nevertheless, an armed struggle for independence there certainly was. I have, at various points, used both terms.

Black and Tans and Auxiliaries

British ex-servicemen recruited from 1920–1 to reinforce the RIC. The Black and Tans were so called because of the khaki trousers and dark-green tunics that they initially wore due to a shortage of proper uniforms. The Auxiliaries, which were recruited from officers, arrived a few months later than the Black and Tans. While technically an auxiliary division of the RIC, in practice Auxiliaries tended to operate independently. Both groups of men rapidly became known – and hated – for their undisciplined and brutal behaviour.

Irish Civil War

This lasted from 28 June 1922 until 30 April 1923. However, outbreaks of violence both preceded and followed the war itself. The conflict was between those members of Sinn Féin and the IRA who supported the Anglo-Irish Treaty and those who were only prepared to settle for a republic. The majority of the population were in favour of the terms of the Treaty and the Free Staters emerged the winners. Although the Republicans lost, the war never officially ended, as there was no negotiated peace, only a ceasefire.

Irish Republican Army (IRA)

From 1919 onwards the Irish Volunteers became increasingly known as the IRA, although individual members retained the title of Volunteer. Following the founding of Dáil Éireann, the IRA became the official army of the Republic and Volunteers swore allegiance to the Dáil government. However, a spirit of independence lived on. In the Civil War of 1922–3 the IRA split. Some of its troops joined the Free State Army, while the majority, known to their opponents as 'Irregulars', fought against the new state for a republic. In 1925, after its defeat in the Civil War, the IRA, still inspired by the notion of its own independence, split from Sinn Féin, the political wing of Republicanism. As an autonomous military body it managed to cause a good deal of trouble, and in 1936 it was banned by de Valera as head of government.

Irish Volunteers, Cumann na mBan (League of Women), National Volunteers

In 1913 the Irish Volunteers were founded as an armed force (despite a serious shortage of arms), to promote Home Rule and provide a counterbalance to the militantly unionist Ulster Volunteer Force. The next year Cumann na mBan, a women's auxiliary corps, was set up. Many of its members, despite, or perhaps in some cases because of, the chauvinism of the male Volunteers, played an active, fearless and often radical role. After the outbreak of the war with Germany, the Volunteers split when John Redmond, leader of the Nationalist Party, called on all Irishmen to support the British war effort. Redmond's supporters, who were the vast majority, formed the National Volunteers. The remainder of the Irish Volunteers, predominantly led by the Irish Republican Brotherhood, organised the Easter Rising of 1916. Within a few years the movement developed into the Irish Republican Army.

Royal Irish Constabulary (RIC)

This was founded in 1836 as a national, centrally controlled, paramilitary force. However, from the Famine onwards, it gradually became more like a conventional police force. By the time of the Troubles, with many Catholic constables and little military training, it was ill-equipped to deal with guerrilla warfare. Following the Anglo-Irish Treaty it was disbanded.

The Troubles

This term, used to describe the conflicts which lasted in Ireland roughly from 1918 until the end of the Civil War in 1923, has now mostly fallen into disuse. It is hard to find it mentioned in any recent publication on the period. However, until quite lately it was widely employed. For instance, A. J. P. Taylor, in his *Oxford History of England 1914–1945* (published in 1965), wrote at some length on 'the "troubles" as they were called'. One difficulty with using the term is that the phrase is vague; it also fails to reflect an Irish view of what happened. However, it still has some advantages: it was widely used at the time, it described how many ordinary people felt about what was going on, it is non-partisan and it encompasses the whole dramatic and historic period during which the south of Ireland gained freedom. For all these reasons, I have referred to that period as 'the Troubles' in this book. It is also the phrase which I always heard my family, and many others, use.

POLITICS

The Anglo-Irish Treaty, the Irish Free State, the Republic of Ireland

The Anglo-Irish Treaty was signed in London in December 1921, by representatives of the Dáil and the British government. The Treaty, establishing an Irish Free State as a self-governing dominion within the Commonwealth, was agreed in January 1922 by the Dáil. However, a significant minority, led by de Valera, voted against ratification, because the Treaty did not establish a republic. Within months this profound disagreement led to civil war. Under the new constitution of 1937, introduced by de Valera, the Free State was abolished and southern Ireland (Éire) became a republic in all but name. The head of government, previously president of the Executive Council (Cabinet), became Taoiseach and an elected president became head of state, replacing the British-appointed Governor General. In 1948 the state was formally declared to be the Republic of Ireland.

Blueshirts

The Blueshirts were a political movement founded in 1932, mainly from Free State ex-servicemen. It rapidly gained in popularity, was strongly opposed to Fianna Fáil and took on many of the appearances of a European fascist party. While its uniform proved very popular with members, its demand for uniformity was greeted less enthusiastically. In 1933, after losing a humiliating confrontation with de Valera and the government, it merged with other parties to form Fine Gael.

Cumann na nGaedheal (Party of the Irish)

Cumann na nGaedheal was launched in 1923 to support the Anglo-Irish Treaty. Led by William Cosgrave, with Kevin O'Higgins as his able right-hand man, the party won the 1923 Dáil election and remained in power until 1932. Through skilful leadership and a commitment to democracy and the rule of law, it laid the foundations for a successful independent state. However, it tended to neglect bread-and-butter party politics and became exhausted after a decade of power. In 1933 it amalgamated with other centre parties to form Fine Gael.

Dáil Éireann (Council of Gaelic elders)

The first Dáil consisted of the seventy-three Sinn Féin candidates elected to the British House of Commons in the 1918 general election. Refusing to take their seats, these members set up their own assemby in Dublin (sitting as Teachtaí Dála, usually known as TDs or deputies.) In 1919 the British government declared the Dáil an illegal organisation, but it continued to function, more or less successfully. It set up its own army (the IRA), legal system and various government ministries, in particular local government and agriculture. Following the Anglo-Irish Treaty and the Civil War, it was accepted legally as the parliament for southern Ireland. The constitution of the Irish Free State (1922) required that all elections to the Dáil be by proportional representation. This gave minority interests a fair chance of representation. The Dáil met, and continues to meet, in Leinster House, in central Dublin, formerly the residence of the Dukes of Leinster.

Farmers' Party and National Centre Party

The Farmers' Party mainly represented the interests of larger farmers in the south and east; from the start it was close to Cumann na nGaedheal. It first contested a general election in 1922; from 1923 to 1932 the seats it won declined from fifteen to three. It was absorbed into the very similar National Centre Party just before the election of January 1933: the latter, in turn, amalgamated before the end of the year with the newly founded Fine Gael.

Fenians (ancient Irish warrior caste)

This term originated in the later nineteenth century. They were revolutionaries, more or less formally organised, dedicated to founding a democratic Irish republic.

Fianna Fáil (Soldiers of Ireland)

Fianna Fáil was founded by de Valera in 1926. Unlike Sinn Féin, it was prepared to work towards establishing a republic within the framework of the Irish Free State, provided the oath of allegiance to the British Crown, agreed under the Anglo-Irish Treaty of 1921, was scrapped. The ambiguous position of Fianna Fáil led to some complicated political manoeuvring from 1927 to 1933. However, once de Valera formed a government in 1932, he moved successfully to remove the oath. Thereafter, the party established itself as the dominant force in Irish politics.

Fine Gael (Gaelic Tribesmen)

In September 1933 Cumann na nGaedheal, the National Centre Party (incorporating the Farmers' Party) and the Blueshirts merged to form Fine Gael. A centrist party committed to the Free State, it was to all intents and purposes a development of Cumann na nGaedheal. It established itself as the second major party in the southern Irish state, but has seldom managed to surpass Fianna Fáil in popularity.

(Irish) National League

The National League was a political party founded in 1926 under William Redmond, son of the former leader of the Nationalist Party, John Redmond. In many ways a successor of the Nationalist Party, it supported the Free State and pursued right-of-centre policies. It won eight seats in the June 1927 general election but was reduced to two in the election of September that year. It was dissolved in 1931, (no connection with National League founded 1882).

Irish Republican Brotherhood (IRB)

The IRB was a secret society which grew out of the Fenian movement and shared its aims. It only began to exert real influence in the years immediately leading up to the Easter Rising of 1916.

Labour Party

The Labour Party first contested a general election in 1922, under Thomas Johnson as leader, when it won seventeen seats. It never again achieved similar success. Apart from a brief period in 1927, when it looked as if it might hold the balance of power and join a Fianna Fáil government, it remained of marginal significance in Irish politics.

Land League

The Land League was founded in 1879, with Parnell as its president, to promote peasant proprietorship. Pressure from the League helped secure the 1881 Land Act, but its aggressive methods resulted in its being hounded by the British government. It was disbanded in 1882.

Nationalist Party, United Irish League, Molly Maguires

The Nationalist (or Irish Parliamentary) Party was dominant in Irish politics from the 1870s until the First World War. The party was led, throughout most of those years, by Parnell (1880–1890) and Redmond (1900–1918). Their followers were often referred to as Parnellites and Redmondites, respectively. Committed to democracy and maintaining the union with the United Kingdom, the Nationalists' chief aim was the achievement of Home Rule in a united Ireland. The party also acted as the main representative of Catholic and tenant farmer interests. The United Irish League was founded in 1898, in effect replacing the defunct National League as the Nationalist Party's constituency organisation. Within a few years it was actively supported by the Molly Maguires (officially, the Ancient Order of Hibernians). This was a strongly, even narrowly, Catholic and nationalistic organisation. It developed into a formidable, ruthless and at times violent political machine.

O'Brienites and the All for Ireland League

O'Brienites were followers of the maverick Corkman William O'Brien, a journalist and politician. A prominent Nationalist Party MP, O'Brien turned against Parnell when the party split in 1891 over the leader's divorce case. In 1909 O'Brien left the Nationalist Party and set up the All for Ireland League, pursuing a policy of conciliation with Unionists and active agricultural reform. Popular in his native Cork, O'Brien won eight seats in the general election of 1910. However, the O'Brienites never broke out of their southwestern stronghold. After 1916 the All for Ireland League, and its leader, rapidly faded as a political force. O'Brien became sympathetic to Sinn Féin.

Protestants

In the late nineteenth and early twentieth century there was no major party representing the interests of Protestants in the south of Ireland. Nevertheless, many were politically active. They mostly fell into two readily recognisable groups: Unionists, who opposed any measure of Home Rule, and Home Rulers, who supported it. Both groups were loyalists; i.e. supported the government of the United Kingdom and wished to maintain some form of constitutional link with it. Particularly during the Troubles, Republicans tended to lump all loyalists together, seeing their hostility to a fully independent Ireland as their main characteristic. Republican Protestants had existed, if only in small numbers, since at least the late eighteenth century, with some taking leading roles in Irish history. However, they played little or no part in the life of County Cork during the later years of British rule.

Sinn Féin (Ourselves Alone)

Sinn Féin, a radical nationalist party, was founded in 1905. In 1917 de Valera was elected president, and Sinn Féin espoused Republicanism. In the 1918 general election Sinn Féin won 73 out of 105 seats and replaced the Nationalist Party as the dominant voice of Irish nationalism. The party refused to accept the Anglo-Irish Treaty of 1921 and in 1926 it split, with significant numbers joining de Valera in Fianna Fáil. Sinn Féin, refusing to recognise the Irish Free State, entered the political wilderness. Although the party remained active, in the south it never regained its previously dominant position.

Land Legislation

From the late nineteenth century until the outbreak of the First World War, the British government introduced a series of Land Acts, which initiated a significant transfer of land ownership from landlords to tenants. The process was virtually completed under the Irish Free State.

Gladstone's Land Law Act, 1881

This act granted the 'three Fs': Fair Rents, Fixity of Tenure and Free Sale. It also set up a Land Commission, which could adjudicate on fair rents and make loans to enable tenants to purchase their holdings.

Balfour Land Act, 1891

This act made the transfer of land easier and set up the Congested Districts Board, which had powers to relieve overcrowding in impoverished areas.

Wyndham Land Act, 1903

This act introduced arrangements whereby entire estates could be transferred from landlords to tenants. Backed by government money, the terms were financially beneficial to both parties. The act, which was very popular, greatly accelerated the growth of peasant ownership of land.

Land Act, 1923 (Irish Free State)

This introduced the compulsory transfer of remaining tenanted land and abolished the Congested Districts Board.

Land Annuities

These were yearly repayments by tenants to the British government of loans made under various acts for the purchase of land. Following the Anglo-Irish Treaty, the Irish Free State agreed to collect this money and transfer it to the British government. De Valera opposed making any further repayments, and when Fianna Fáil came to power in 1932 they were duly suspended. The British government retaliated with various economic sanctions.

KEY DATES

1872	Jasper born in Skibbereen (August)
1879	Parnell elected chairman of the Nationalist Party
1881	Anti-landlord riot in Skibbereen
	Gladstone's second Land Act grants the 'three Fs'
1882	Irish National League founded
1883	Jasper attends the Bishop's School, Skibbereen
1888	Jasper apprenticed as a solicitor
1890	Parnell ousted as leader of Nationalist Party following his divorce
1891	Balfour Land Act
1893	Jasper wins first place, and gold medal, in final All-Ireland Law Exams
1895	J. Travers Wolfe & Co. founded
1898	Jasper marries Minnie Vickery
	Irish Local Government Act
	United Irish League founded (local organisation of Nationalist Party)
1903	Wyndham Land Act
1905	Sinn Féin founded
	Liberal Party wins UK general election
1907	*Ne Temere* (decree on mixed marriage) promulgated by Pope Pius X
1908	Jasper and family move to Norton
1909	William O'Brien founds All for Ireland League
1910	United Kingdom general election. In Ireland, Nationalist Party remains dominant; O'Brienites win eight seats in County Cork. In Britain, the Liberals under Asquith retain power
1911	Jasper's son, Travers, born. Willie Wood Wolfe, Jasper's brother, marries Dollie O'Shea
1912	Jasper makes successful speech in London at Irish Protestant demonstration supporting Home Rule
	Third Home Rule Bill introduced in House of Commons
1913	Irish Volunteers founded
1914	UK declares war on Germany (August)
	Home Rule enacted (September), but suspended until war is over
1916	Easter Rising in Dublin. Proclamation of Irish Republic (April)
	Jasper appointed Crown Solicitor for the West Riding and City of Cork (June)
	Lloyd George becomes prime minister, at the head of a war government, with a powerful representation of Tory and Unionist interests (December)
1917	Sinn Féin commits itself to Republicanism and elects de Valera president
1918	Conscription crisis
	Sinn Féin becomes dominant party in Ireland following victory in UK general election
1919	First Dáil meets in Dublin (January)
	Anglo-Irish War/War of Independence begins (January)

Irish Volunteers becoming known as IRA and, in theory at least, subject to the political control of the Dáil government

The Dáil, Sinn Féin and the IRA declared illegal by the British government

1920   Jasper appears for the Crown at the inquest into the murder of Tomás MacCurtain, Lord Mayor of Cork (April)

Black and Tans and Auxiliaries start arriving in Ireland

1921   Tom Barry and his IRA flying column attack Skibbereen (February)

Failed IRA attempt to capture Jasper near Skibbereen, at Caheragh (February)

Truce ends Anglo-Irish War (July)

Jasper kidnapped by IRA and condemned to death (October). Released on intervention of Father McCarthy

Anglo-Irish Treaty signed in London (December)

1922   Jasper targeted in killings of Protestants by IRA Volunteers, but he is in Cork and escapes to England (April)

Irish Civil War starts between Irregulars (IRA supporters of a Republic) and Free Staters (supporters of the Anglo-Irish Treaty and the Free State) (June)

Irregulars invade Skibbereen. Jasper taken captive and told he will be shot; he is released on the intervention of Father McCarthy and again escapes to England (July)

Michael Collins shot dead after leaving a meeting in Skibbereen (August)

Irish Free State formally established (December)

1923   End of Irish Civil War (April)

Cumann na nGaedheal founded

Free State general election (proportional representation); Cumann na nGaedheal victory; Cumann na Gaedheal candidate Neilus Connolly tops poll in West Cork (August)

Land Act, Irish Free State

1924   Cobh shooting of unarmed British soldiers and civilians, allegedly by IRA

1925   IRA splits from Sinn Féin

1926   Sinn Féin splits and de Valera sets up Fianna Fáil

1927   General election (June); Cumann na nGaedheal victory

In West Cork, Jasper stands as an Independent and is elected to the final place

Kevin O'Higgins assassinated (July)

Jasper successfully defends suspects accused of the Cobh shootings of 1924 (August)

Jasper plays a key role in the Dáil in securing the abstention of Alderman Jinks, and so helps save the Cumann na nGaedheal government from defeat in a vote of No Confidence proposed by Fianna Fáil (August)

General election; Cumann na nGaedheal victory (October)

In West Cork, Jasper again stands as an Independent candidate. He is elected top of the poll (on first preferences)

1932   Dáil general election. De Valera and Fianna Fáil win (February)

In West Cork, Jasper slips to second place (first preferences)

1933   General election; Fianna Fáil win and begin to emerge as the dominant political force in Irish politics (January)

In West Cork, Jasper does not stand and ends his political career

Fine Gael founded. Before long, Jasper joins the new party

Jasper's daughters, Dorothy and Ray, get married from Norton

1936   De Valera bans the IRA

1937   New Irish constitution establishes a Republic in all but name

1940   Jasper elected president of the Law Society of Ireland

1946   Death of Jasper's son, Travers

1948   Republic of Ireland formally established
1952   Jasper dies at home in Norton (August)

Notes and References

CHAPTER 1. JASPER AND MINNIE WOLFE

1. Anecdote about Murty and the butcher is from Pat O'Donovan.

CHAPTER 5. METHODISTS

1. My account of the Methodists in Skibbereen and West Cork is based on:
    Dudley Livingstone Cooney, *The Methodists in Ireland*, Columba, 2001.
    Rev. W. E.Cullen (ed.), *Skibbereen Methodism 1798–1938* (booklet), 1938.
    John Dowse, *Methodism in the Far West of Cork*, Mizen Journal, 1995.
    Christian Advocate, 'Skibbereen Circuit', 15 December 1891.
    Irish Christian Advocate, 'Skibbereen Methodist Church Centenary Services' 19 May,
    2 June, 1933.
    Irish Christian Advocate, 'Skibbereen, a Methodist Garden' 20, 27 November 1936.
    Irish Christian Advocate, 'Some Reminiscences of the Skibbereen Circuit' 12, 19, 26
    February, 5, 12 March 1937.

CHAPTER 7. TRIBES

1. Seamus Crowley, 'Rossa – Legendary Rebel', *Southern Star Centenary Supplement 1889–1989*. 1989.
2. The Bence Jones riot and National Land League rally are described in Pat Cleary, 'Skibbereen – No Puny Village', *Southern Star Centenary Supplement 1889–1989*.
3. The full title of the *Eagle* was first the *Skibbereen Eagle*, and from around 1900 the *Cork County Eagle*. To avoid confusion I refer to it throughout as the *Eagle*, which in fact is the name by which it was popularly known.

CHAPTER 8. THE BISHOP'S SCHOOL

1. Christopher Peters, (Dean of Ross), 'St Fachtna's College,' in *St Fachtna's Cathedral, Ross: a history*, Select Vestry, Ross Union of Parishes, c. 2001.
2. From 1929–1931 Jim Burke, using the pen-name 'Finnerty', published a series of reminscences about the Bishop's, or Upper and Intermediate School, which in turn provoked further memories from various correspondents. All this appeared in the *Southern Star*, of which Burke was editor at the time.

CHAPTER 9. SOLICITOR'S APPRENTICE

1. Quoted in Pat Cleary, *Nineteenth Century Skibbereen*, Seanchas Chairbre, no. 2, December 1983.

CHAPTER 11. 'A THIN, RESTLESS YOUTH, WITH EARS LIKE THE HANDLES OF AN URN'

1. Maurice Healy, *The Old Munster Circuit*, Wiley and Son, 2001.
2. E. OE. Somerville and Martin Ross, 'The Boat's Share', in *The Irish R. M. and his Experiences*, Faber and Faber, 1928.
3. Anecdote about the Baltimore ship case is from Gerald O'Brien.
4. The *Cosmopoliet* case. Tim Cadogan, who has researched this incident in detail, drew my attention to it, and kindly provided me with relevant papers. I made particular use of the *Eagle* cuttings, (1, 8, 15, 22 June, 7 July 1907; 20 June, 1908).

CHAPTER 12. PROTESTANT HOME RULER

1. Joseph O'Brien, *William O'Brien and the course of Irish Politics 1881–1918*, University of California Press, 1976.
2. Patrick Maume, *The Long Gestation: Irish Nationalist Life 1891–1918*, Gill & Macmillan, 1999.
3. The southern Protestant Movement in favour of the third Irish Home Rule Bill hardly receives a mention in the historical literature dealing with the period. I only came across it when relevant newspapers and other documents turned up in Jasper's desk, now owned by Jim O'Keeffe, TD.

CHAPTER 13. A MIXED MARRIAGE

1. *Ne Temere*: I found the requirements of this papal decree, and the way it was applied in practice, quite difficult to pin down. After reading the original, as well as consulting various individuals and publications, I relied mainly on; J. A.Corriden, Thomas J. Green, and Donald E. Heintschel, (eds.). *The Code of Canon Law: a text and commentary*,Geoffrey Chapman, 1985.
2. Anecdote about Willie Wood Wolfe's conversion to Catholicism is from Janet Connell.

CHAPTER 14. CROWN SOLICITOR

1. R. B. McDowell, 'Ch. 4. The Courts of Law', in *The Irish Administration 1801–1914* Routledge, 1964.

CHAPTER 15. 'YOUR GRANDAD PUT MY DAD IN GAOL!'

1. Anecdote about the gaoled Dad is from Derek Walton.
2. Florence O'Donoghue, 'Tomas McCurtain', The *Kerryman*, 1958.

CHAPTER 18. GUNRUNNING

1. Liam O'Regan, son of Joe O'Regan, told me the story of the gunrunning episode.

CHAPTER 19. 'SLOUCHING THROUGH LIFE MEEK AND TAME'

1. My account of IRA activities in and around Skibbereen is based on:
   Tom Barry, *Guerrilla Days in Ireland*, Anvil Books, 1989.
   Meda Ryan, *Tom Barry: IRA Freedom Fighter*, Mercier Press, 2003.
   Liam Deasy, *Towards Ireland Free: The West Cork Brigade in the War of Independence 1917–1921*, Royal Carbery Books, 1973.

CHAPTER 20. NEILUS

1. Much of this chapter relies on an unpublished memoir which Neilus Connolly wrote towards the end of his life.

CHAPTER 21. 'THE PURSUIT BECAME SO HOT'

1. Anecdote about Harry Wolfe and the IRA Arms Fund is from Gerald O'Brien.
2. Liam O'Regan, *The Imperialistic Bishop of Ross and his political influence*, Mizen Journal, 1997.
3. Anecdote about Jasper's escape from the IRA in Baltimore is from Penny Weir.

CHAPTER 22. 'THE IRA OFFERED THE SERVICES OF THE PARISH PRIEST'

1. The story of Eddie Swanton's kidnapping by the IRA is based on his father Richard's and Jasper's applications to the Irish Grants Committee, as well as on the report, (the *Eagle*, January 28, 1922), of his appeal for compensation heard in the Skibbereen Quarter Sessions.
2. J. P. Casey , 'Republican Courts in Ireland 1919–1922', *Irish Jurist*, 1970, and Cahir Davitt, 'The Civil Jurisdiction of the Courts of the Irish Republic', *Irish Jurist*, 1968.
3. Garnishee Orders were explained to me by Arthur Weir, a barrister.

CHAPTER 23. 'THEY WANT TO TERRORISE THE LANDLORDS'

1. The dealings of the Skibbereen Urban District Council with The Town Tenants' League and the Dáil Éireann Minister for Local Government are covered in papers included in the Dáil Éireann Local Government file, (National Archives, Ireland). In particular I refer to Council minutes, Council correspondence with the Minister, and The Town Tenants' League resolution on Landlords.

CHAPTER 24. LANDLORDS OF CASTLEFREKE

1. My account of the Carberies of Castlefreke, (later spelt 'Carberry' by some members of the family), is based on:
    Juanita Carberry, 'Child of Happy Valley', *Ardfield/Rathbarry Journal*, 2000–1.
    Paddy O'Sullivan, 'High Cross of Castlefreke', *Ardfield/Rathbarry Journal* 2000–1.
    Jeremy Sandford (ed.), *Mary Carbery's West Cork Journal 1898–1901*, Lilliput Press, 1998.
2. Anecdote about Willie Wood Wolfe and the sale of Cononagh timber is from John Murphy.
3. Tim O'Neill, 'Michael Collins and the Castlefreke Estate', *Ardfield/Rathbarry Journal*, 2002–3.
4. Details of William Wood's problems with the IRA are taken from his application for compensation to the Irish Grants Committee (National Archives, Kew).

CHAPTER 25. 'A LEADING PROFESSIONAL MAN IS MISSING'

1. Anecdote about Jasper drinking with the would-be IRA burners of Norton is from Val Walton .
2. For the killings, attempted murders and other events of 27–29 April 1922 I have relied, in the first place, on family memories, and on Jasper and William Wood's applications for compensation to the Irish Grants Committee, (National Archives, Kew). For the more general context I have referred to Peter Hart's *The IRA and its enemies* and Meda

Ryan's *Tom Barry: IRA Freedom Fighter*. The events of those few days remain controversial. The attempted attacks on Jasper and William Wood in Skibbereen have, as far as I know, not previously been publicly known. These facts, and the background to them, can suggest further perspectives on what happened, why, and how.

CHAPTER 26. 'I WAS INFORMED I WOULD BE SHOT'

1. Anecdote about the IRA and the Norton horse is from Penny Weir.
2. The siege of Skibbereen was described in detail in the *Cork Examiner* (4 and 5 July 1922), the *Southern Star* (8 July 1922), the *Eagle* (8 July 1922), and by Pat Cleary in 'Skibbereen – no puny village', (*Southern Star Centenary Supplement 1889–1989*). I also made use of family memories, (particularly Dorothy Wolfe's), Neilus Connolly's memoir, and Jasper's application to the Irish Grants Committee, (National Archives, Kew).
3. Anecdote about the burning of Glencurragh House is from Gerald O'Brien.

CHAPTER 27. 'MY WARMEST FRIENDS'

1. Anecdote about Jasper's meeting with Neilus Connolly in Cork is from Philip O'Regan.
2. Finbarr O'Driscoll spoke with me at length about his father Seán, and his family.

CHAPTER 31. 'FROM A FEW FRIENDS'

1. Mary Kotsonouris, *Retreat from Revolution; the Dáil Courts 1920–24*, Irish Academic Press, 1994.

CHAPTER 33. COUNSEL FOR THE IRA

1. Anecdote about Jack Wolfe and the Republican boxer from John Murphy.

CHAPTER 34. THE COBH SHOOTING

1. My account of the Cobh shooting is based on:
   Cork Examiner (22, 24, March, 14 May, 29 October, 5 November, 1924).
   Southern Star (29 March, 1924).
   Kieran McCarthy and Maj-Britt Christensen, *Cobh's Contribution to the Fight for Irish Freedom 1913–1990*, Oileann Mor, 1992.
   Maryann GialanellaValentis, *Almost a Rebellion; the Irish Army mutiny of 1924*, Tower Books, 1985.

CHAPTER 35. INDEPENDENT CANDIDATE FOR THE DÁIL

1. J. Anthony,Gaughan, *Thomas Johnson 1872–1963; first leader of the Labour Party in Dáil Éireann* , Kingdom Press, 1980.

CHAPTER 36. ''TWAS JASPER, AND NOT JINKS, SAVED THE IRISH NATION'

1. F. S. L. Lyons, in *Ireland since the Famine*, published the now widely accepted view that it was the editor of *The Irish Times* and an Independent deputy from Sligo who persuaded Jinks to abstain in the No Confidence motion. This version of events is not at odds with the part played by Jasper. It is quite possible that, while Jasper was speaking in the Dáil, R. M. Smyllie and Major Cooper TD persuaded Jinks to leave

Leinster House. They may, or may not, have subsequently wined and dined him. Indeed, they may have started their efforts at hospitality earlier in the day. Anyway, they almost certainly put him as soon as conveniently possible on the train home.

CHAPTER 38. 'I REMAIN, AS FROM THE BEGINNING, A SUPPORTER OF THE IRISH TREATY'

1. Anecdote about Brian Wolfe and de Valera is from Janet Connell.

CHAPTER 41. GAELIC TRIBESMAN

1. For information about the Skibbereen Blueshirt rally; see the *Southern Star Millenium Supplement*, p.8.

CHAPTER 42. 'AN EXCELLENT MEMBER OF THE PROFESSION'

1. Anecdote about the lawyers charged with drinking after hours is from John Murphy and Gerald O'Brien. I failed to find a newspaper report of this event, which must have excited much local interest, not to mention hilarity. However, having been told the story separately, by two unrelated people, I have no doubt it occurred.
2. Anecdotes, Alfie Regan and the land boundary, the woman with a crippled arm, and the paternity case of the ugly baby were remembered by Willie Wood Wolfe's family, and told to me by John Murphy and his brothers. The latter case was also reported in the *Southern Star*, 15 October 1938.
3. The paternity case involving Eugene McCarthy and the complicated sequence of court cases and assaults which resulted were reported in much detail by the *Southern Star*, (12 November 1938, 16 November, 7 and 21 December 1940, 25 January 1941); and by the *Cork Examiner*, (8, 18 January 1941).

SOURCES AND BIBLIOGRAPHY

Libraries and archives

Bodleian Central and Law Libraries, Oxford University; Clonakilty Museum; Colindale Newspaper Library, British Museum; Cork City Library; Cork County Library; National Archives, Ireland; National Archives, Kew; National Library of Ireland; Skibbereen Heritage Centre; Skibbereen Registration Office; Society of Genealogists, London; *Southern Star* Newspaper Archive

Unpublished correspondence, diaries, memoirs and other documents

Neilus Connolly's memoir; Irish Grants Committee, Applications for compensation from R. Swanton, W. W. Wolfe, J. T. Wolfe and W. G. Wood (National Archives, Kew); Ministry of Finance, Irish Free State, Compensation Claim from J. T. Wolfe (National Archives, Dublin); Minutes of The Southern Star Ltd; miscellaneous correspondence from family sources; report, 1924, of Circuit Court Judge in Cork County on compensation claim from J. T. Wolfe (National Archives, Dublin); Skibbereen Urban District papers 1921, from Dáil Éireann Local Government file (National Archives, Dublin); Dorothy Wolfe's diary for 1927 (any other diaries are lost); Wolfe family correspondence; Jasper Wolfe papers found in his desk, now owned by Jim O'Keeffe TD; Rachel Wood Wolfe diaries, 1888, 1911, 1912 (other diaries are lost.)

Newspapers and periodicals

Belfast Telegraph; *Catholic Times*; *Christian Advocate* (later *Irish Christian Advocate*); *Cork Examiner*; *Daily Chronicle*; *Daily News*; *Eagle* (Skibbereen, later Cork County); *Freeman's Journal*; *Gazette of the Incorporated Law Society of Ireland*; *Irish Press*; *Irish Statesman*; *Southern Reporter*; *Southern Star*; *Southern Star* Centenary Supplement 1889–1989; *Southern Star* Millenium Supplement 2000; *The Times*; *Ulster Guardian*; *West Cork People* Commemorative Edition, 22 August 2002.

PUBLICATIONS

While I have made use of a range of publications, there are some on which I have regularly relied. I list these below. Where I have turned to particular books and articles for information relevant to specific chapters, they are detailed under 'Notes and References'. I cite the editions I have actually used, frequently paperbacks subsequent to the original date of publication.

General histories

Campbell, Colin, *Emergency Law in Ireland 1918–1925*, Oxford University Press, 1994.
Coogan, Tim Pat, *De Valera: Long Fellow, Long Shadow*, Hutchinson, 1993.

Coogan, Tim Pat, and George Morrison, *The Irish Civil War*, Weidenfeld & Nicolson, 1998.

Ferriter, Diarmaid, *The Transformation of Ireland*, Profile Books, 2005.

Foster, R. F. (ed.), *The Oxford History of Ireland*, Oxford University Press, 1992.

Jackson, Alvin, *Home Rule: An Irish History 1800–2000*, Phoenix, 2004.

Kee, Robert, *The Green Flag*: vol 2, *The Bold Fenian Men* and vol 3, *Ourselves Alone*, Penguin, 1989.

Lee, J. J., *Ireland 1912–1985: Politics and Society*, Cambridge University Press, 1989.

Lyons, F. S. L., *Ireland since the Famine*, Fontana Press, 1985.

McCardle, Dorothy, *The Irish Republic*, Corgi Books, 1968.

Regan, John M., *The Irish Counter-Revolution 1921–1936*, Gill & Macmillan, 2001.

County Cork

Abbeystrewry, a Parish Memoir, Forum Publications, 1991.

Barry, Tom, *Guerilla Days in Ireland*, Anvil Books, 1989.

Campbell, Fergus, *Land and Revolution in Nationalist Politics in the West of Ireland 1891–1921*, Oxford University Press, 2005.

Coogan, Tim Pat, *Michael Collins*, Pimlico, 1990.

Deasy, Liam, *Towards Ireland Free: The West Cork Brigade in the War of Independence 1917–1921*, Royal Carbery Books, 1973.

De La Salle Past Pupils' Union, *And Time Stood Still: A Pictorial History of Skibbereen and District*, De La Salle Past Pupils' Union, 2002.

Hart, Peter, *The IRA and Its Enemies: Violence and Community in Cork 1916–1923*, Oxford University Press, 1999.

Kingston, Willie, 'From Victorian Boyhood to the Troubles', *Skibbereen and District Historical Journal*, 2005.

Ryan, Meda, *Tom Barry: IRA Freedom Fighter*, Mercier Press, 2003.

Ó Faolain, Seán, 'The South West', in *An Irish Journey*, Longmans, Green & Co., 1940.

Wright, Jane, *She left her heart in China: The story of Dr Sally Wolfe*, Cloverhill Press, 1999.

Records and references

Boylan, Henry (ed.), *A Dictionary of Irish Biography*, Gill & Macmillan, 1999.

Cadogan, Tim, and Jeremiah Falvey (eds.), *A Biographical Dictionary of Cork*, Four Courts Press, 2006.

Censuses of Ireland, 1901, 1911.

Connolly, S. J. (ed.), *The Oxford Companion to Irish History*, Oxford University Press, 1999.

Dáil Éireann Parliamentary Debates: Official Reports 1927–1932, vols. 19–45, Dublin.

Hodges, Rev. Richard J., and W. T. Pike (eds.), *Cork and County Cork in the Twentieth Century; Contemporary Biographies*, W.T. Pike, 1911.

O'Day, Alan, and John Stevenson (ed.), *Irish Historical Documents since 1800*, Gill & Macmillan, 1992.

Walker, Brian M. (ed.), *Parliamentary Election Results in Ireland 1801–1922*, Royal Irish Academy, Dublin, 1978.

Walker, Brian M (ed.), *Parliamentary Election Results in Ireland 1918–1992*, Royal Irish Academy, Dublin; Institute of Irish Studies Belfast.

Wylie, J. C. W., *Irish Land Law*, Professsional Books, 1975.

Journals

Ardfield/Rathbarry Journal; Irish Law Times and Solicitors' Journal; Irish Jurist; Mizen Journal; Skibbereen and District Historical Society Journal.

INDEX

Page numbers in **bold** refer to entries in glossary.